The Business of Japanese Foreign Aid

Japan is now the world's largest donor of Official Development Assistance (ODA), distributing one-fifth of all world-wide foreign aid. Concentrating heavily on infrastructure projects in Asia, Japanese ODAs have predominantly taken the form of concessional loans, raising many questions about the aims and motives of the Japanese foreign aid programme.

The Business of Japanese Foreign Aid brings together five case studies focusing on the procedures, methodologies and business mechanisms at the implementation level of ODA, suggesting that there are many more factors influencing the process than might have been anticipated at the policy-making level in Tokyo. Examining such countries as China, Thailand, Indonesia and the Philippines, these studies explore the process not only of giving but also of receiving aid, arguing that many of the recipient countries exert considerable influence over the distribution of Japanese foreign aid.

Marie Söderberg is Senior Research Fellow at the European Institute of Japanese Studies, Stockholm.

European Institute of Japanese Studies East Asian Economics and Business Studies Series
Edited by Jean-Pierre Lehmann
Director, European Institute of Japanese Studies

The centre of gravity of the global economy is now firmly in the Asia Pacific region. The European Institute of Japanese Studies East Asian Economics and Business series analyses some of the reasons for and implications of this fundamental shift. Edited by Jean-Pierre Lehmann, and calling on contributors from across the world, the series will showcase the first-class research instigated by the Institute in Stockholm. *The Business of Japanese Foreign Aid* is the first book to be published in the series.

The Business of Japanese Foreign Aid
Five case studies from Asia
Edited by Marie Söderberg

The Business of Japanese Foreign Aid

Five case studies from Asia

Edited by Marie Söderberg

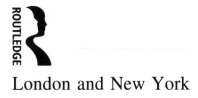

London and New York

First published 1996
by Routledge
11 New Fetter Lane, London EC4P 4EE

Simultaneously published in the USA and Canada
by Routledge
29 West 35th Street, New York, NY 10001

© 1996 The European Institute of Japanese Studies, selection and editorial
matter; individual chapters, the contributors

Typeset in Times by
J&L Composition Ltd, Filey, North Yorkshire
Printed and bound in Great Britain by
TJ Press (Padstow), Padstow, Cornwall

British Library Cataloguing in Publication Data
A catalogue record for this book is available from the British Library

Library of Congress Cataloging in Publication Data
The business of Japanese foreign aid: five case studies from Asia/
edited by Marie Söderberg
1. Economic assistance, Japanese–Asia–Case studies.
I. Söderberg, Marie.
HC412.B867   1996
338.9'15205—dc20   96-5527

ISBN 0–415–13878–7 (hbk)

Contents

Series editor's preface

One of the defining issues of the turn of the century will be the international role that Japan will assume. The current circumstances and trends indicate that the role will be defined primarily by Japan's financial power, rather than by ideology. In the post cold-war age, this quality in principle should make Japan well equipped for approaching matters from a predominantly pragmatic viewpoint.

Having emerged in this decade as the world's biggest provider of overseas aid to developing countries, by definition Japan's role looms large. It has also aroused controversy. As Japan is generally suspected of pursuing economic objectives according to mercantilist principles, the accusation has been that Japan's aid business is business for Japanese business.

The research undertaken by Dr Marie Söderberg and her team makes a significant contribution by addressing these questions from a detailed and concrete perspective. And it comes up with some surprising answers, proving that conventional wisdom may be off the mark.

Having ascertained the principles and guidelines emanating from the relevant bodies in Tokyo, the book focuses on what actually happens. *The Business of Japanese Foreign Aid* delves in depth into the mechanics and dynamics of the transactions from governments to business in specific instances in China, Indonesia, Thailand and the Philippines. In so doing, the practices and prospects for European companies are described and discussed.

It is a pleasure to have this book as the first in the series jointly launched by the European Institute of Japanese Studies at the Stockholm School of Economics and Routledge. The series focuses on the economics and business of the East Asian region and in particular the driving forces, trends and developments in intra-regional cross-border flows of capital, goods and technologies. The Asia Pacific region is presenting the international business community with new bases of competition. The objective of the series is to provide sound analysis on these forces in a manner that will provide enlightenment and practical assistance to business executives, government officials and academics, to policy-makers and to policy-thinkers.

Japanese aid in East Asia is one of the major integrative forces. In light of the significant sums it represents and will represent, it has major implications for European corporations. The detail and depth of Marie Söderberg's work will significantly enrich their strategies. It also provides an excellent launch for this new series.

Jean-Pierre Lehmann

Figures

Maps

Tables

APPENDICES

Contributors

Magnus Berg is a graduate of the East Asia Study Program at Stockholm University.

Åsa Malmström is a graduate of Stockholm School of Economics and a research assistant at the European Institute of Japanese Studies.

Ben Warkentin is a PhD candidate at Duisburg University, Germany. At present he is based at Dokkyo University in Japan.

Gang Zhang is a PhD candidate at Stockholm School of Economics.

Abbreviations

ADB	Asian Development Bank
AfDB	African Development Bank
Asahi	*Asahi Shimbun*
ASEAN	Association of South East Asian Nations
AWSJ	*Asian Wall Street Journal*
B&W	Babcock and Wilcox
BAPPEDA	regional development planning board (Indonesia)
BAPPENAS	national development planning agency (Indonesia)
BKPM	investment co-ordinating board (Indonesia)
BOI/DTI	Board of Investment/Department of Trade and Industry (Philippines)
BOT/BOO	Build–Operate–Transfer/Build–Operate–Own
BW	*Business World*
CALABARZON	the provinces of Cavite, Laguna, Batangas, Rizal and Quezon (Philippines)
CE/MC	Combustion Engineering/Mitsubishi Corporation
CGI	Consultative Group on Indonesia
CNIMIEC	China National Industrial Machinery Import and Export Corporation (a subsidiary of CNMIEC)
CNMIEC (CMC)	China National Machinery Import and Export Corporation
CNTIC	China National Technical Import and Export Corporation
DAC	Development Assistance Committee
DENR	Department of Environment and Natural Resources (Philippines)
DOH	Department of Highways (Thailand)
DTEC	Department of Technical and Economical Co-operation (Thailand)

EBRD	European Bank for Reconstruction and Development
ECC	environmental compliance certificate, to be issued by EMB (Philippines)
ECD	Economic Co-operation Department (of Mitsui & Co. Ltd, Japan)
ECFA	Engineering Consulting Firms Association (Japan)
EIA	environmental impact assessment, application for ECC (Philippines)
EIS	environmental impact statement (system); sometimes refers to the whole system including EIA and ECC (Philippines)
EKUIN	co-ordination ministry for economy, finance, industry and development supervision (Indonesia)
EMB	Environmental Management Bureau of DENR (Philippines)
E/N	Exchange of Notes
EPA	Economic Planning Agency (Japan)
ETA	Expressway and Rapid Transit Authority (Thailand)
FCTIO	Foreign Capital and Technical Import Office (China)
FEER	*Far Eastern Economic Review*
FGD	flue gas desulphurization (equipment)
F/S	feasibility study
GDP	gross domestic product
GOJ	Government of Japan
GOP	Government of the Philippines
IBRD	International Bank for Reconstruction and Development (World Bank)
ICB	international competitive bidding
ICC	Investment Coordination Committee
IDB	Inter-American Development Bank
IGGI	Intergovernmental Group on Indonesia (now superseded by CGI)
IHT	*International Herald Tribune*
IS	international shopping
JAIDO	Japanese International Development Organization
JETRO	Japan Export and Trade Organization (Japan)
JICA	Japan International Co-operation Agency (Japan)
LA	loan agreement

LCB	local competitive bidding
LDC	less-developed country
LGU	Local Government Unit (Philippines)
LLDC	least among less-developed countries
Mainichi	*Mainichi Shimbun*
MAI/PAP	Multilateral Assistance Initiative/Philippine Assistance Program
MB	*Manila Bulletin*
MEAO	Machinery and Electric Appraisal Office (China)
MERALCO	Manila Electric Company (Philippines)
MITI	Ministry of International Trade and Industry (Japan)
MOA	memoranda of agreement
MOF	Ministry of Finance (Japan)
MOFA	Ministry of Foreign Affairs (Japan)
MOFTEC	Ministry of Foreign Trade and Economic Co-operation (China)
MOR	Ministry of Railways (China)
NEDA	National Economic and Development Authority (Philippines)
NESDB	National Economic and Social Development Board (Thailand)
NEWJEC	New Japan Engineering Consultants Inc.
NGO	non-governmental organization
NIC	newly industrializing country
Nikkei	*Nihon Keizai Shimbun*
NPC	National Power Corporation (Philippines)
ODA	Official Development Assistance
OECD	Organization for Economic Co-operation and Development
OECF	Overseas Economic Co-operation Fund (Japan)
OPEC	Organization of Petroleum Exporting Countries
PCI	Pacific Consultant International
P F/S	preliminary feasibility study
PLN	Persahaan Listrik Negara (state electricity company – Indonesia)
PMTDP	Philippine Medium Term Development Plan
RDC	Regional Development Council, local subdivision of NEDA and highest regional government body (Philippines)
RIDA	Research Institute of Development Assistance (Japan)

SAPROF	Special Assistance for Project Formation (an OECF programme)
SC	State Council (China)
SPC	State Planning Commission (China)
TAC	Technical Appraisal Centre (part of MOR)
UNDP	United Nations Development Programme
USAID	United States Agency for International Development
Yomiuri	*Yomiuri Shimbun*

NOTE ON CURRENCIES

The research undertaken in compiling this volume involved a number of countries with different currencies. To make it easier for the reader these have been translated into US dollars. When the yen is used the dollar amount is given as well. US dollars are not used exclusively because the loans were actually given in yen. With the significant fluctuations that occur in exchange rates over time, the picture of Japanese ODA portrayed in dollars is radically different from the one given in yen. The exchange rates used for calculations of currencies from OECD countries are those used by DAC. As for the recipient countries, the yearly average exchange rates found in the IMF publication *International Financial Statistics* have been used.

Introduction:

Time to look at Japanese aid in practice

Marie Söderberg

There have been a number of studies on Japanese foreign aid during recent years. This is understandable as since 1989 (with the exception of one year) Japan has been the world's largest donor and with its budget of more than $11 billion contributes around one-fifth of all the official development assistance (ODA)[1] from the industrialized world. The interest in Japanese ODA can be further understood considering the gloomy picture of foreign aid in general. The recession in many of the 21 OECD Development Assistance Committee (DAC)[2] countries has led some of them to reduce spending on foreign aid. This reduction is coupled with a renewal of the debate on whether aid is useful at all, or only profits the dominant group in society,[3] and whether the liberalization of trade barriers would be much more effective in helping developing countries.[4]

There is but one exception of this gloomy picture, namely, Japan. In contrast with other donors it has been raising its target for foreign aid spending. Whereas $50 billion was spent on ODA during the period 1988–92, $70–75 billion is expected to be spent during 1993–97. This will further strengthen Japan's dominant position in the field. No wonder there is an interest in Japanese foreign aid.

Besides its size, the fact that Japanese ODA is radically different from that of other donors makes it interesting. When compared with other OECD countries (see Chapter 1) it is evident that Japanese aid has a high priority on funding economic infrastructure, such as roads, railways, telecommunication and power projects. Japanese ODA also has a higher percentage of aid loans[5] and a lower percentage of grants[6] than other donors.

So far, however, the approaches used in analysing Japanese ODA are rather traditional. The models used to date, although they all shed light on different aspects of Japanese ODA, do not give the full picture. As will be shown by this research project, they are actually far from enough to tell us anything substantial at all about how Japanese aid is working in reality.

THE SHORTCOMINGS OF PREVIOUS RESEARCH ON JAPANESE ODA

A lot of the literature so far has been made up of attempts to evaluate Japanese aid and come up with conclusions on whether it is 'good' or 'bad', a model to follow or a form of aid that should be strongly rejected.

There is a substantial group of Japanese researchers who are highly critical of Japanese ODA in general. They are critical of large-scale economic infrastructure projects which, they assert, only profit people in developing countries who are already financially well-off. Alternatively, these projects are regarded as being of most benefit to Japanese companies. The researchers' studies portray infrastructure projects as environmentally destructive and provide numerous examples of people who have been forced off their land because of construction of a project and thus lost the ability to support themselves. Many of these researchers, who have close connections to some non-governmental organizations (NGOs), oppose industrialization as a solution to the problems of the poor in the developing world. They believe 'small is beautiful' and advocate a more people-to-people based approach to ODA.[7]

In contrast, another group of researchers is extremely proud of the 'Japanese way' of providing aid. To them the high level of loans reflects the Japanese philosophy of giving 'help to self-help', which is based on Japan's own experience and includes considerable government intervention in the economic development process. They view the economic development in South East Asia as proof of the effectiveness of Japanese aid policy, claiming Japanese credit for such rapid economic growth.[8] According to researchers in this group, Japan should be seen as a model for others to follow. Recently attempts have been made to attract international attention for these views.[9]

The problem with research which evaluates aid in terms of 'good' or 'bad' is that the results are predictable and will vary according to the ideological standpoint the research starts from. Such studies will not really tell us much about the working of Japanese aid processes.

Another approach is to study Japanese aid from a comparative perspective. This has been done both on Japanese aid in general[10] and aid to Asia[11] in particular. This does not tell us very much about

Japanese aid *per se*, either. The only thing we learn is in what sense it is different from or similar to that of aid from other countries.

Some researchers have tackled different aspects of the Japanese aid policy-making process, such as the role of the bureaucrats,[12] the politicians,[13] the business community[14] and external influences.[15] These studies tell us a lot about the policy-making process of Japanese aid. They tell us nothing of how aid functions in reality; neither do studies that look at different rationalities behind Japan's decision to provide ODA on the scale it does today. Some researchers view aid as a contribution by Japan to fulfil its obligations to international society. Others consider it as a way of gaining international influence. It has also been discussed in the terms of 'burden sharing' (*yakuwaribuntan*) according to which Japan should take greater responsibility in the field of aid to compensate for the United States' global security umbrella.[16] Another rationale for aid is that it can be seen as a means to secure natural resources or as a strategic tool within the concept of comprehensive security.[17]

All the above approaches have one thing in common. They only look at ODA from a donor perspective. Japanese aid is seen as something that is formed in Tokyo. Its content may vary depending on the strength of the different bureaucratic actors or the Japanese rationale for giving aid at the time but it is executed from Tokyo according to a standard pattern, irrespective of which country is the recipient. This is an outdated colonial approach that has nothing to do with the realities of today.

To examine Japanese ODA from an economic perspective does not give a full picture, either. One might conclude that the high level of ODA loans is more probably the result of a small Japanese state budget than of any particular aid philosophy.[18] This does not tell us anything about the way Japanese aid works. Neither do the studies that have been done from a business perspective. Although officially almost all aid loans are untied, there are scholars who assert that official statistics do not provide an accurate picture and that there is a strong connection between aid and Japanese companies as well as Japanese private direct investment.[19]

On the other hand, a list of companies that have won contracts worth more than ¥1,000 million ($10 million) for construction work and ¥100 million ($1 million) for consulting services is now published by the Overseas Economic Co-operation Fund (OECF), the Japanese bureau responsible for implementation of ODA loans. This list shows that a considerable number of foreign companies have actually succeeded in winning Japanese ODA orders.[20]

4   *Marie Söderberg*

As the interest for becoming involved in this sort of contract work has grown among the international business community, so have the activities of both Japanese agencies and foreign embassies in Tokyo. The OECF publishes *Guidelines for procurement under OECF loans* and *Guidelines for the employment of consultants by OECF borrowers* in English. The Danish Embassy in Tokyo has recently completed a report on how to obtain orders financed by Japanese foreign aid.[21] Several embassies have arranged seminars on ODA from a business perspective and the Swedish Embassy provides help for companies that want to win orders.[22] The American Chamber of Commerce in Tokyo even has a special ODA Committee that meets regularly to discuss ODA from a business perspective.

All these are Tokyo-centred activities. With the exception of a few journalistically styled 'documentary' reports on individual projects which focus mainly on environmental or humanitarian issues, studies on Japanese ODA to date have primarily been concluded from desktops or libraries in Japan, the United States, Australia or other industrialized countries. The material used has mainly been official statistics, policy declarations, different white papers and organizational schemes of the bureaucracy. The value of all these is limited when it comes to explaining what is happening out there, in reality. This is true for any country, but might be especially so for Japan, where policy principles in different areas are not always intended to be implemented but are rather seen as valuable instruments to please domestic as well as international opinion.[23]

Although many researchers have suggested it and pointed out the importance, no major study, until this one, has looked at Japanese ODA where the action takes place, that is, at the implementation level.

SCOPE OF THIS STUDY

The starting-point for this study is not to see Japanese aid as something directed from Tokyo alone. The fact that Japanese aid is request-based has been taken seriously. Therefore this study looks at aid both from a donor and a recipient perspective. It does not see aid as something static, but as a process that needs to be investigated in more detail, not only at the policy level but further down the pipeline.

This volume examines Japanese ODA at the implementation level. It encompasses a business studies perspective and it is large-scale, capital-intensive, economic infrastructure projects that are studied. The purpose is to study the processes from the initiation of a project until the conclusion of contracts, both from a recipient and a donor perspective.

By understanding the processes, the various parties involved, i.e., including government agencies and the private sector in Japan, other DAC countries and developing countries, should gain a better understanding of how the Japanese aid system functions and which strategic options that are available within the system. The question of whether this type of aid is effective or not, or if it should be recommended to other donors is not addressed. Neither are alternative solutions to the infrastructure projects studied, although these surely exist. This is not because these questions are not considered important but simply because it is beyond the scope of this research project.

WHY ECONOMIC INFRASTRUCTURE PROJECTS?

Japanese aid has many faces. Besides loan-aid, which is mainly used for economic infrastructure projects, there is also grant assistance. This encompasses other forms of aid often of the so-called soft type that is tied to humanitarian considerations. There is grant aid for food and disaster relief but also for constructions related to health, education, welfare and communications. Then there is technical assistance, under which heading money is provided to pay for many of the Japanese experts dispatched to developing countries. These help in technical training and overall planning. Technical assistance can include various training facilities in the recipient countries as well as money to pay for the large number of trainees sent to Japan.

In the multilateral field Japan participates actively through providing money to the Asian Development Bank, the World Bank and numerous other organizations as well as hosting large international conferences.[24]

Why did this study then choose to concentrate on economic infrastructure projects? There are several reasons. One is simply that financing of economic infrastructure, as will be shown in Chapter 1, is the most common form of aid given to the main recipients. This is where the bulk of the aid money goes. Another reason is that it is this emphasis on economic infrastructure that makes Japanese bilateral aid different from that of other donors. When compared to other countries this can be seen as a specific feature of the 'Japanese type' of aid, or economic co-operation, as the Japanese prefer to call it. Economic infrastructure plays an important role in this concept which, besides ODA, also encompasses other official flows as well as private direct investment. It is a key element in Japan's belief in development through industrialization.

It is also in this area that the debate has been focusing. Do the infrastructure projects contribute to sustainable development or do they cause environmental destruction, dependency and indebtedness in the recipient countries? Economic infrastructure projects are where the promotion of Japanese business interests is most often suspected, at the same time as Japanese authorities claim that the projects are almost completely untied. This is also the area where the international business community has shown the greatest interest.

The choice of economic infrastructure projects also leads inevitably to a decision on the type of aid studied, namely, loan aid. This is the one almost exclusively used to finance capital-intensive projects like power plants, roads, railways and ports. The great amount of loan-aid is another outstanding feature of Japanese ODA. Loan aid has its own characteristics. It has a different type of decision-making with different actors involved than, for example, grant aid, as is shown in Chapter 1. It has its own implementing agency, namely, OECF, with specific concepts on how aid is to be implemented. It is also treated differently from other forms of aid by the recipients. These differences in how loan aid is looked upon both in Japan and in the recipient countries are likely to affect the implementation process.

METHODOLOGY

Case studies

The research is based on case studies and major loan-financed infrastructure projects are targeted. The merits and shortcomings of the case-study method have been debated among political scientists for a long time. To study what is happening at the implementation level, however, is a very useful method which can generate a considerable amount of information. With this method there is of course always a risk of failing to distinguish between what is unique in one case and what applies in general. To circumvent this weakness a mutual analytical framework was created for this study. This consisted of three independent factors, each factor being a set of variables pointing in one direction. These factors to a varying degree depending on the case, affected the implementation process. In these case studies the factors are used as analytical tools to explain what happens as well as why certain things happen during the process.

Country-specific factors

The country-specific factor is what is specific for each country. Each recipient country has its own historical and cultural background. Each has its own ideas and plans of how the country should be developed. Each has its own administrative systems, business practices, laws and regulations as well as particular ways of thinking. This affects the kinds of projects that a country requests as well as the way it handles aid during the implementation process.

Project-specific factors

The project-specific factor is what is specific for a special project. The way a project is dealt with and the kind of problems that might occur depend on what kind of project it is. The project-specific factor implies that there might be similarities between certain types of projects although they are implemented in different countries. Two similar projects in different countries might actually have more in common than two different projects in the same country. Some projects are more detrimental to the environment than others. The level of impact a project has on the daily life of people varies and so does the technological sophistication of a project and the likely involvement of foreign companies.

ODA loan factor

The ODA loan factor, is what is specific for ODA loan projects as compared to projects with other official (domestic or foreign) or private financing. This might imply diplomatic considerations as well as different control systems and a number of conditions established by the donors. Within this category there are also some OECF-specific variables, that is, variables that are found in OECF loans but not in other ODA loans. This can be the result of different philosophies, different ways of operating as well as differences in the number and background of staff.

The choice of projects

One of the most crucial methodological questions was the sample, that is, which countries and which projects to use as case studies. A goal was to obtain five reasonably detailed case studies, involving instances in which Japanese companies were the contractors; cases of collaboration between Japanese and other DAC foreign partners; and cases where the major contractor was a local company and, if possible, a European company. The cases studied should be projects within the category of economic infrastructure and preferably different types of projects. The initial focus was on which countries to chose. Since almost 80 per cent of all the Japanese loan aid went to Asia in 1993[25] and there was a significant concentration on certain countries it soon became obvious that the countries in the study should be in Asia and that they should be the major recipients of Japanese ODA.

Indonesia, stands in a class of its own as it has cumulatively received more loan aid than any other country and was, therefore, an obvious choice. China was another such choice, as after a temporary interruption of new projects following the Tiananmen Square incident when a number of people were massacred, it was once again on the list as the largest aid recipient in 1993. Thailand and the Philippines, two countries with differing relations with Japan but both among the top five on the list of countries receiving most aid, were also chosen.

Project selection was based on whether it was a representative and valid major project for that country. The first step was to find out in which sectors in each country Japanese loan aid was most commonly found. In doing this priority was given to the amount of money, rather than to the number of projects.

Projects also needed to be fairly recent cases since Japanese ODA is constantly evolving and has changed considerably in recent years. Availability of data was another reason for choosing more recent cases, so that there was a greater likelihood that the people involved in the selected project were still working in the area and could be used as a source of information. Projects were excluded if the contracting process was still largely incomplete, due to the relative scarcity of information at an earlier stage of a project.

The OECF list of companies that have received orders was one of the tools used in case selection. The list was arranged by recipient country. Information given in the list was project name, type of project, total sum of money provided by OECF as well as the name and nationality of contractors. It soon became apparent that this list was incomplete and did not include all projects and contractors, for example, some contractors listed in 1993 suddenly disappeared from the list in 1994. The list was subsequently complemented by additional lists of projects obtained from the recipient countries.

Every endeavour was made to select as 'typical' cases as possible.

One of the projects first selected was later found to be exceedingly controversial due to environmental considerations and it was, therefore, discarded because information became difficult to obtain. The companies involved would not discuss the project when first contact took place even at an initial level in Tokyo. This was the Kotapanjang Hydroelectric Power and Associated Transmission Line Project in Indonesia. It was deemed prudent to find a substitute case which would be more open to analysis since the purpose of this study was to describe the decision-making process up to the signing of contracts rather than to assess the effects of the project on the environment. Another power project was sought since this sector has received 25 per cent of the Japanese loan aid to the country. The choice fell on Renun Hydroelectric Power Project in northern Sumatra.

In Thailand the road projects have received more money than any other type of project. Therefore, a road project was needed and the choice was made to study the Chonburi–Pattay New Highway. This was the first case study and served as a model for the others. Analysis focused on, among other things, how the project was conceived, progressed, approved, tendered and finally the basis for appointment of contractors. The model was not to be so strictly applied to other countries such that information of importance would be disregarded or that parameters could not be changed depending on the particular circumstances of the case. The Thai case study was instead established as a model to ensure some level of consistency between the cases studies, which was particularly important as there were several people involved in the analysis.

When the Thai case was presented at a very early stage the question was raised as to whether any general conclusions could be drawn from a solitary case in one country. It was, therefore, decided to study two different cases in at least one of the countries. China with its enormous population and land mass was the obvious choice. Two case studies of different types of economic infrastructure in different parts of the country were undertaken in China. One was the Shenzhen Dapeng Bay Yantian Port Project and the other was the Henshui–Shangqiu Railway Construction Project.

In the Philippines, Calaca II, a coal-fired thermal power plant, was chosen for several reasons. One reason was that the researcher was already well-acquainted with the area. Another was simply that this has been the largest OECF-financed economic infrastructure project in the Philippines to date.

RESEARCH PROGRESS

Case studies as a method are of course only fruitful if people and organizations involved are willing to hand out information. This has not always been the case with Japanese ODA, as is clearly shown in earlier research work such as that of Margee Ensign.[26] It is probably also one of the main reasons why studies so far have been largely conducted through white papers and other official documents and not at the implementation level.

The timing of this project seemed fortunate since it happened to coincide with a government campaign for more 'open' access to ODA information. Although somewhat hesitantly at the beginning, an amazing amount of information was finally handed out. This is true both for Japanese officials in Tokyo and those working in the various countries where case studies were conducted. Many of them had a number of meetings with the researchers and their supportive attitude was essential.

The researchers got a surprising amount of information from the officials in recipient countries as well. This was mostly not handed out at first request but required a considerable amount of persistence and confidence-building measures. Numerous interviews were conducted off the record and many of them outside the regular offices.

Besides interviews with officials directly or indirectly involved in the implementation process, in each of the cases a considerable number of interviews where also held with business people, politicians, journalists, NGOs and academics. Relevant written material was collected and analysis of various statistical data undertaken. The study does not rely solely on Japanese statistics, but also on statistics from DAC and other international organizations as well as those from each of the recipient countries. This implies a considerable amount of footwork from all the researchers involved. That is probably another reason why no similar research project has been undertaken so far. It is time-consuming and requires a considerable amount of effort to collect information at the implementation level. This project could not have been undertaken by one person. What was required was a group of researchers working systematically and collecting information on a massive scale.

As the cases were researched, both in Tokyo and in the recipient countries, preliminary drafts were presented at seminars at the European Institute of Japanese Studies in Stockholm. Drafts of all the case studies were also presented to the OECF in Tokyo which then distributed them to the responsible departments and their respective offices in the recipient countries. The comments received from the OECF have, where considered appropriate, been included in the final version. The comments received from some of those involved in the aid administration in the recipient countries have also been included. Various scholars have also read the preliminary drafts and added comments as well as additional information.

In April 1995 a workshop was held in Stockholm in which the cases were presented and discussed with people from the business community with actual experience of ODA projects in Asia, as well as representatives from DAC, OECF and scholars from the recipient countries.

The research method chosen had some limitations. All relevant information was not always obtained. So called 'hidden business costs', or bribes, are, for example, not discussed or are given rather superficial treatment. This is not because they do not exist but rather because there is a lack of reliable information about them. Several enquiries were made but only produced information about 'hidden business costs' in general. In the case of the Philippines, where bribery was investigated by Parliament, certain information could be included.

However, even if the research method was not 100 per cent perfect, which they seldom are outside the textbooks, this study was different in the sense that it was the first that tried to look at aid processes where the action takes place, that is, at the implementation level. The researchers adhered to academic standards as far as possible and got behind the scenes while maintaining independent judgement.

The study is a revolution in analytical perspectives in the sense that it looks at Japanese aid both from a recipient's as well as a donor's point of view. It shows that policy studies carried out so far only explain what is happening at the policy-making level, and bear little relevance to what is actually happening in the recipient countries. If this is what matters, the study is bound to set new standards in the ODA literature on Japan.

STUDY OUTLINE

The first chapter puts Japanese ODA into context. It provides a history of Japanese ODA implementation and a general description of its current status. An analysis is made of the recipients and what kind of aid they have been receiving. The policy-making process, the actors involved and their motives are explored. Comparisons are made between the Japanese approaches and those of other aid donors.

The second chapter is about OECF, the agency responsible for the implementation of the yen loans. Its foundation and development up to the present are analysed. Economic realities of OECF, its personnel, and its organization as well as how this affects its operation in general are discussed. The yen loans are also examined, including who the recipients are, what type of projects and what conditions are imposed. The implementation process as it should work according to the OECF operational manual is also described.

The third chapter addresses the question of how Japanese business responds to ODA. It takes up Keidanren's view on ODA and the significance of aid to the general business of Japanese companies. It looks at ODA versus private investment in Asia. The roles of engineering consulting firms and the trading houses are considered and there is a case study of how one company approaches aid.

Chapter 4 is the Thai case study, Chapter 5 the Indonesian, Chapter 6 the Philippine one and Chapters 7 and 8 the Chinese cases. These chapters constitute the main part of this book in which the implementation of ODA is described in detail. In each chapter conclusions are drawn on the specific case.

In Chapter 9 a comparison is provided between the cases and conclusions are drawn about how the process works in general and what the roles of the different actors are. Contrary to conventional wisdom, there appears to be considerable diversity within Japanese aid and room for outsiders to act. Knowledge of the processes should be of help for researchers, business people, environmentalists, aid administrators, politicians and others interested in the field whether they want to work within the system or to change it.

NOTES

1 Aid will be defined here according to the same rules as ODA within the OECD's Development Assistance Committee (see note 2) which means that it should be: (1) resources provided by official agencies or by their executing agencies; (2) the main objective being the promotion of the economic development and welfare of developing countries; (3) its concessional character is due to the effort to avoid placing a heavy burden on developing countries, and thus consists of a grant element of at least 25 per cent.
2 The Development Assistance Committee is OECD's special committee to deal with foreign aid. Its 22 members are Australia, Austria, Belgium, Canada, Denmark, Finland, France, Germany, Ireland, Italy, Japan, Luxembourg, The Netherlands, New Zealand, Norway, Portugal, Spain, Sweden, Switzerland, the United Kingdom, the United States and the Commission of the European Communities.

3 Rehman Sobhan, *From Aid Dependence to Self Reliance*, BIDS-UPL, Dhaka,1990.

4 OECD calculations suggest it would be worth twice the annual flow of foreign aid see 'Empty promises', *Economist*, 7 May 1994.

5 To be considered as ODA these loans must have conditions (that is, interest rates and periods of grace) that are soft enough to correspond to a grant element of 25 per cent, although in the end the recipient still has to pay the whole sum of the loan back.

6 That is, ODA that the recipient does not have to pay back.

7 See for example Kazuo Sumi, *ODA Enjo no Genjitsu*, Iwanami Shinshō, Tokyo, 1989 or Yoshinori Murai, *Musekinin Enjo Taikoku Nihon*, JICC, Tokyo, 1989.

8 See for example Masamichi Hanabusa, 'A Japanese perspective on aid and development' in Shafique Islam (ed.), *Yen for Development: Japanese Foreign Aid and the Politics of Burden-Sharing*, Council on Foreign Relations Press, New York, 1991.

9 See for example a 400-page report presented by the World Bank, *The East Asian Miracle, Economic Growth and Public Policy*, Oxford University Press, New York, 1993. Financial assistance for the report was given by the Government of Japan.

10 Takako Doi, Yoshinori Murai and Keiichi Yoshimura, *ODA Kaikaku, Kanada Gikai kara no Teigen to Nihon no Genjō*, Shakaishisōsha, Tokyo, 1990.

11 Department of International Development Co-operation, Ministry of Foreign Affairs, Sweden, *In Support of Asian Development*, Stockholm, 1992.

12 Alan Rix, *Japan's Economic Aid: Policy-making and Politics*, Croom Helm, London, 1980.

13 Kenji Suzuki, *Kokusaiha Giin to Riken no Uchimaku*, Yell Books, Tokyo, 1989.

14 David Arase, *Buying Power: The Political Economy of Japan's Foreign Aid*, Lynne Rienner Boulder, CO, 1995.

15 Robert M. Orr Jr, *The Emergence of Japan's Foreign Aid Power*, Columbia University Press, New York, 1990.

16 Shafique Islam (ed.), op. cit.

17 Dennis Yasutomo, *The Manner of Giving: Strategic Aid and Japanese Foreign Policy*, Lexington Books, Lexington, 1986. (This study was completed before the end of the Cold War.)

18 Akira Nishigaki and Yasutami Shimomura, *Kaihatsu Enjo no Keizaigaku*, Yuhaikaku, Japan, 1993.

19 A recent example is the work by Margee Ensign, *Doing Good or Doing Well? Japan's Foreign Aid Program*, Columbia University Press, New York, 1993.

20 This list was first published in 1992. For the one from 1994 see Appendix I.

21 Ministry of Foreign Affairs, *How to Gain Access to Japanese Financing of Official Development Assistance (ODA)*, Copenhagen, 1994.

22 The Swedish Embassy has a special programme for informing about coming Japanese ODA projects as well as helping Swedish companies get acquainted with appropriate officials and organizations. The Swedish

Export Council hosted a seminar under the title 'Japanese ODA Seeks Help from Swedish Companies' in September 1994.

23 Marie Söderberg, 'Japanese Development Aid: Trendiness versus Reality', *Japan Forum*, 5(2), Oxford University Press, 1993, pp. 217–31.

24 For more information on Japanese multilateral aid see Dennis T. Yasutomo, *The New Multilateralism in Japan's Foreign Policy*, Macmillan, London, 1995.

25 Figures according to OECF, *Annual Report 1994*.

26 Margee Ensign, op. cit.

APPENDIX I

Principal contractors under OECF loans to foreign governments (FY 1993)

Country	Project name	Loan agreement		Principal contractor
		Date of approval	Amount of approval (¥ million)	Principal contractors in FY 1993
Asia				
Bangladesh	Greater Dhaka Telecommunications Network Improvement Project (II)	28 May 1992	14,761	Nippon Telecommunications Consulting (Japan)*
China	Hengyang–Guangzhou Railway Transportation Reinforcement Project (IV)	6 July 1987	8,789	Sunkyong Ltd (Korea)
	Wuqiangxi Hydroelectric Power Project (I)	3 Aug. 1988	2,470	Hunan Provincial Machinery Import & Export Group Corp. (China), Electric Power Development (Japan)*
	Wuqiangxi Hydroelectric Power Project (II)	23 May 1989	6,020	Hunan Provincial Machinery Import & Export Group Corp. (China), Mitsubishi Corp. (Japan)
	Hengshui–Shangqiu Railway Construction Project (I)	28 Mar. 1991	5,695	Hainan Flywheel Industries Trading Co. (China)
	Wuqiangxi Hydroelectric Power Project (IV)	4 Oct. 1991	8,100	Hunan Provincial Machinery Import & Export Group Corp. (China), Mitsubishi Corp. (Japan)
	Yunnan Fertilizer Plant Construction Project (II)	4 Oct. 1991	5,690	China National Chemical Construction Corp. (China)

APPENDIX I *continued*

Country	Loan agreement			Principal contractor
	Project name	Date of approval	Amount of approval (¥ million)	Principal contractors in FY 1993
China	Nine Provinces and Cities Telecommunication Network Expansion Project (II)	4 Oct. 1991	11,576	Sumitomo Corp. (Japan), Marubeni Corp. (Japan)
	Shenmu–Shuoxian Railway Construction Project (II)	4 Oct. 1991	9,940	Shenzhen Hua Shen Material & Equipment (China), China Resources Metals & Minerals (Hong Kong)
	Hengshui–Shangqiu Railway Construction Project (II)	4 Oct. 1991	6,550	Hainan Flywheel Industries Trading Co. (China)
	Tianshengqiao First Hydro Power Project (I)	4 Oct. 1991	4,367	Teshmont Consultants Inc. (Canada)*, Electric Power Development/Nippon Koei (Japan, Japan)*
	Nanning–Kunming Railway Construction Project (I)	4 Oct. 1991	5,461	Voest-Alpine Schienen GmbH (Austria)
	Luzhai Fertilizer Plant Construction Project (I)	4 Oct. 1991	2,898	Technip Division Technip Speichim Tour Technip (France), Siry Chamon Impianti SpA (Italy)
	Wuqiangxi Hydroelectric Power Project (V)	15 Oct. 1992	5,400	Mitsubishi Corp. (Japan)
	Nine Provinces and Cities Telecommunication Network Expansion Project (III)	15 Oct. 1992	14,358	Nissho Iwai (Japan)

Project	Date	Amount	Company
Air Navigation and Air Traffic Control Modernization Project (III)	15 Oct. 1992	9,896	Itochu Aviation (Japan)
Baoji–Zhongwei Railway Construction Project (III)	15 Oct. 1992	12,901	Marubeni Corp. (Japan), ABB Transformers AB (Sweden), Mitsubishi Corp. (Japan), Empresa Nacional Siderurgica SA (Spain), Voest-Alpine Schienen GmbH (Austria)
Nanning–Kunming Railway Construction Project (II)	15 Oct. 1992	9,904	
Luzhai Fertilizer Plant Construction Project (II)	15 Oct. 1992	3,069	Siry Chamon Impianti SpA (Italy)
Inner Mongolia Fertilizer Plant Construction Project (IV)	25 Aug. 1993	4,509	Snamprogetti SpA (Italy), Toyo Engineering (Japan)
Yunnan Fertilizer Plant Construction Project (III)	25 Aug. 1993	5,745	China National Chemical Construction Corp. (China)
Hengshui–Shangqiu Railway Construction Project (IV)	25 Aug. 1993	6,407	Sumitomo Corp. (Japan)
Tiansehngqiao First Hydro Power Project (III)	25 Aug. 1993	16,647	Electric Power Development/Nippon Koei (Japan, Japan)*
Luzhai Fertilizer Plant Construction Project (III)	25 Aug. 1993	3,700	Siry Chamon Impianti SpA (Italy)
Jiujiang Fertilizer Plant Construction Project (III)	25 Aug. 1993	9,757	Snamprogetti SpA (Italy), Toyo Engineering (Japan)
Fujian Province Zhang Quan Railway Construction Project	25 Aug. 1993	6,720	China Resources Metals & Minerals (Hong Kong)
India			
Assam Gas Turbine Power Station and Transmission Line Construction Project (II)	10 Feb. 1988	13,552	Hyundai Corp. (Korea), Bharat Heavy Electricals (India)

APPENDIX I *continued*

Country	Loan agreement			Principal contractor
	Project name	Date of approval	Amount of approval (¥ million)	Principal contractors in FY 1993
India	Anpara B Thermal Power Station Construction Project	13 June 1991	19,318	Tokyo Electric Power Services/Tata Consulting Engineers (Japan, India)*, Bharat Heavy Electricals (India), SAE (India), Asea Brown Boveri Ltd India (India), Crompton Greaves (India)
	Ajanta–Ellora Conservation and Tourism Development Project	9 Jan. 1992	3,745	Pacific Consultants International/Tata Consulting Engineers (Japan, India)*
	Anpara B Thermal Power Station Construction Project (IV)	3 Dec. 1992	13,224	EPDC International/Tokyo Electric Power Services (Japan, Japan)*
	Gandhar Gas Based Combined Cycle Power Project (III)	21 Dec. 1992	19,538	Marubeni Corp. (Japan)
	Bakreswar Thermal Power Project	24 Jan. 1994	27,069	EPDC International (Japan)*
	Anpara B Thermal Power Station Construction Project (V)	24 Jan. 1994	17,638	EPDC International/Tokyo Electric Power Services (Japan, Japan)*, Mitsui & Co. (Japan)
Indonesia	Jabotabek Area Railway Project (VI)	8 Dec. 1987	13,565	Pacific Consultants International/Japan Transportation Consultants/Japan Electrical Consulting/PT Intra Era Cipta (Japan, Japan, Japan, Indonesia)*
	Rehabilitation of Diesel Railcars Project	5 July 1988	4,819	Sumitomo Corp./PT Humpuss Trading (Japan, Indonesia)

Project	Date	Amount	Contractors/Consultants
Road Rehabilitation Project	21 Oct. 1988	29,538	PT Abun Sendi (Indonesia), PT Kaliraya Sari (Indonesia)
Jabotabek Area Railway Project (VII)	22 Dec. 1989	10,381	Pacific Consultants International/Japan Transportation Consultants/Japan Electrical Consulting/PT Intra Era Cipta (Japan, Japan, Japan, Japan, Indonesia)*
Rehabilitation of Irrigation and Flood Alleviation Works	22 Dec. 1989	21,518	Kumagai Gumi/PT Kadi International/PT Nindya Karya/Hitachi/PT Ruhaak Phala Industri (Japan, Indonesia, Indonesia, Japan, Indonesia)
Bila Irrigation Project (I)	14 Dec. 1990	6,460	PT Wijaya Karya (Indonesia)
Ujung Pandang Port Urgent Rehabilitation Project	14 Dec. 1990	6,658	Wakachiku Construction/Sumitomo Corp./PT Jaya Sumpiles Indonesia (Japan, Japan, Indonesia)
Maritime Transportation Sector Loan in Eastern Indonesia (I)	25 Sep. 1991	8,499	Japan Association for Aid to Navigation/PT Waskita Perdana Konsultan (Japan, Indonesia)*, Pacific Consultants International/PT Diagram Triproporsi/PT Intiera Cipta (Japan, Indonesia, Indonesia)*, Overseas Shipbuilding Cooperation Center (Japan)*, Overseas Shipbuilding Cooperation Center/PT Tomo & Son (Japan, Indonesia)*, Overseas Shipbuilding Cooperation Center/PT Bina Cita Mayapada (Japan, Indonesia)*, Pacific Consultants Internation/PT Peicinal/PT Wiratman & Associates/PT Bita Enarcon Engineering (Japan, Indonesia, Indonesia, Indonesia)*

APPENDIX I *continued*

| Country | Loan agreement | | | Principal contractor |
	Project name	Date of approval	Amount of approval (¥ million)	Principal contractors in FY 1993
Indonesia	Kotapanjang Hydroelectric Power and Associated Transmission Line Project (II)	25 Sep. 1991	17,525	Sumitomo Corp. (Japan), Elin Energieversorgung (Austria), Kvaerner Boving (United Kingdom)
	Java–Bali Power Transmission Line and Substation Project (East Java)	25 Sep. 1991	7,671	Lucky Engineering (Korea)
	Heavy Loaded Road Improvement Project	25 Sept. 1991	11,992	PT Teguh Raksa Jaya/PT Bumi Redjo (Indonesia, Indonesia)
	Junction Network for Expanded Jakarta Exchange Area Project	25 Sep. 1991	3,556	Tomen Corp. (Japan)
	Way Sekampung Irrigation Project (I)	8 Oct. 1992	7,653	Nippon Koei/Sinotech Engineering Consultants/PT Bhakti Werdhatama Konsultan/PT Indra Karya/PT Virama Karya/PT Yodya Karya/PT Wiratman & Associates/Indec & Associates (Japan, Taiwan, Indonesia, Indonesia, Indonesia, Indonesia, Indonesia, Indonesia)*
	South Sumatra Swamp Improvement Project	8 Oct. 1992	5,577	Euroconsult/Pacific Consultants International/Indec & Associates/PT Nusvey/PT Bias Reka (Netherlands, Japan, Indonesia, Indonesia, Indonesia)*

Project	Date	Amount	Consultants
Bili–Bili Multipurpose Dam Project (II)	8 Oct. 1992	20,798	CTI Engineering/PT Virama Karya/PT Indra Karya/PT DDC Consultants (Japan, Indonesia, Indonesia, Indonesia)*, Hazama Corp./PT Brantas Abipraya (Japan, Indonesia)
Java–Bali Power Transmission Line and Substation Project (II)	8 Oct. 1992	6,862	New Jec (Japan)*, Lucky Engineering (Korea)
Development Project of Institute of Technology in Bandung (I)	8 Oct. 1992	1,609	Pacific Consultants International/Nissoken Architects & Engineers/Yamashita Sekkei/PT Wiratman & Associates/PT Bita Enarcon Engineering (Japan, Japan, Japan, Indonesia, Indonesia)*
Semarang Port Development Project (II-2)	8 Oct. 1992	3,590	Japan Port Consultants/PT Wiratman & Associates (Japan, Indonesia)*
Jabotabek Area Railway Project (IX)	8 Oct. 1992	15,347	Pacific Consultants International/Japan Transportation Consultants/Japan Electrical Consulting/PT Intra Era Cipta/PT Kutami & Associates/PT Jaya CM Manggala Pretama (Japan, Japan, Japan, Indonesia, Indonesia, Indonesia)*
North Java Line Track Rehabilitation Project (I)	8 Oct. 1992	3,302	Japan Transportation Consultants/Pacific Consultants International/PT Intra Era Cipta (Japan, Japan, Indonesia)*
Engineering Services for Sipansihaporas Hydroelectric Power Project	30 Nov. 1992	820	Tokyo Electric Power Services (Japan)*
Engineering Services for Central Sumatra Forest Rehabilitation Project	30 Nov. 1992	426	Japan Overseas Forest Consultants Association/Pacific Consultants International/PT Tri Tunggal Konsultan/PT Aero Karto Indonesia (Japan, Japan, Indonesia, Indonesia)*

APPENDIX I *continued*

Country	Loan agreement			Principal contractor
	Project name	Date of approval	Amount of approval (¥ million)	Principal contractors in FY 1993
Indonesia	Engineering Services for Surabaya Airport Construction Project	30 Nov. 1992	519	Japan Airport Consultants (Japan)*
	Surabaya Urban Development Project (I)	26 Feb. 1993	11,251	Pacific Consultants International (Japan)*
	Rehabilitation of Radio and Television Networks (II)	4 Nov. 1993	708	NHK Integrated Technology (Japan)*
Korea	Seoul Subway Construction Project (II)	31 Oct. 1990	72,000	Kangwon Industries (Korea), Hyundai Precision & Ind. (Korea)
	Livestock Feedmills Construction Project	31 Oct. 1990	5,414	Hanil Development (Korea)
	Meat Processing Plant Construction Project	31 Oct. 1990	1,728	Intercool Food Technology (Denmark)
Malaysia	Higher Education Loan Fund Project (HELP)	28 May 1992	5,493	Japan–Indonesia Science and Technology Forum (JIF) (Japan)*
	Port Klang Power Station (III)	28 May 1992	31,966	EPDC International (Japan)*
Mongolia	Railway Transportation Rehabilitation Project	26 Nov. 1993	3,321	Pacific Consultants International/Japan Railway Technical Service/Japan Transportation Consultants (Japan, Japan, Japan)*

Country	Project	Date	Amount	Contractors
Pakistan	Rural Electrification Project	1 Nov. 1988	20,738	Face (PVT) (Pakistan)*, Pakistan Engineering Services (Pakistan)*, Indus Associated Consultants (Pakistan)*, Jafri and Associates/Engineering Services (Pakistan, Pakistan)*
	Indus Highway Project	30 Mar. 1989	8,516	Saitagumi (Japan)
	Daudkhel Fertilizer Plant Modernization Project	30 Mar. 1989	18,598	Toyo Engineering Corp. (Japan)
	Metropolitan Water Supply Project (Simly)	30 Mar. 1989	5,750	Taisei Corp. (Japan)
	Indus Highway Project (II)	14 Jan. 1991	20,778	Frontier Works Organization (Pakistan), China Petroleum Engineering Construction (China), Pacific Consultants International/ Nippon Koei (Japan, Japan)*
	Bin Qasim Thermal Power Station Extension Unit 6 Project (I)	6 Mar. 1992	13,551	Marubeni Corp. (Japan), Interhom (PVT) (Pakistan)
	Track Circuits at 94 Mainline Stations Project	6 Mar. 1992	3,221	Marubeni Corp. (Japan)
	On-Farm Water Management Project	6 Mar. 1992	8,230	Halcrow Rural Management (England)*
Philippines	Metro Manila Circumferential Road No. 5 and Radial Road No. 4 Construction Project	27 Jan. 1988	4,837	E. Ramos Construction (Philippines)
	West and Northwest Leyte Road Improvement Project (II)	26 May 1989	5,500	F.T. Sanchez/Kimwa/Socor Construction (Philippines, Philippines, Philippines)
	Pampanga Delta Development Project, Flood Control Component (I)	9 Feb. 1990	8,634	Hanil Development (Korea), Leadway Construction (Philippines)

APPENDIX I *continued*

Country	Loan agreement			Principal contractor
	Project name	Date of approval	Amount of approval (¥ million)	Principal contractors in FY 1993
Philippines	Maritime Safety Improvement Project	16 July 1991	3,516	Kanematsu Corp. (Japan)
	Fishing Ports Development Project (II)	20 Mar. 1992	7,655	Engineering Equipment Inc./J.E. Manalo (Philippines, Philippines)
	Provincial Cities Water Supply Project (II)	26 May 1992	1,094	Nippon Jogesuido Sekkei (Japan)*
	Regional Telecommunication Development Project (III) in Regions I & II, Phase C	19 Aug. 1993	3,803	Nippon Telecommunications Consulting (Japan)*
Sri Lanka	Transmission System Augmentation and Development Project	22 Nov. 1988	4,360	Marubeni Corp. (Japan), Sri U-Thong/Itochu Corp. (Thailand, Japan)
	Towns East of Colombo Water Supply Project	28 Mar. 1990	1,997	China National Overseas Engineering Corp. (China)
	Greater Colombo Telecommunication Network Improvement Project (II)	18 Mar. 1991	10,968	Sumitomo Corp. (Japan)
	Port of Colombo Extension Project (II)	18 Mar. 1991	11,021	Tomen Corp. (Japan)
	Port of Colombo Extension Project (III)	31 Mar. 1992	21,055	Tomen Corp. (Japan)

	Project	Date	Amount	Consultants/Contractors
	Greater Colombo Flood Control and Environment Improvement Project	31 Mar. 1992	11,198	Kajima Corp./Keang Nam Enterprises (Japan, Korea)
	Upper Kotmale Hydroelectric Power Project (Engineering Services)	31 Mar. 1992	1,482	Chuo Kaihatsu Corp./Nippon Koei Corp./EPDC International/Central Engineering Consultancy (Japan, Japan, Japan, Sri Lanka)*
	Port of Colombo Extension Project (IV)	12 Aug. 1993	7,728	Tomen Corp. (Japan), Overseas Coastal Area Development Institute of Japan/Japan Port Consultants (Japan, Japan)*
Thailand	Map Ta Phut–Sattahip Water Pipeline Project	22 Nov. 1988	1,459	CTI Engineering/Sanyu Consultants Inc./Team Consulting Engineers (Japan, Japan, Thailand)*
	Klong Sip Kao–Kaeng Khoi Railway Project	20 Feb. 1990	8,158	Pacific Consultants International/Japan Electrical Consulting/Thai Professional Engineering Consultants (Japan, Japan, Thailand)*
	Telephone Network Expansion Project (Local Cable Network)	11 Sep. 1990	15,318	Sumitomo Electric Industries/Thai Sumiden Engineering & Construction/PDTL Trading (Japan, Thailand, Thailand)
	Outer Bangkok Ring Road (East Portion) Construction Project (I)	7 Dec. 1990	12,958	Prayoonvisava Engineering (Thailand), L.C.C. Limcharoen (Thailand), Metropolitan Concrete Products (Thailand), The Civil Engineering (Thailand), Rojsin Construction Engineering (Thailand)

APPENDIX I *continued*

Country	Loan agreement			Principal contractor
	Project name	Date of approval	Amount of approval (¥ million)	Principal contractors in FY 1993
Thailand	Bangkok–Chonburi Highway Construction Project (I)	7 Dec. 1990	15,497	Sermsanguan Construction (Thailand), Namprasert Construction (Thailand), The Construction Sahaphandh (Thailand), Thaipipatana Limited Partnership (Thailand), Vianini Lavori SpA/Vianini Thai Construction and Development/Nawarat Patanakarn (Italy, Thailand, Thailand), Ch. Karnchang/Ch. Karnchang-Tokyu Construction/Tokyu Construction (Thailand, Thailand, Japan)
	Bhumibol Hydroelectric Project Unit 8	18 Sep. 1991	7,854	Kvaerner Energy AS/ABB Power Generation (Norway, Switzerland)
	Ramindra-Atnarong Expressway Project	18 Sep. 1991	14,804	Vichitbhan Construction/See Sang Karn Yotah (1979)/Krung Thon Engineers (Thailand, Thailand, Thailand), Tokyu Construction/Ch. Karnchang/Ch. Karnchang–Tokyu Construction (Japan, Thailand, Thailand), Vianini Lavori SpA/Nawarat Patanakarn/Vianini Thai Construction and Development (Italy, Thailand, Thailand), Bhrom Vivat/Metropolitan Concrete Products (Thailand, Thailand), Pacific Consultants International/Epilson/Southeast Asia Technology/Thai Engineering Consultants

Thailand	The Fourth Bangkok Water Supply Improvement Project (I)	18 Sep. 1991	8,638	Italian Thai Development (Thailand)
	Map Ta Phut Port Project (III)	18 Sep. 1991	3,395	Sahaisant (Thailand)
	Chonburi–Pattaya New Highway Construction Project (II)	18 Sep. 1991	5,670	Thaiwat Engineering/Vanitchai Construction (1979) (Thailand, Thailand)
	The Sirikit Hydroelectric Project Unit 4	29 Jan. 1993	4,404	Mitsubishi Corp. (Japan), Acres International (Canada)*
	Ramindra–Atnarong Expressway Construction Project (II)	29 Jan. 1993	21,850	Pacific Consultants International/Epsilon/ Southeast Asia Technology/Thai Engineering Consultants (Japan, Thailand, Thailand, Thailand)*
	Fourth Bangkok Water Supply Improvement Project (Phase II) and The Fifth Bangkok Water Supply Improvement Project	29 Jan. 1993	16,969	Asano Engineering (Japan), SAFEGE Consulting Engineers/Team Consulting Engineers (France, Thailand)*
	Nong Pla Lai–Nong Kho Water Pipeline Project	29 Jan. 1993	6,362	Sanyu Consultants/Team Consulting Engineers (Japan, Thailand)*, Summit Grade Ltd, Partnership (Thailand)
Middle East				
Iran	Godar-e-Landar Hydroelectric Power Project	2 June 1993	38,614	Nippon Koei/Moshanir Power Engineering Consultants/Lahmeyer International GmbH (Japan, Iran, Germany)*
Jordan	Road Improvement Project	26 Jan. 1989	13,424	Consulting Engineering Center (Jordan)*
Syria	Jandar Power Station Project	11 June 1991	51,598	Ekono Energy Ltd (Finland)*
Turkey	Renovation and Widening Project for the Golden Horn Bridge	5 Apr. 1991	13,763	Ishikawajima-Harima Heavy Industries/ Enka Insaat/Bayindir Insaat (Japan, Turkey, Turkey)

APPENDIX I *continued*

Country	Loan agreement			Principal contractor
	Project name	Date of approval	Amount of approval (¥ million)	Principal contractors in FY 1993
Africa				
Ghana	Telecommunication Expansion Project (II)	14 Dec. 1988	10,508	Marubeni Corp./Itochu Corp. (Japan, Japan), Telecommunications Consultants India (India), Marubeni Corp. (Japan)
Kenya	Mombasa Airport Improvement Project	30 Mar. 1990	9,010	Takenaka/Mitsubishi Corp. (Japan, Japan)
	Cement Plant Rehabilitation Project	30 Mar. 1990	7,674	Tomen Corp. (Japan)
Latin America and Carribean				
Bolivia	Patacamaya–Tambo Quemado Road Improvement Project	21 Oct. 1992	3,955	Empresa Constructiones y Comercio Camargo Correa SA (Brazil)
Brazil	State of Goias Rural Electrification Project	5 Sep. 1991	12,832	Alcoa/Alcun/Furukawa (Brazil, Brazil, Brazil), Electric Power Development (Japan)*, Internacional de Engenharia SA (Brazil)*
	Santos Port Development Project	5 Sep. 1991	28,889	Pacific Consultants International (Japan)*

Country	Project	Date	Amount	Company
Chile	Laja–Diguillin Irrigation Project	20 Nov. 1991	12,477	Minmetal Ltda/Chuo Kaihatsu Corp./Black and Veatch International (Chile, Japan, USA)*
	Railway Rehabilitation Project	20 Nov. 1991	6,412	Pacific Consultants International/Japan Railway Technical Service/Libra Ingenieros Consultores Ltda (Japan/Japan/Chile)*
Columbia	Bogata Water Supply Improvement Project	5 Dec. 1991	8,375	Cogefarimpresit Costruzioni Generali SpA (Italy)
El Salvador	Power Sector Emergency Improvement Project	19 Mar. 1993	8,817	Harza Engineering Company International L.P. (USA)*
Guatemala	Metropolitan Guatemala City Telecommunication Expansion Project	9 Feb. 1990	5,875	NTT International (Japan)*
Jamaica	North Coast Development Project	29 Oct. 1991	8,606	DHV International (UK) Ltd (Holland)*, Stanley Consultants Inc. (USA)*
Mexico	The Mexico City Sulfur Dioxide Emission Reduction Project	7 Nov. 1990	69,338	Snamprogetti SpA (Italy)
	Monterrey Water Supply and Sewerage Project	20 Oct. 1992	13,482	Desarrollo y Construcciones Urbanas SA de CV (Mexico), Atlatec, SA de CV (Mexico), Sumitomo Corp. (Japan)
	Mexico Metropolitan Area Reforestation Project	20 Oct. 1992	10,403	Chuo Kaihatsu Corp. (Japan)*
Paraguay	Agricultural Sector Strengthening Project	26 Aug. 1987	11,847	Ecomipa S.A./Estructura Ingenieria SRL (Paraguay, Paraguay)

APPENDIX I   *continued*

Notes 1 ● Publication of the contractors' names is subject to the approval of recipient countries
● Names of contractors listed above received contract amounting to more than ¥100 million or equivalent value for consulting services, or ¥1,000 million or equivalent value for others

2 Contractors with* are consulting firms which deal with consulting services of the project

3 Contractors under OECF Commodity Loan and Two-Step Loan are not listed above

1 Japanese ODA – what type, for whom and why?

Marie Söderberg

In January 1995 the city of Kobe in Japan was shaken by an earthquake which made 300,000 people homeless and took more than 5,000 lives. Reaction on the stock market was immediate: stocks associated with construction and glass production rose quickly while insurance companies' stocks slumped. The news media also responded swiftly by sending up helicopters to view the catastrophe.

Official initiatives to help the stricken population were not so timely. It took two full days before 13,000 troops from the Self Defence Forces could be deployed to the disaster area as bureaucrats and politicians bickered over the precise wording of the official request for assistance. There was a shortage of water in the area yet it took several days before neighbouring provinces decided to help by sending in supplies.[1] Several weeks after the earthquake there were still people camping out in parks without shelter even though the temperature was near freezing point. Help from American doctors and a Swiss rescue team of dog handlers that could have arrived within hours was delayed for days due to bureaucratic red tape. When Japan finally accepted help offered from countries such as the Philippines and South Korea, the government legitimized it by stating that acceptance would ease these countries' ability to accept future aid from Japan. It took a number of days before the Japanese Prime Minister visited the area. He was shown on television meeting the victims, urging them to struggle on (*gambatte kudasai*). Hospitals were overcrowded and influenza epidemics raged among the survivors.

A few months earlier another major catastrophe had happened, this time in the Baltic Sea. The passenger ship *Estonia* sank to the bottom of the sea, killing more than 800 people. This was the worst sea accident ever experienced in this part of the world. The reaction was immediate. Within hours the Swedish Prime Minister had flown to

Helsinki to meet his Finnish and Estonian counterparts and to be directly involved in the rescue operation. In most towns groups were promptly formed by church members, private citizens and doctors to help the relatives and friends of those killed as well as the few survivors.

These two incidents are very different and are, therefore, difficult to compare. However, the differences in the implementation of 'official aid' between Japan and other developed countries can be highlighted – differences that are of importance to the concept of foreign aid and that are rooted in two markedly different cultural backgrounds.

In the West there is a tradition of helping people in other countries that extends back at least a century. The Church has often played a central role and numerous voluntary organizations have been active in the field at home as well as in the recipient countries. A decision not to take immediate action and 'send in the marines' during the *Estonia* catastrophe would have been unthinkable in the West. Indeed, a Prime Minister who did not engage himself personally in the rescue operations would have been politically dead.

The same is true for many other aid activities, that is, the provision of social, health and public services, within Swedish society and many other Western countries. For example, anyone seriously ill is given immediate treatment at a Swedish hospital whereas in Japan patients are expected to prove that they are able to pay the bill before treatment is given.

These values, based on human life being considered sacred, have always been fundamental to Western foreign aid, even if they do not always dominate other government considerations such as ideology, foreign policy, defence strategy and business concerns.

Christians are quite obviously not the only ones who help others. There are numerous examples of how they have not helped at all, the Nazis in Germany who claimed to be Christians being one of the most extreme examples. The European crusaders that colonized other peoples in the name of Christ are another example. Of course Japanese people helped others in connection with the Kobe earthquake. There are numerous stories of how local people worked day and night trying to dig out victims trapped under collapsed houses. Japanese people have helped each other on a number of other occasions as well.[2]

However, the situation with the Japanese government is a little different. The victims in Kobe did not receive new houses but instead received loans enabling them to build houses for themselves. Rather than grants they were given 'help to self-help', a concept and a way of thinking that influences Japanese foreign aid as well.

The basis for official aid and the way it is implemented in Japan and in the West are different. The Church has been at the forefront of Western foreign aid. Missionaries have often accompanied this aid, which means that besides providing physical aid there have been definite ideas of how other people should live their lives, build their societies and what their beliefs should be. They have intervened dramatically in local societies, using both the carrot and the stick approaches to dealing with what they thought was right and wrong. Japan has not had such a tradition of intervention.

Among DAC members, Japan is the only country that is not dominated by Judeo-Christian values.[3] In comparison to other countries it has very few people working with foreign aid either on a voluntary or professional basis, although it provides almost one-fifth of all the ODA. Japan's history of providing aid is also relatively short.

HISTORICAL BACKGROUND

In 1994 Japan celebrated the fortieth anniversary of its ODA programme, according to the Foreign Ministry.[4] As the term 'ODA' did not exist 40 years ago one must assume that what was meant was the fortieth anniversary of Japan's foreign aid programme, or rather economic co-operation programme. The term foreign aid is not used in Japan and up till 1958 the distinction was never made between 'aid' and other forms of economic co-operation, a concept that includes official flows in general as well as private direct investment.

Although foreign aid today has a distinct budget of its own, it is still seen within this concept. ODA is one of three avenues of Japan's economic co-operation with developing countries. The others are other official flows and private direct investment.

In 1954 Japan became a donor through a $50,000 contribution to the Colombo Plan. War reparation is also presented as an origin of 'aid', although it was not presented as such at the time. Agreements on war reparations were signed with Burma in 1954, the Philippines in 1956 and Indonesia in 1958. These war reparations were given to build up what had been damaged during World War II, that is, mainly the infrastructure. Money was 'tied' and rather than aid, it can be regarded as the promotion of exports from Japanese industry. It was given to the countries which suffered under Japanese aggression during the war but not to the People's Republic of China, because of the communist take-over and Japan's alliance with the USA, and was not given to South Korea until 1965.

Major government economic co-operation began with the yen loan programme of 1957 in which priority was initially given to South East Asia. Between 1957 and 1964 16 of 21 loan agreements were for India or Pakistan. These were all loans from the Export-Import Bank of Japan and were based on interest rates that would not have qualified them as ODA within the present definition.[5] The emphasis was on co-operation and to a large extent this money, besides filling certain needs in the developing countries, also served the purpose of establishing Japanese industry in Asia. During the 1960s the Japanese economy became strong enough to establish the country as an international power. Japan joined OECD and provided the first grant aid in the same year, 1969, as the Development Assistance Committee (DAC) introduced the concept of ODA.[6]

Aid in the 1960s was almost totally confined to Asia and overwhelmingly served commercial purposes, but this pattern changed with the oil crisis of 1973. Japan's vulnerability due to heavy energy imports became obvious when the Organization of Petroleum Exporting Countries (OPEC) placed an oil embargo on the USA and its allies who had, at least morally, supported Israel during the Yom Kippur War.

It was at this time that the implementation of aid became politicized. Aid was used as a diplomatic tool to restore neutralist credibility in the Arab world. A Japanese mission, endowed with a huge aid package, was sent out to placate Arab anger. As a consequence of the oil crises the stable supply of natural resources became another ingredient of Japanese aid policy. It also gave rise to the unofficially adopted 7:1:1:1 regional distribution doctrine in which 70 per cent of aid is earmarked for Asia and 10 per cent each for the Middle East, Latin America and Africa.[7]

By the end of the 1970s the Japanese Ministry of Foreign Affairs (MOFA) had two motives as justification for aid. One was that Japan should contribute to peace and stability in the world. As a 'peace' country (that is, a country without military power[8]) the only means to do this was through economic aid. The second motive was related to the first and had to do with Japan's image of itself as a country poor in natural resources. Trade was a prerequisite to obtain resources and Japan recognized its significant interdependence with the developing countries. A certain amount of infrastructure was needed to conduct trade effectively and to extract natural resources in Asia. That was why Japanese aid money should be spent on economic infrastructure. At this time aid was regarded as a necessary cost for acheiving a more secure and peaceful world and Japan's own prosperous development in the future. In 1977 Prime Minister Fukuda announced the first of a number of aid-doubling plans that would eventually make Japan the world's leading provider of ODA. These aid-doubling plans gave another motive to Japanese ODA, namely, the wish to be respected in the international community where considerable 'Japan bashing' was occurring. It was also a way to improve Japan's image in Asia where Japanese business activities had left far from favourable images of the country. This was the start of the so called gift-giving diplomacy (*omiyage gaiko*), which since then has been extensively used by Japanese Prime Ministers touring in Asia.

Humanitarian considerations, as reasons for aid, did not appear with any weight until the late 1970s. They were mentioned as one of five main considerations for Japan's economic co-operation policy by MOFA in 1978 together with international economic security, Japan's duty as an economic power, economic self-interest and what was called 'normal diplomatic necessity'.[9]

For a number of years an obsession with the quantity of aid was evident until Japan in 1989 became the world's biggest donor of ODA.

JAPANESE ODA TODAY

Since 1989, (with the exception of one year) Japan has continued to be the world's biggest donor of ODA. Considering that substantial increases have not been announced by any other country, this places Japan in a class of its own as the world's leading donor nation. If it is viewed in this way, Japan appears to be a responsible nation with a strong social conscience. Indeed, a new leadership role for Japan in this field is envisaged by some government officials.

An analysis of Japanese ODA statistics reveals another picture. Despite being the number one donor in absolute terms, Japan gives only 0.26 per cent of its GNP which is well below the average of DAC countries. In fact, it places Japan in seventeenth place among 21 DAC countries. Although it has adopted the UN goal of using 0.7 per cent of GNP for ODA, no time frame has been decided upon. Recent progress towards this goal is slow and Japanese ODA as a percentage of GNP decreased during 1992 and 1993 (see Table 1.1) and then increased again in 1994 but only marginally.

Table 1.1 ODA performance of DAC countries in 1992–93 ($ million, per cent of GNP)

Country	1992 $[a]	1993 $[a]	Percentage of GNP 1992	1993	Percentage change in $ value	Change in real terms[b]
Denmark	1,392	1,340	1.02	1.03	−3.7	1.6
Norway[c]	1,273	1,014	1.16	1.01	−20.3	−10.8
Sweden[c]	2,460	1,769	1.03	0.98	−28.1	−6.0
Netherlands[c]	2,753	2,525	0.86	0.82	−8.3	−4.6
France[c]	8,270	7,915	0.63	0.63	−4.3	−0.2
Finland	644	355	0.64	0.45	−44.8	−31.2
Canada	2,515	2,373	0.46	0.45	−5.7	−0.1
Belgium[c]	870	808	0.39	0.39	−7.1	−2.9
Germany[c]	7,583	6,954	0.39	0.37	−8.3	−6.4
Australia[c]	1,015	953	0.37	0.35	−6.1	0.3
Luxembourg	38	50	0.26	0.35	31.9	34.6
Switzerland	1,139	793	0.45	0.33	−30.4	−28.6
Italy	4,122	3,043	0.34	0.31	−26.2	−9.2
United Kingdom[c]	3,243	2,908	0.31	0.31	−10.3	1.4
Austria[c]	556	544	0.30	0.30	−2.2	−0.2
Portugal	302	246	0.36	0.29	−18.5	−8.8
Japan[c]	11,151	11,259	0.30	0.26	1.0	−12.3
New Zealand	97	98	0.26	0.25	0.6	−1.0
Spain	1,518	1,213	0.27	0.25	−20.1	−5.0
Ireland	69	81	0.16	0.20	18.4	34.4
United States[c]	11,709	9,721	0.20	0.15	−17.0	−19.0

Notes
(a) At current prices and exchange rates
(b) At 1992 exchange rates and prices
(c) Includes forgiveness of non-ODA debt in 1992 as follows: (i) Export credit claims ($ million) Australia 4, Austria 25, Belgium 30, France 109, Germany 620, Japan 32, Netherlands 11, Norway 47, Sweden 7, United Kingdom 90 (ii) Military debt, United States 894
Source: DAC

During 1993 Japanese ODA increased in dollar terms, but actually decreased by more than 12 per cent if calculated in yen. The importance of the yen–dollar exchange rate should always be kept in mind when considering Japanese ODA. The huge increases that have occurred in the Japanese ODA budget are to a large extent the result of the increasing value of the yen. In dollars the amount has tripled but in real terms, or yen, the increase is slightly less than 30 per cent for the years 1983–93 (see Table 1.2).

Table 1.2 Japanese ODA, net disbursement in $ million and ¥ billion

Year	$ million	¥billion
1983	3,761	893
1984	4,319	1,026
1985	3,797	906
1986	5,634	950
1987	7,454	1,078
1988	9,134	1,170
1989	8,965	1,236
1990	9,069	1,313
1991	10,952	1,473
1992	11,151	1,413
1993	11,259	1,252

Source: Japanese Foreign Ministry official white paper on aid, 1994

LOW QUALITY

The total sum of Japanese ODA in 1993, $11.3 billion, is impressive. If this sum is disaggregated, the picture is less impressive. If ODA is calculated on a per capita basis, the Japanese contribute $88 each while the Swedes, for example, contribute $233 and the Norwegians $276. On the other hand, Americans only contribute $37 each. Consequently, the Japanese rank somewhere in the middle among the DAC countries.[10]

The quality of the aid among DAC countries is not often measured in terms of the success of a project. Judging which projects are successful or not is difficult and opinions might differ. Instead, the quality of aid is measured solely in economic terms. Quality is measured by grant share (i.e. the amount of grant aid compared with loan aid) and grant element (i.e. grant aid plus that part of loan aid which is considered to be a grant). Japan finishes at the bottom of both those lists.[11] With a grant share of 43.8 per cent it is far below most other countries. Average among the DAC countries is a grant share of 77.1 per cent. This clearly demonstrates one of the peculiarities of Japanese aid. It is to a large extent based on loans and the recipients are expected to repay them.

If the grant element of Japanese aid is considered, that is, grant aid plus what the concessional conditions of the loans are worth, the figure is 76.6 per cent. This means that if foreign aid was more narrowly defined and consisted only of the grant element, and did not include the sums of the loans included in the ODA figures compiled by DAC, Japan would no longer be the largest donor nation in the world. Japanese foreign aid would then be $8.7 billion, well

Table 1.3 Grant share and grant element of total ODA among DAC countries (1992–93 average; percentage, excluding debt re-organization)

Country	Grant share	Grant element
Australia	100	100
Austria	72.8	88.1
Belgium	(97.0)	(99.5)
Canada	95.7	99.3
Denmark	99.8	99.8
Finland	82.3	90.4
France	(74.8)	(87.5)
Germany	80.2	92.7
Ireland	100	100
Italy	80.9	92.6
Japan	43.8	76.6
Luxembourg	100	(100)
Netherlands	98.4	99.5
New Zealand	100	100
Norway	99.3	99.5
Portugal	97.3	(98.6)
Spain	(44.3)	(80.3)
Sweden	100	100
Switzerland	100	100
United Kingdom	(92.2)	(96.5)
United States	97.9	99.1

Source: DAC (figures within ( ) are incomplete)

below the US figure of $9.7 billion with a grant element of 99.1 per cent (see Table 1.3).

However, one cannot avoid the fact that Japanese ODA represents a huge amount of money. As will be shown in the case studies, it has been essential in building up large parts of the economic infrastructure in the main recipient countries.

During years 1992–93 the amount of Japanese bilateral loans have decreased from the level reached in 1990 and 1991. Those were somewhat exceptional years and a large part of the increase in 1991 was money paid to the Middle East after the Kuwait crisis. Otherwise, loan aid has been fairly stable and there is no sign of any substantial decrease in the amount of loan aid being paid out (see Figure 1.1).

If one looks at figures for net disbursement, however, Japanese loan aid seems to decrease and grant aid and technical assistance to increase. The main reason for this is that repayment of the loans given in the beginning of the 1980s has already begun. Assuming that developing countries are repaying promptly,[12] money flowing back to the OECF from the developing world is likely to increase year by

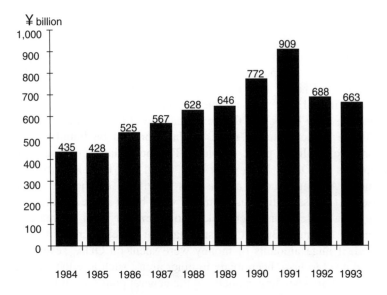

Figure 1.1 OECF loan disbursements, 1984–93
Source: OECF

Table 1.4 Japanese ODA, 1992, 1993 (net disbursement, $billion, ¥billion)

Type of aid	1992 ($)	1992 (¥)	1993 ($)	1993 (¥)	Percentage change $ (¥)
Grant aid	1.733	219.5	2.019	224.4	+16.5 (+2)
Technical assistance	2.132	269.9	2.602	289.2	+22.1 (+7)
Loan aid	4.620	585.2	3.544	393.4	−23.3 (−33)
Multilateral assistance	2.848	360.7	3.310	367.4	+16.2 (+2)
Total	11.332	1435.2	11.474	1275.6	+1.3 (−11)

Source: Japanese Foreign Ministry official white paper on aid, 1993 and 1994
Note: These are Japanese figures as opposed to DAC figures given in the text – there is a slight difference but the trends are still clear.

year from now on. In particular, between 1985 and 1991 the sum of loans extended each year actually doubled, even in yen, and the repayment of those has now commenced. If the money being repaid is deducted from what is being paid out, net disbursements are likely to continue to decrease, even if the amount being paid out remains the same (see Table 1.4).

WHY QUALITY HAS BEEN LOW

There are differing explanations as to why the quality of Japanese aid is so much lower than aid from other countries. At the policy-making level, the most common explanation is from an ideological viewpoint – that Japan's aid policy reflects the Japanese philosophy of help through 'self-help', that is, it is better to give loans than grants because it will make the recipient countries more careful with the money as they know that they eventually will have to pay it back.

At the implementation level, explanation can be found from an economic, realistic point of view. The politicians promised huge increases of ODA. Money for this could not be taken from the General Account Budget as this was heavily in deficit after the oil crises. At the same time as promises were being made for increased foreign aid, decisions were taken to freeze or even decrease the General Account Budget. Assuming that taxes were not to be raised, if huge amounts of money were spent on ODA, severe cuts would need to have been made in other areas, such as education and social welfare spending, something the general public would not have liked.

ODA was allowed to grow more than any other item in the General Account Budget (see Figure 1.2) but only about 50 per cent of the money comes from this budget. The remainder is from the Fiscal Loan and Investment Programme which consists of money from postal savings, pensions and other civilian savings which people expect to be repaid with interest. That makes it difficult to give money in the form of grants.[13] The OECF budget (which will be analysed in Chapter 2) relies, to a particularly high extent, on loans itself.

THE RECIPIENTS

Even though Japanese aid is more widely dispersed than before, Asia remains the main recipient, receiving, in 1993, 60 per cent of all bilateral Japanese ODA. By geographic region, Africa occupied second place with 12 per cent of the aid, Central and Latin America received 9 per cent and the Middle East 6 per cent. Eastern Europe is a low-priority region and received only 1.5 per cent.

The top five countries receiving most aid are all Asian and together they received 48 per cent of total bilateral Japanese aid (see Table 1.5). As will be highlighted in the case studies, all these countries, except China, who followed a policy of self-reliance until 1978, have

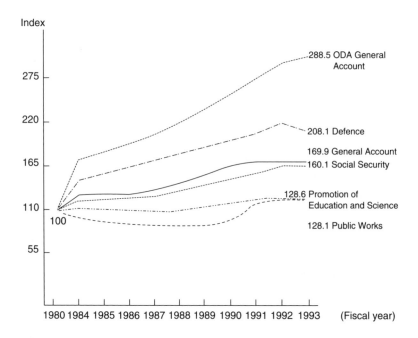

Figure 1.2 Trends in growth of ODA and other budgets (index: FY 1980 = 100)
Source: Japanese Foreign Ministry

Table 1.5 Main recipients of Japanese ODA in fiscal 1993 (disbursement, $ million)

Country	Amount of bilateral aid	Share of total (%)
China	1,350.67	16.54
Indonesia	1,148.89	14.07
The Philippines	758.39	9.29
Thailand	350.15	4.29
India	295.94	3.62

Source: Japanese Foreign Ministry official white paper on aid, 1994

had a long post-war history of economic co-operation with Japan. Besides ODA, China, Indonesia and Thailand are also receiving a considerable amount of Japanese private investment. In all of these countries financing of economic infrastructure projects is the dominant form of aid. The top recipients mainly received loans, which constituted 78 per cent of all aid to China, 80 per cent of that to

Indonesia, 68 per cent to the Philippines, 54 per cent to Thailand and 84 per cent to India. Japan was the most significant donor to all these countries giving sometimes five times more than the next-largest donor and never less than twice as much as any other country. The predominate form of aid to the Asian countries is loan aid. They received 80 per cent of all the Japanese loan aid.[14]

Loans limit the kind of projects that can be considered feasible. The OECF has to reassure itself that it will get the money back. Of course, all aid projects do not directly generate money but many of them, especially in the field of infrastructure, do.

From a humanitarian point of view it may seem logical to give most aid to the poorest countries in the world which have a greater need of aid, but such consideration is not shown in Japanese aid implementation. Japan gives less than other countries to the least among less-developed countries (LLDC[15]), that is, the poorest countries in the world. Of the 21 DAC member countries only Spain gives less than Japan to these countries. (See Table 1.6 for the largest donors.)

Table 1.6 Percentage of aid to the LLDCs by a selection of DAC members, 1993

Japan	USA	UK	France	Germany	Italy	Canada	DAC total
17	23	27	23	27	24	23	24

Source: DAC

One reason for the comparatively low proportion of aid to the poorest countries in the world is the heavy priority Japan gives to certain countries in Asia which have seen tremendous economic growth. As will become clear from the case study, Japan is nowadays almost the only country that extends bilateral aid on any scale to Thailand, as that country has reached such a level of development that it is debatable whether further aid is needed. (Japanese ODA to countries of various income groups is shown in Table 1.7.) Another reason is probably the low priority that 'soft' questions like poverty alleviation get within Japanese ODA, if not on the policy level at least during the implementation stage. The large amount of loans are a proof of this. Loans are considered unsuitable for the poorest countries of the world as their ability to repay debt appears doubtful. This is the reason grant assistance predominates in Japanese aid to Africa, where many of the poorest countries are located.

Table 1.7 Japanese bilateral aid recipients divided into income groups, 1993 (disbursement, $ million)

LLDCs	1,198.0 (14.7%)[a]
LICs (low-income countries[b])	3,754.4 (46)
LMICs (lower middle-income countries[c])	1,933.4 (23.7)
UMICs (upper middle-income countries[d])	238.1 (2.9)
HICs (high-income countries[e])	32.6 (0.4)
Not classified	1,007.9 (12.3)
All together	8,164.3 (100)

Source: Japanese Foreign Ministry official white paper on aid, 1994
Notes
(a) Figures differ slightly from those given above as they are from a different source
(b) GNP per capita income of less than $676 (excluding the LLDC group)
(c) GNP per capita income of more than $676 but less than $2,696
(d) GNP per capita income of more than $2,696 but less than $8,355
(e) GNP per capita income of more than $8,355

TIED VERSUS UNTIED AID

An examination of DAC statistics shows that Japan has a higher than average percentage of untied aid, 58.5 per cent of total bilateral ODA, compared to the average among DAC countries of 43.7 per cent. Japan ranked fifth in percentage of untied aid following Austria, New Zealand, Sweden and the United States. The ratio of untied aid to tied aid is extremely high in the field of Japanese loan aid. According to OECF's own calculations, 97 per cent of loan aid is now untied.[16]

For grant aid programmes contracts should be signed 'with Japanese nationals (a consulting firm and contractors) relative to the detailed design, supervision of work, construction, and equipment procurement, and the project commence [*sic*]'.[17]

General grant assistance is considered 'partly untied' which means that non-Japanese companies can obtain such orders if the recipient governments request that the Japanese government procure non-Japanese products. MOFA will only approve such aid in those circumstances where no Japanese products exist; where there is only one Japanese product and no competition; where Japanese products are extremely disadvantageous or where there are other special conditions applicable such as the need of emergency procurement. This means that grant aid and technical assistance are, with minor exceptions, tied. That Japanese aid still registers such a high percentage of untied aid for its total ODA is to a large extent dependent on the fact that this is calculated on commitment basis.

The yen loan commitments are much larger than the sum actually disbursed.

THE CONTENT OF JAPANESE AID

A comparison of the content of Japanese ODA with other countries clearly shows an emphasis on economic infrastructure. In 1992, 41 per cent of all bilateral aid went to that sector, whereas the equivalent figure for US aid was 4 per cent, for Britain 29.8 per cent, France 15.7 per cent and Sweden 9.8 per cent. Of the DAC countries' total aid, 20.6 per cent went to economic infrastructure[18] (see Table 1.8).

Within the category 'economic infrastructure' transport received the most money, followed by the energy sector. The transportation sector received 19 per cent of Japan's total ODA.[19] Within this sector 90 per cent of all the aid was loan aid, with 98 per cent channelled to Asia and only 2 per cent to Africa.[20] These figures demonstrate dramatically that these kinds of capital-intensive projects are almost exclusively reserved for Asia.

Road building received 50.1 per cent of the loan aid for transportation in 1993, railway 30.0 per cent, airports 10.6 per cent and ports 8.2 per cent. The energy sector received 16 per cent of Japan's total ODA. Of all this aid, 90 per cent was in the form of loans and most of it went to Asia. Of the nine countries that received commitments for projects in 1993, only one, namely Iran, was not what, by Japanese aid authorities, would be classified as an Asian country. The communication sector received 4 per cent of Japan's bilateral ODA and again Asia was the main recipient receiving 78 per cent of the aid.

Table 1.8 Major aid uses by individual DAC members in 1992 (percentage of total commitment)

	Japan	USA	UK	France	Sweden	DAC total
Social infrastructure	12.3	15.2	24.0	31.8	26.1	19.2
Economic infrastructure	40.7	3.5	29.8	15.7	9.8	20.6
Agriculture	9.4	2.9	8.6	7.0	10.1	6.7
Industry and other production	8.9	3.3	7.0	8.1	18.5	8.1
Food aid	0.3	7.3	1.6	0.4	–	3.1
Programme assistance and other	28.4	67.9	29.0	37.0	35.5	42.4

Source: DAC

THE ODA CHARTER

The 1990s witnessed a new trend in Japanese ODA in that, at least verbally, it became more politicized and more environmentally conscious. To a certain extent this followed the trends of the time, although the Japanese verbal commitments were more explicit than others. The Gulf crisis had called attention to the question of armaments in developing countries and in 1991 Prime Minister Kaifu announced four anti-militaristic principles for ODA. The following year these principles were confirmed and strengthened by the so-called 'ODA Charter' which called for consideration of the following four principles in aid implementation:

1 Environmental conservation and development should be pursued in tandem.
2 Any use of ODA for military purposes or for aggravation of international conflicts should be avoided.
3 Full attention should be given to trends in recipient countries' military expenditures, their development and production of mass-destruction weapons and missiles, their export and import of arms.
4 Full attention should be given to efforts for promoting democratization and the introduction of a market-oriented economy, and the situation regarding the securing of basic human rights and freedoms in the recipient country.

The first principle was going to have implication for the Philippine case study, as will be shown in Chapter 6. The enviromental problems with the project did not fit in well with Japan's intention of profiling itself as an enviromentally conscious country, which it tried to do through promises of sharp increases in enviromentally related ODA at the United Nations Conference on Environment and Development in Rio in 1992.[21]

The validity of the principle at the implementation level can be questioned as Japan's emphasis is on economic infrastructure, which usually in itself implies a certain amount of enviromental destruction.

The anti-militaristic and, in particular, the human rights principles are in line with international trends concerning aid. In Japanese implementing processes the principles have been promptly enforced in countries like Haiti, Sierra Leone and Malawi. These countries are, however, of minor importance to Japan. When it comes to larger neighbours in Asia, such as Indonesia, Thailand and India, the principles have not been reflected in the implementation of ODA. Japan has satisfied itself with explaining its principles and policies and expressing concern about things that are not in accordance with those principles, rather than taking any direct action. The only exception is China. Under pressure from public opinion at home Japan cut grant aid in August 1995 in protest at Chinese nuclear testing. The cutting must be considered rather mild punishment as the grant aid part in Japanese aid to China only is around 4 per cent.

There is a part of one of the principles that seems to be given priority and which matches well with Japanese aid at the implementation level as well at the country's own experience and its belief in development through industrialization, that is, the introduction of a market economy. This is reflected in the introduction of new recipients such as Vietnam, Cambodia and Mongolia. Economic infrastructure is a prerequisite for the introduction of a market economy in developing countries.

Japan's cautious attitude towards implementing the rest of the principles in neighbouring countries is likely to continue unless flagrant violations occur[22] and international or domestic pressure is applied. One of the reasons for this caution, besides a lack of tradition of telling governments in other countries how they should act, is the anti-Japanese feelings that exist in many Asian countries. Triggered by some Japanese action they could easily surface, which would be fruitful neither for diplomatic nor business interests. In addition, many Japanese do not believe that a tougher attitude would yield productive results. It did not in China, where the business of nuclear testing goes on as usual.

Another reason for the cautious attitude towards Asian neighbours is, as can be understood from the case studies and from Chapter 3 'Japanese ODA – the business perspective', that there are other interests at stake which might weigh heavier than the political ones. This leads to the questions of who rules the process of Japanese ODA and what motives steer them.

HOW POLICY IS FORMED

As a rule, Japanese aid policy-making is not controversial. There are few politicians with an in-depth knowledge and interest in the field. Public opinion polls show that Japanese people are, in general, positive towards foreign aid, but that interest is rather low. Japan does not have large numbers of people or groups that voluntarily take a special interest in ODA.[23]

The ODA budget is dealt with by the Diet every year without any political debate or deliberation on its content. It is only the total amount of the budget that is decided by the Diet. The actual detailed allocation of the budget is usually determined later by the bureaucrats. Japanese politicians do not gain votes on ODA questions and, therefore, these have low priority.[24] Questions arise in the Diet, however, when there is any form of scandal involved, for example, when aid money is diverted into the pockets of President Marcos of the Philippines or when ODA projects are likely to lead to environmental destruction on a massive scale, such as the coal-fired powered plant highlighted in our Philippine case study. On such occasions politicians are likely to intervene in the implementing process and might actually, as in the Calaca case, stop it at least temporarily.

There are individual members of the Diet who are interested in ODA but there is no powerful group, (a so-called *zoku*), with a special interest in aid as with other areas, such as defence (*bōeizoku*). The closest substitute is probably the country-based so-called parliamentarian friendship associations (*giinrenmei*) that endeavour to promote contacts with certain countries and, in so doing, also take an interest in aid.[25] More often, however, the policy-making process itself is mostly left in the hands of the bureaucrats. This does not mean that aid policy formulation is a clear-cut and easy process. Japan does not have one ministry or bureau responsible for ODA but about 20 different government bodies that may be involved, depending on the subject-matter. This gives room for considerable inconsistency and infighting within the bureaucracy.[26] Among the twenty or so bodies there are four 'main ones' with more responsibility than the others: the Ministry of Finance (MOF), Ministry of Foreign Affairs (MOFA), Ministry of International Trade and Industry (MITI) and the Economic Planning Agency (EPA).

Under the policy-making bodies there are two main implementing agencies. As will be shown in the case studies, this is where a lot of the actual work is done. They are the ones in charge of the implementing process. They have one interest in common with the bureaucrats. They are interested in smooth, scandal-free operations that do not involve the politicians. Such involvement usually complicates the process and makes effective operations more difficult. The two agencies are: (1) Japan International Co-operation Agency (JICA) which is formally placed under MOFA. It deals with grant aid and technical assistance; (2) the Overseas Economic Co-operation Fund (OECF) which is formally placed under the Economic Planning Agency but is actually governed by 'the Four-Ministry System'[27] which, in addition to EPA, consists of MOF, MITI and MOFA.

This study focuses on OECF which is the agency handling the economic infrastructure projects and all the loan aid. JICA will only be marginally dealt with to the extent that it affects OECF projects. The co-operation and co-ordination, or rather lack of them, between the two, will also be dealt with in the case studies.

Each body within 'the Four-Ministry System' has different motives and considerations governing its handling of foreign aid. Every year it is not just one white paper that is published on ODA policy but, in fact, three different papers, one each written from the distinct perspectives of MOFA, MITI and EPA. Policy is generally formulated as a result of pluralistic conflict and consensus-building between the bodies. Their interests in ODA and from which aspects they look at it can be summarized in the following schedule.[28]

1 Ministry of Foreign Affairs
   Foreign-policy related economic co-operation
2 Ministry of Finance
   Economic co-operation related to public finance and to international monetary policy
3 Ministry of International Trade and Industry
   Economic co-operation related to trade and the national economy
4 Economic Planning Agency
   Formulation of basic policies on economic co-operation, and general co-ordination

Each body has the right to block a decision it does not agree with. In addition to domestic requests and individual goals, input is received from world trends in ODA as well as from requests submitted by recipient countries. Loan aid policy is mainly formulated as a result of consultations, confrontations and compromises between the four bodies. OECF should not be forgotten in the process, either. Although it is only an implementing agency, and thus only active in the implementing process, it has now been in existence for more than 20 years and includes not only a number of officials seconded from other ministries but also a large body of people raised within the organization and who during the years have not only gathered a lot of knowledge about ODA but also about how to govern the aid-giving process. Policy formulation in Tokyo is one thing but what happens at the implementation level may be quite different, as will be shown in the case studies. There, the implementing agencies have to adjust to existing realities. OECF will be dealt with in the next chapter.

NOTES

1 Meanwhile water was sent all the way from Yokohama (600 km away from Kobe) by a private initiative of the mayor of that city.
2 When the house of a friend of mine in a small Japanese village burned down almost all the inhabitants of the village made substantial financial contributions to help in building a new one.
3 Less than 1 per cent of the Japanese population is Christian.
4 As stated in the Japanese Foreign Ministry's white paper, *Waga Kuni no Seifu Kaihatsu Enjo 1994* (official white paper 1994) as well as in the OECF *Annual Report 1994*.
5 The loans had interest rates of 5.75–6.0 per cent and were firmly tied to purchases from Japan, see Alan Rix, *Japan's Foreign Aid Challenge*, Routledge, London and New York, 1993.
6 Japanese Foreign Ministry, op. cit.
7 Robert Orr, *The Emergence of Japan's Foreign Aid Power*, Columbia University Press, New York, 1990.
8 According to the present constitution Japan cannot have any military forces and does not possess the right to solve international conflicts by military means. This does not prevent the country from maintaining defences and a Self Defence Force of 245,000 men and one of the largest military budgets in the world. Notwithstanding the Japanese defence cost is only around 1 per cent of GNP which is lower than in most other industrialized countries.
9 Alan Rix, *Japan's Economic Aid: Policymaking and Politics*, Croom Helm, London, 1980.
10 DAC press release issued in 1992.
11 Spain actually has a lower grant share but here the figures are not complete.
12 This may not occur in every case, but most recipients are Asian countries that have experienced positive economic development which should make it possible for them to afford repayment.
13 Akira Nishigaki, *Kaihatsu Enjo no Keizaigaku*, Yuhaikaku, Tokyo, 1993.
14 Japanese Foreign Ministry, op. cit.
15 There were 47 countries in this category according to UN calculations.
16 For more information on the OECF loans see Chapter 2.
17 JICA, *Annual Report 1993*; the so-called non-project grant assistance for structural adjustment support is an exception as it is untied. As a proportion of the grant aid budget it amounts to roughly 2 per cent.
18 Japanese Foreign Ministry, op. cit.
19 It had a share of over 30 per cent of the OECF loans in 1993.
20 Japanese Foreign Ministry, op. cit.
21 Japan promised to increase environmentally related aid to ¥1 trillion ($8 billion) over a five-year period starting from fiscal 1992.
22 An example of this was the 1989 Tiananmen Square incident in China which happened before these principles were adopted but where Japan actually took action.
23 For more information on the role of NGO's in Japanese aid policy see Marie Söderberg, 'Enskilda Organisationers roll i japansk biståndspolitik', a paper presented at a seminar at Stockholm University, 1992.

24 Interview with Yukio Nakamura, Liberal Democratic Party's Policy Affairs Research Council, March 1994.
25 Myanmar is a case in point here. The Myanmar (or Burma) lobby is said to be very strong in the Japanese Diet. In the autumn of 1995 a decision was taken to restart aid to Burma again although the opposition leader Aung San Suu Kyi claimed it was too early and asked Japan to wait.
26 For a more detailed overview of the policy-making process see Orr, op. cit.
27 Actually three ministries and one agency.
28 MITI description.

2 OECF and the implementation process

Marie Söderberg

By July 1994, the outstanding balance of OECF loans and equity investments exceeded ¥8 trillion, approximately half that of the World Bank group and more than the combined total of four regional development banks (the Asian Development Bank, the Inter-American Development Bank, the African Development Bank and the European Bank for Reconstruction and Development). OECF has become one of the world's major development finance institutions as well as a principal executing agency of Japan's ODA.[1]

HISTORICAL BACKGROUND – HOW IT BECAME WHAT IT IS TODAY

By the end of the 1950s Japanese business and government circles were dissatisfied with the limited amount of government funding that existed for overseas development projects. The Exim Bank,[2] established in 1950, was criticized for being too commercially oriented and its export promotion aim for being too restrictive for many of the development projects. This led Prime Minister Nobusuke Kishi to set up the Asian Development Fund in 1957. The charters of this fund required that other countries should also contribute to it, but this did not happen, and, therefore, the fund was never drawn upon. The money from the fund was instead used as the basis for another new organization, OECF, which was established in 1961.[3] It took several years for the fund to begin effective operations and it was not until 1965 that it made its first government loan, as a part of Japan's newly established relationship with South Korea.

Administrative control over the organization posed a problem as three ministries (MOF, MOFA and MITI) all considered that it should be within their jurisdiction. To avoid any conflict between the ministries, supervisory responsibility was instead given to EPA. EPA was to act as a co-ordinator between the three ministries. Unfortunately, EPA was domestically weak and this weakened OECF from the outset. It became subordinate to bureaucratic interests rather than what was espoused in the OECF legislation, namely, the development of recipient countries. One of the effects of this was that there was no new recruiting for OECF until 1964. Instead it was staffed by personnel from the ministries. There were also several early attempts to merge the fund with the Exim Bank.

OECF's loan department was headed by an officer from the Bank of Japan and its two divisional directors were from the Exim Bank and the Japan Development Bank, with desk-level staff transferred from the Exim Bank. This, in effect, made the fund's Loan Department an extension of the bank.

Following complaints that the fund was too small and that the division of functions between the fund and the bank should be more explicit, an investigating committee was formed in 1963. Some commentators, such as the newspaper *Asahi Shimbun*, demanded a bigger role for OECF whereas MOF proposed that its duties should be taken over by the Exim Bank.

The committee findings were in favour of an independent body. OECF gradually became more powerful and in 1968 it was given sole responsibility for funding the Indonesian aid programme. At this time there was no clear demarcation between OECF loans and loans provided by the Exim Bank and it was not until 1975 that OECF was given responsibility for all ODA loans.

The real boost for OECF was the first of four medium-term targets or so called 'aid-doubling' plans presented by Japan in 1978. To reach those targets ODA loans were going to be an important tool. During the four plans between 1978 and 1992, OECF provided almost 50 per cent of all aid, and its budget increased five times in dollar terms. Loan aid was the form of aid that was going to be most frequently used to achieve the increase in Japanese ODA spending. Most of the money went to building up economic infrastructure in Asia.

LOANS THAT FINANCE LOANS

As was pointed out in the last chapter, there was a limit due to political considerations on the amount ODA could increase within the General Account Budget. Money had to be found somewhere else and the solution chosen was to borrow it from the general public's savings. OECF was already borrowing money in 1978. It had started

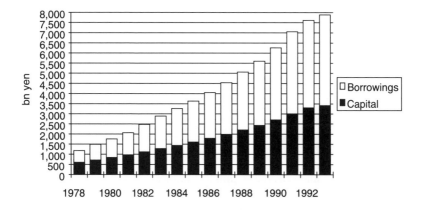

Figure 2.1 Changes in capital and borrowing balance
Source: OECF

to borrow from the Fiscal Loan and Investment Program in 1965 but there was limit placed on the amount as OECF legislation prohibited it from borrowing more than its own capital and reserve fund. This was insufficient to pay for the increase in ODA that Japan had committed itself to undertake. Something had to be done and in 1979 the OECF legislation was amended to enable OECF to borrow three times the sum of its capital and reserve fund. Consequently, as loans increased, borrowings as a percentage of OECF's financial resources also increased (see Figure 2.1). In addition, due in part to international pressure, the terms and conditions of the loans became more favourable to recipients. The increasing cost of the funds for OECF, at the same time as the return was lowered, led to a negative spread after fiscal 1980. Since 1984 this negative spread has decreased, due, to a certain extent, to lower interest rates for OECF borrowing as a result of falling interest rates in the financial markets.

LOW STAFF NUMBERS

A significant difference between OECF and other organizations disbursing ODA loans is its limited staff numbers. OECF's outstanding and disbursed loans marginally exceeded the combined total of the Asian Development Bank (ADB), the Inter-American Development Bank (IDB), the African Development Bank (AfDB) and the European Bank for Reconstruction and Development (EBRD). Staff numbers in these organizations are 1,898 in ADB, 1,818 in IDB, 1,244 in AfDB and 795 in EBRD. OECF is in a class of its own with a staff of only 315 (in 1993 – see Table 2.1).[4] The World Bank, with loans slightly more than double those of OECF, has a staff of 6,197.

Table 2.1   Total number of OECF officers and staff

Year	1984	1988	1992	1993
Number	249	267	303	315

OECF has an extremely small number of staff moving large amounts of money and this situation does not appear likely to change. As will be shown in the case studies (which were all done in countries where OECF has offices of its own), the small number of staff has implications for the implementing processes.

Why is it that there are so few people working in OECF? It is sometimes claimed that this is the result of influence from MOF which wants to keep the OECF's own operational budget at a modest level. This may be true to a certain extent, especially during those years when the Japanese state budget was heavily in deficit. It may also be because the Japanese type of loan aid is somewhat different from that of other countries. A large amount of money is disbursed but with a low degree of interference in the affairs of other countries. Aid is to be requested by the recipient countries themselves. OECF does not have a large number of staff giving advice on what should be done in different developing countries. Rather than development experts, their staff are economists and bureaucrats who know how to handle requests for loans.

The shortage and type of staff also affects the type of projects that OECF is likely to support. It leads to a preference for 'large-scale projects' where a considerable amount of money can be spent at one time with minimal administrative effort. It is much easier for OECF to manage a project with one big power plant then ten smaller ones in different countries. One of the constant problems for OECF staff is how to disburse money as quickly and effectively as possible, and to a certain degree their work is evaluated on this basis. The status of OECF in the world community is connected to the amount of money that it manages. If OECF fails to find suitable projects it loses prestige and may suffer the risk of a budget decrease the following year. This also means that large infrastructure projects that require disbursements of large sums at one time with minimal administrative effort are a solution to OECF's problems.

Another effect of OECF's low number of staff, and also a result of the fact that aid is request-based, is that it has created room for other groups of actors to become involved in the aid process. This is clearly shown in the case studies. Which other actors that are likely to be involved vary somewhat with the country as well as project-specific factors. One group consists of Japanese companies. There are numerous accounts of how Japanese companies have 'helped' governments in recipient countries to find suitable projects and then submit aid requests to Japan. The interest in doing so, at least with loan-financed projects, appears to have decreased considerably (see the next chapter) since loan aid became untied and there is no longer any guarantee of a certain company obtaining a specific order.[5] The untying of loans has also, theoretically, allowed companies from other countries to assist governments in recipient countries in finding suitable projects.

Another important group of players performing work caused by the lack of OECF staff is made up of administrators and planners in the developing countries. Many of these, especially in Asia, have had considerable experience in dealing with OECF and have substantial knowledge of the process and how to submit requests. This will become especially obvious in the China case studies. Japan International Co-operation Agency (JICA), to a certain extent, also fills the gap. Although JICA is a separate organization it carries out a number of development studies, master plans and feasibility studies on a grant-aid basis which are sometimes used for OECF projects. It also dispatches a number of technical experts to various ministries or govenment agencies in the recipient countries. In Indonesia, in particular, there seem to be considerable numbers of technical experts, as will be clear from the case study.

With regard to OECF staff, 49 are stationed in overseas offices[6] together with 90 locally employed staff. The tradition of transferring staff to OECF from the Four Ministries still exists and some are in managerial positions. The Managing Director of the Co-ordination Department comes from the Ministry of Finance and the Deputy Manager from MITI.[7] There are a number of officials seconded at a lower level as well. At the same time, OECF now also has its own staff, that is, a group of people who have worked solely for OECF and are making a career within the organization. Some of them are now becoming fairly senior with many years' experience and knowledge within the field of aid. They have also become fairly powerful with their expertise and understanding of how the system operates. This group tends to act as go-betweens for, on one side, Japanese formal decision-makers, that is, MOF, MITI, MOFA and EPA, and on the other, the recipient countries' decision-makers.

The officials of the Japanese ministries which deal with yen loans do not, in general, have lengthy experience in the aid field. They rotate between the different departments of their ministries and do not stay more than a few years in the same position. Work with yen loans is but one of many postings that they pass through during their careers. Their expertise is not in development but in finance, trade, foreign affairs or economic planning, depending on which ministry they belong to. They may not have any idea of how things work in the recipient countries, what those countries really need or what projects will contribute most effectively to development. Consequently, these officials seek the advice of OECF staff who are experts in this field, many of them having been stationed abroad, working directly with the recipients.

The situation in most of the recipient countries is similar. An official, for example, in a railway ministry in a developing country may know a great deal about railway construction but may not necessarily be an expert on requesting OECF loans. Indeed, even if that official has applied for such a loan previously he or she may not be aware of new trends or regulations that have been issued in Tokyo and therefor advice from the experts at OECF is sought.

As is evident from the case studies, there is a continuous contact between OECF representatives and bureaucrats at certain ministries in the recipient countries. The OECF representatives become aware of likely projects long before any requests are made. They can then advise the officials from the recipient countries on whether or not these projects are likely to receive loan aid. OECF officials are the people who, initially provide guidance and information and subsequently check that the loan agreements are signed and the projects implemented.

OECF'S ORGANIZATION

OECF is formally governed by an executive board consisting of six members and one auditor. The chairman[8] is Akira Nishigaki who comes from the Ministry of Finance. The last three chairmen have all been officials from the Ministry of Finance which suggests that they tend to dominate this position. The other five members of the board include one representative of each of the four ministries, that is, MOF, MITI, MOFA and EPA plus one representative from OECF who acts as first vice-president. The auditor is an official from EPA. Reporting to the board is a Secretariat Office led by a Special Adviser to the President, the Research Institute, 17 overseas offices and eight different departments.

The Co-ordination Department is responsible for planning and administration. It is also responsible for public relations, co-financing, overseas office administration and project co-ordination. At the operational level the control of this department is important because the head of it clears the annual budget request. MOF appointees occupy the complete chain of command in this department from the top down to the detailed work of the budgeting and accounting divisions.[9] The responsibilities of the Accounting and General Services Department and Controller's Department are implied by their titles.

There are three Operations Departments which are divided into a number of sections directly responsible for specific countries. There is at least one overseas office connected to the activities of each of those sections and it is in these offices that the greatest concentration of OECF career staff is found. From these sections, the main part of the work related to countries in the developing world takes place. In the case studies presented in this book there have been a number of sections involved. Thailand is dealt with by the first section of Operations Department I (which also deals with Singapore, Laos and Cambodia), Indonesia by the second section (which also deals with Malaysia) and the Philippines by the third section (also responsible for Oceania). China is dealt with by the first section in Operations Department II (which also is responsible for Korea and Mongolia).

Since 1993, the Project Development Department, apart from planning and monitoring projects, has also included a section for Environment and Social Development. OECF's Technical Department is responsible for technical appraisal and supervision. This department is constantly understaffed. As is obvious from the case studies, technical expertise is frequently borrowed from different ministries depending on the type of project. There is also a newly formed Research Institute of Development Assistance (RIDA) established within OECF. This is to a large extent staffed by people from the business community, seconded to work for OECF for a limited period. Not surprisingly, many of these people have more experience with business than with helping developing countries.

MERGER OF OECF AND EXIM BANK

In March 1995 the Japanese government announced that OECF would be merged with the Exim Bank in 1999. It was one of a series of administrative reforms announced during the spring of 1995. The newspapers described it as the result of the government coalition's desire to restrict the power of the mighty Japanese Ministry of Finance.[10] The ministry currently appoints retired officials to well-paid jobs at both institutions and through the merger such chances would be reduced.

As described above, plans for a merger between the two organizations are not new and last time the Ministry of Finance itself was the driving force behind such plans. Exim Bank officials were understood to be relieved at the latest plans because they are less drastic than earlier proposals to dismember the bank entirely. The Exim Bank and OECF occupy the same building in Tokyo but otherwise have different jurisdictions. The Exim Bank lends to a mixture of private companies and state institutions but, unlike OECF, provides almost no ODA. In 1994 the Exim Bank, with a staff of 550, provided a greater loan amount than OECF. According to the government, the new, merged, institution will maintain a clear division between trade finance and aid. It is still too early to know the form of the new organization and who will profit or lose from the changes. To a certain extent the activities of the two are similar. They both finance a considerable number of economic infrastructure projects in Asia. They are both major players, that is, both have substantial financial resources which they are willing to lend to certain projects in developing countries. Although the conditions of the ODA loans are leaner, it does happen that they are 'competitors' for the same project. They might also be complementing each other, as in our Philippine case, where the first of the power plants was financed by money from the Exim Bank and the second by OECF.

From ODA's point of view it may seem more logical to merge OECF with JICA instead of the Exim Bank, since both these organizations operate in the aid field. This has not happened nor is it likely to in the near future. Their type of work is actually quite different and their opinion of each other's works not always very high, as found out during this research project.

At present it seems likely that the merger will lead to a more blurred borderline between ODA and other official flows. The decision in 1996 to allow OECF loans in connection with Build–Operate–Transfer/Build–Operate–Own (BOT/BOO) projects points in that direction.

BUDGET SIZE AND FINANCIAL CONDITIONS

On a gross disbursement basis OECF loans amounted to ¥663 billion ($6 billion) in 1993, a slight decrease, of 4 per cent, from 1992. Commitments were considerably higher and amounted to ¥1,010 billion ($9 billion). There are several reasons for the difference between commitments and disbursements (see Figure 2.2). One reason already mentioned is shortage of OECF staff. The heavy workload experienced can sometimes lead to difficulties and delays in disbursements. This is especially true for projects located in countries where there is no OECF office and where no annual consultations take place. In those countries it takes considerably longer to move projects through the pipeline.[11]

Another reason why OECF suffers from a constant 'pipeline' problem lies on the recipient side. Although all the loans that OECF commits are based on requests from recipient countries, things do not always progress according to schedule. For instance, local opposition can put an end to a project, governments or the priorities of governments as well as economic conditions and plans can change, or OECF sometimes has problems persuading a recipient country to fulfil its part of the deal so that money can be disbursed.

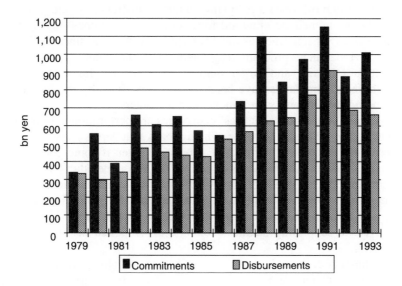

Figure 2.2   OECF loans, 1979–93
Source: OECF

The terms and conditions of loans vary with the economic capabilities of the recipient countries. The stronger economies receive less favourable conditions than the weak ones, but even for the stronger economies interest rates are far below the market rate. The average interest rate was 2.65 per cent in 1993 (as compared to 2.61 per cent in fiscal 1992). The average repayment period for loans committed in 1993 was 28 years and 6 months. Repayment is carried out on a straight line amortization basis with a general grace period of 9 years and 1 month.[12] The grant element of the Japanese bilateral ODA loans[13] was 57.1 per cent in 1993 which was a slight decrease from 1992's figure of 59.9 per cent.[14] The constantly increasing value of the yen has made the loans less favourable than expected in many recipient countries. OECF loans are all in yen and in the more advanced of the developing countries, such as Thailand, governments have started to hedge against increases in the yen through the currency market.[15]

Countries that have problems meeting payments can reschedule them (according to the Paris Club agreement[16]). Substantial loan rescheduling characterised 1992, mainly because Egypt rescheduled a large amount at one time.[17] However, loans cannot be written off which may be partly explained by the fact that to a large extent OECF borrows its money. Although recipient countries cannot have their loans written off, once a recipient country in distress has paid, it can receive an immediate grant aid for another project amounting to the same sum. Special schemes for this have been available since 1987.[18]

The repayment problem may increase if the value of the yen continues to rise and larger amounts become due for repayment each year. Complaints have been raised many times by the Indonesian and the Chinese governments, among others.

Many of the Asian countries' economies are performing extremely well at the moment, however, which means that Japan's chances of receiving repayment in full appear positive, even if some countries complain about the problem's of repayment. If, on the other hand, the economic development of the Asian countries entered into a deep depression (which nothing at the moment indicates), OECF is likely to get into trouble. There is, therefore, a considerable Japanese interest in supporting healthy economic development in the area in general.

A number of the older borrowers in Asia are reliable payers and the disbursement rate of ¥663 billion in 1993 can be compared with a repayment rate of almost ¥200 billion.[19] Repayment has been increasing every year and, assuming that the developing countries continue paying their debts, the repayment rate is likely to increase considerably during the late 1990s when grace periods for the large loans granted at the end of the 1980s expire.

TIED VERSUS UNTIED

In the beginning all loans were tied. The concentration of tied loans in Asia together with heavy Japanese private business investment from the end of the 1960s to the beginning of 1970s created a good deal of tension. DAC also pushed Japan to improve the quality of its aid and international co-ordination for the untying of loans commenced. LDC untying[20] was promised by Japan in December 1972 and to allow this both OECF and Exim Bank legislation had to be amended. Following DAC agreements, all loans concluded after January 1975 were, in principle, LDC untied. During the 1980s there was a gradual shift to allow more and more of the loans to become general untied.[21]

Until the early 1990s all consultants employed in development projects had LDC untied conditions, which meant that they were usually Japanese, since there was a shortage of people with high technological qualifications in the developing world. Current bidding for consultancy is on a case-by-case basis also done on general untied conditions. In 1993 almost 97 per cent of the OECF loans were under general untied conditions (see Table 2.2) with contracting occurring mainly through international competitive bidding arranged by the executing agency in the recipient country and not by OECF (see the section 'Operational guidelines for OECF loans' p. 65). This arrangement, that the recipient country is in charge of the purchasing, affects the procurement process and makes it different in each country, as will become clear from the case studies.

The switch to untied conditions was also in part a result of requests from developing countries reluctant to accept tied loans to finance certain projects since the tying usually meant that they had to pay considerably more than if they had used international competitive bidding (ICB). It was also a result of the constantly rising value of the

Table 2.2 Tying status of OECF loans (commitment basis, per cent)

Year	1984	1986	1988	1990	1992	1993
General untied	54	52	74	84	91	97

Source: OECF

yen which made many Japanese goods uncompetitive. Another factor was discussions within DAC which led to commitments from the members to restrict tying. A system of monitoring the tying of aid was established. As the percentage of untied aid increased, Japanese companies started losing orders (see Table 2.3).

Whether a company belongs in the category of LDC, Japan or OECD (other than Japan) depends, according to OECF, on what it is regarded as by the recipient country. The categories are not as distinct as they seem. Joint ventures between local companies and companies from OECD countries (including Japan) are classed as LDC if they are considered to be local. This is irrespective of what share of the joint venture the local company owns. In some countries it is common business practice by companies of OECD countries to put up 'local' companies through joint ventures since this appeals to the decision-makers in the recipient countries and might lead to more favourable treatment.

Another problem is that only the main contractor is registered with OECF. This contractor might then use a number of sub-contractors from other countries. As will become clear from the case studies, this may even be a precondition to an order. In construction work the local content is likely to be fairly high, even if the winner of the contract is a company from an OECD country. A contract won by a Japanese trading house will be registered as a Japanese contract, but might include only a few or even no Japanese sub-contractors at all. This places the validity of the figures in Table 2.3 in question but trends can still be detected. The Japanese figure of 29 per cent of all orders must be regarded as high considering that loans are 97 per cent untied. Japan does not usually secure that high a percentage on

Table 2.3 Nationality of companies receiving contracts financed by OECF loan aid (figures given as percentage of total amount)

Year	LDC*	Japan	OECD (other than Japan)
1986	24	67	9
1988	41	43	16
1990	52	27	21
1992	52	35	13
1993	53	29	18

Source: OECF

Note: * All countries that are not OECD members are grouped together in this category, i.e. even countries such as Hong Kong, Taiwan and Singapore. This seems like an odd grouping today but probably did not when it was first created. It is the one still used by OECF other orders made through ICB. One explanation could be that Japanese companies find out about OECF projects before companies from other countries and then compete more aggressively for them. Another explanation could be that the figures simply do not show an accurate picture.

WHICH COUNTRIES RECEIVE LOANS?

Asia is where Japan considers it has a special responsibility. However, the quality[22] of aid that flows to Asia is much lower than aid granted to other countries. Asia only received 48 per cent of the grants, but almost 80 per cent of the loans in 1993. To a certain extent this results from the fact that many of the countries in Asia have reached a higher level of development and thus are considered to have the ability to afford repayment. This may not be completely logical throughout Asia, however. India, with a GNP per capita income of $310[23] receives 84 per cent of its aid from Japan in the form of loans whereas Thailand, with a GNP per capita income of $1,840, only receives 54 per cent as loans and the rest as grant aid or technical assistance. Another possible explanation is that economic infrastructure projects are concentrated in Asia and these require such a large amount of money that it has to be covered by loans (as explained in Chapter 1). The sheer volume of loans has placed many of the countries heavily in debt to Japan, with Indonesia, the largest borrower of all, in a class of its own (see Table 2.4). The five largest recipients of OECF loans are the same as the five largest recipients of Japanese ODA in 1993.

Table 2.4 Total amount of OECF loans received by the ten biggest recipients up to 1993 (¥ billion)

Country	Amount
1 Indonesia	2,413,569
2 China	1,399,102
3 India	1,393,814
4 Thailand	1,149,535
5 The Philippines	1,072,433
6 Pakistan	645,834
7 Korea	645,527
8 Malaysia	584,819
9 Bangladesh	483,593
10 Egypt	432,625

Source: Japanese Foreign Ministry official white paper on aid, 1994

TYPE OF PROJECTS FINANCED

The main part of OECF loans are used for economic infrastructure projects. In 1993 this accounted for 66 per cent of the loans. The single most significant category within infrastructure was electric power and gas development which accounted for almost 30 per cent of the total. This was followed by transportation and telecommunications (see Figure 2.3). The share of commodity loans which, among other things, support international balance of payments and structural adjustments declined to 8.6 per cent from over 30 per cent two years earlier.

Apart from loans to foreign governments, OECF also provides loans to and equity investment in private corporations working in developing countries, but this is only a minor part of its business.[24]

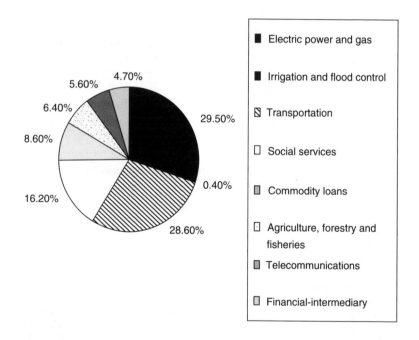

Figure 2.3   Loan commitments by sector, FY 1993
Source: OECF

OPERATIONAL GUIDELINES FOR OECF LOANS

In 1989 the Administrative Management Bureau of the Management and Co-ordination Agency which is under the Prime Minister's office, released a report that dealt with the administration of loan aid. One of its findings was that the responsibility for different loan approval procedures was not clear. This in turn led to delays in making loans, even for countries making requests on an annual basis. The report suggested that basic loan assessment guidelines should be laid down.[25]

OECF has had a range of assessment manuals in use since 1976 but no basic policy guidelines were available for the ministries in their joint decision-making, even though the system had been in operation since the 1960s and huge amounts of money had been disbursed. This situation needed immediate action and the report proposed DAC guidelines of December 1988 as a model to adopt. In March 1991 OECF published its *Operational guidelines on OECF loans* which was based on the DAC precedents and was aimed mainly at borrowers, although it served as a guide for Japan-based decisions also. In this publication the project cycle 'which every development project financed by OECF follows' is described.[26] As will become obvious in the case studies which follow, this is not always the case. This project cycle should rather be seen as a picture of how OECF ideally would like the process to work. It is a theoretical approach constructed from a desk in Tokyo. At the implementing stage it has to be adjusted to local conditions if the money is to be effectively distributed. The guidelines are given here as a point of reference when analysing the case studies.

Officially all projects, should pass through the following stages:

I Identification

This begins with the identifying of a project that will meet key development needs and ends with an initial project screening. Generally it consists of the following steps:

1 Proposing measures to solve major problems, with the setting of clear project objectives and identification of target groups (i.e. those benefiting from the project);
2 Establishing the project concept (with possible alternatives);
3 Assessing of the priority or urgency of the project in the country's economic and social development programme;
4 Determining the adequacy of the executing body and the possibilities for private sector participation;

5 Determining the approximate cost;
6 Establishing the prima-facie feasibility and preliminary assessment of project impact.

A project can be identified by government agencies, bilateral or multilateral aid agencies as well as by public or private companies from the country or from other potential donor countries.

II   Preparation

This involves a more detailed examination of the project's economic, financial and technical feasibility, i.e. a feasibility study. This can be carried out by the recipient or by a bilateral or multilateral aid agency. It can also be carried out by JICA under its technical co-operation scheme on a grant basis or by other Japanese semi-governmental organizations providing project preparation expertise on a grant basis.

The feasibility study should eventually result in a detailed report (normally it takes about six months to prepare). It should cover the following points:

1 Background information on the recent economic situation of the country, the sector targeted by the project, a history of the project formulation, information on the project site and surrounding area;
2 Objectives of the project;
3 Analysis of the need for the project, including supply and demand analysis;
4 Detailed comparison of viable alternatives;
5 Detailed description of the project;
6 Preliminary engineering design and analysis of technical feasibility;
7 Cost estimates for the project (both foreign and local currency components);
8 Implementation schedule;
9 Project implementation, operation and maintenance scheme;
10 Executing agency and institutional arrangements;
11 Evaluation of the technical soundness, economical and financial viability, social aspects (including the place of and effect on women in the development) and environmental impact;
12 Possible project risk;
13 Recommendations, if any.

Once the feasibility report is prepared there is also a need for a project implementation programme. This should contain information about (a) priority of the project, (b) financial and budgetary plans for covering the project cost in addition to any OECF loan, and (c) details of the items for which financing by OECF is desired. Most of the items covered by the implementation programme are similar to those in the feasibility study, but while the study should be based on an objective analysis, the implementation programme concerns itself with the intentions of the recipient. If necessary, OECF has a programme called 'Special Assistance for Project Formation' (SAPROF) to help draw up implementation programmes for projects.

When the feasibility report and the implementation plan have been drawn up, the recipient is in a position to request an OECF loan from the Government of Japan. This is done through the Japanese Embassy in the recipient's country.

III Appraisal

From the Embassy the request is handed over to a consultation group consisting of members of the Four Ministries and OECF. (At this stage OECF has usually already received a copy from its overseas office.) OECF then starts a pre-study of the project and, if necessary, a fact-finding mission can be dispatched; it then reports back to the Four Ministries. The Japanese government then sends a mission to the borrower's country for general consultation on the project in the broad perspective of national development.

After the project has been selected for appraisal by the Japanese government (that is, the Four Ministries), OECF's next step is to send an appraisal mission to examine the economic, social, financial, technical, environmental, organizational and managerial aspects of the proposed project. The mission discusses in detail these aspects with the borrower and also carries out a survey of the project site. In principle, international competitive bidding is required for OECF loans. If other procurement procedures are required then OECF ascertains the reasons for their adoption, for example, the type of work and the availability and capability of local contractors. An appraisal mission usually consists of two people, one responsible for the economical aspects and one for the technical ones; their work usually takes around three weeks. The mission reports, first to the OECF board, and then to the Japanese government. Based on the result of this appraisal the government (that is, the consultation group of representatives of the Four Ministries) arrives at its decision on whether the project is suitable for an OECF loan as well as the amount, terms and conditions of the loan.

IV   Negotiations for exchange of notes and loan agreement

The decision to extend a loan is normally announced at an international conference or by the Japanese Embassy in the country concerned. After this 'Prior Notification' representatives from the two governments begin negotiations. When an agreement has been reached, an Exchange of Notes (E/N) is signed stipulating the name of the project, the amount, terms and conditions of the loan, and other bilateral matters such as tax treatment and marine insurance. For the larger recipients in Asia this Exchange of Notes usually names a number of projects at the same time. After this, OECF and the appropriate body of the recipient country engage in concrete loan agreement negotiations and write a contract. In the loan agreement OECF states its financing commitment, specifies in detail the loan amount with terms and conditions, the purpose, scope and content of the project, the executing agency, procurement procedures, disbursement procedures and general terms and conditions.

V   Procurement and disbursement

When a project enters the construction stage, it is the recipient that arranges procurement. The recipient is also in charge of contracting as well as the execution of the project. The recipient prepares the tender documents and divides the project into different contractual stages if that is considered necessary. A consultant may be employed for this job, although it is not a requirement. The recipient is responsible for the implementation and should follow OECF's *Guidelines for the employment of consultants by OECF borrowers* or in the case of material and equipment *Guidelines for procurement under OECF loans*. In principle, procurement of material and equipment is done through ICB. There are, however, certain exceptions:

1 Where the recipient has adequate reasons for wishing to maintain reasonable standardization of its equipment or spare parts in the interest of compatibility with existing equipment;
2 Where the recipient has adequate reasons for wishing to maintain continuity of service provided under an existing contract awarded in accordance with procedures acceptable to OECF;
3 Where the number of qualified suppliers or contractors is limited;
4 Where the amount involved in the procurement is so small that foreign firms clearly would not be interested, or where the advantages of ICB would be outweighed by the administrative burden involved;

5 Where in addition to the above, OECF deems it inappropriate to follow ICB procedures, e.g. in the case of emergency procurement.

The alternative to ICB can then be limited international bidding and international shopping or direct contracting.

OECF is to review and concur the procurement process at several points. It should review and agree tender documents, tender evaluation and contracts, although as long as guidelines are followed it will not intervene. In this sense the recipient governs the procurement process.

The disbursement of loan funds is made as project construction progresses and in response to requests for disbursement by the recipient.

VI Supervision

During the construction of a project, OECF monitors the progress to ensure successful implementation. This supervision covers both physical implementation of the project and loan procedure. Periodic progress reports on the project prepared by the executing agency as required by the loan agreement are useful for identifying problems at an early stage. OECF discusses with the executing agency how any problem encountered can be solved and, if necessary, difficulties can also be discussed with higher authorities of both governments.

VII Post-evaluation

This is carried out in order to learn lessons from the completed project for better planning and more effective implementation of future projects.

Figure 2.4 illustrates the project cycle of OECF loans.

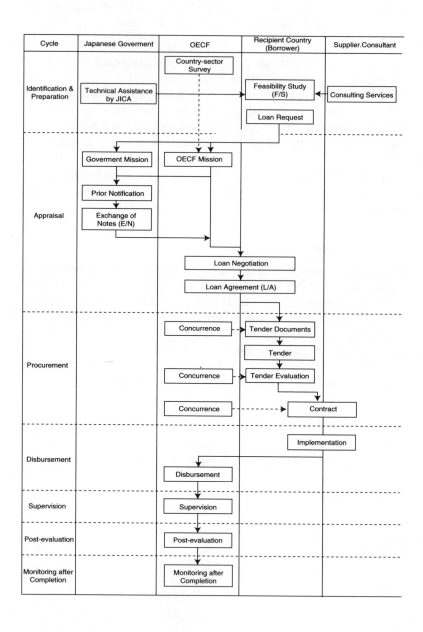

Figure 2.4   OECF project cycle of loans to foreign governments

NOTES

1 Akira Nishigaki, President, Chairman of the Board of OECF in *OECF Annual Report 1994.*
2 The Exim Bank – Export-Import Bank of Japan – is a governmental financial institution that currently deals with other official flows, that is, so-called 'soft loans' which do not have conditions lean enough to qualify them as ODA.
3 For the early part of OECF history, Alan Rix, *Japan's Economic Aid: Policymaking and Politics*, Croom Helm, London, 1980 is relied upon.
4 Figures according to OECF *Annual Report 1994.*
5 This was the way Nippon Koei, the engineering consulting firm working on the Indonesian case, Renun, claimed it was done: It was one of their engineers that passed by the spot and thought it was an ideal place for a hydroelectric power plant. Since the begining of the 1990s, engineering consulting services have also been partly untied.
6 Figures are from July 1994, since then a new office has also been opened in Vietnam.
7 As of April 1995.
8 As of June 1995.
9 David Arase *Buying Power: The Political Economy of Japan's Foreign Aid*, Lynne Rienner, Boulder, CO, 1995
10 Financial Times, 16 March 1995.
11 Alan Rix, *Japan's Foreign Aid Challenge*, Routledge, London and New York, 1993.
12 Figures according to OECF.
13 An explanation of how this is calculated can be found in *DAC Report 1993.*
14 *DAC Report 1994.*
15 Interview with an official at Loan Policy and Planning Sector, Fiscal Policy Office, Ministry of Finance, Thailand.
16 This is an agreement reached among a number of industrialized countries on how the debt of the poorest as well as lower middle-income countries should be rescheduled.
17 This was an unusual case as rescheduling usually covers debts which fail during a certain period (maturity-based).
18 Interview with an official at Co-Financing Division, Co-ordination Department, OECF.
19 Figures from OECF.
20 That means that procurement can be carried out by companies from developing countries or from Japan but not from any other OECD country.
21 General untied means that procurement can be done from companies of any nationality (that is including companies from other OECD countries).
22 That is, quality as measured by DAC in terms of grant share or grant element.
23 1992 figure according to the Japanese Foreign Ministry.
24 The total outstanding loan balance amounted to ¥39 billion and equity investment ¥137 billion in 1993.
25 Rix *Japan's Foreign Aid Challenge*, op. cit.
26 For a more detailed account see the publication itself as only a summary is provided here.

3 Japanese ODA – the business perspective

Marie Söderberg

Embedded in Japan's philosophy of development is the idea that the public and private sectors must work not as adversaries, but as partners in development.[1]

Private companies are given a more prominent position in the Japanese approach to development than in other countries. ODA is not viewed as a separate activity but as one component of the concept of 'economic co-operation'. The present five-year plan which specifies that Japan should increase its ODA to $70–5 billion during 1993–7, is part of a bigger plan for financial co-operation with developing countries in which another $50 billion is to be extended through other official channels, such as loans from the Exim Bank, MITI insurance, etc., during the same period.

While MITI, the prime promoter of the interests of Japanese industry, was against extending assistance that might help developing countries' export industries during the 1970s and early 1980s, this has changed today. As Japanese industry moved some of its production abroad, because of the high value of the yen following the Plaza Accord, MITI became a supporter of export efforts in developing countries.[2] Economic infrastructure was central for such efforts. In this sense ODA became a tool, not only for promoting the export efforts of recipient countries but also for restructuring Japanese industry. A division of labour was to be created in Asia whereby labour-intensive and 'dirty' Japanese production facilities were located abroad. Economic infrastructure, partly paid for by aid, was needed to create new locations for Japanese production.[3]

After a concerted struggle against the untying of loans, the measure is now said by MITI to have raised the financial efficiency of loan aid. In the choice of projects, priority is no longer attached to whether a specific Japanese company will receive the order or not. The sole criterion, apart from the project benefiting the recipient country, is whether it will promote trade between Japan and the recipient country, that is, whether it is beneficial for Japanese trade in general.[4]

ODA V. PRIVATE INVESTMENT IN DEVELOPING COUNTRIES

In many Asian countries direct investment by Japanese companies is substantial, yet ODA also plays an important role in the country's relations with the developing world. While Japanese ODA represents 20 per cent of DAC total, its private capital flows in 1994 represents only 10 per cent of the total of the DAC members. Contrary to the image of Japanese companies expanding all over the world, Japanese direct investment in developing countries is not as significant as its ODA is in comparison with other DAC countries.

In 1994 the sum of Japanese private flows was lower than its ODA for the third consecutive year (see Table 3.1).

1990 and 1991 witnessed very high Japanese direct investment in developing countries. In 1991 total private flows were actually greater than total ODA flows. After that there was a sharp decrease in 1992 and 1993 in Japanese private flows to developing countries. This was in sharp contrast to the general trend in which net resource flows from DAC members to developing countries in 1993 increased and accounted for 56 per cent of total flows.[5] Net flows of private capital from Japan to developing countries and multilateral organizations were only 0.01 per cent of GNP which was far below the 1993 DAC average of 0.33 per cent.[6]

Even though the value of the yen increased during 1992 and 1993, this did not seem to have led to a corresponding increase in direct investment in developing countries. One reason for this might have been the general recesssion in the Japanese economy which actually led many companies to refrain from investing abroad.

In 1994 the situation changed again. Private flows increased drastically and actually became almost as high as the ODA. As a percentage of GNP it amounted to 0.26 which is still below the 0.45 that is the DAC average.[7]

ODA V. PRIVATE INVESTMENT IN ASIA

The 'emerging markets' in Asia are the developing countries that receive most of the private flows from the DAC members. These flows are also increased considerably during recent years. While in

Table 3.1 Total flow of financial resources from Japan to developing countries (net disbursements $ million)

	1991	1992	1993	1994
I Official development assistance	11,034	11,332	11,474	13,469
1 Bilateral assistance				
(a) Grants	1,525	1,733	2,019	2,403
(b) Technical assistance	1,870	2,132	2,602	3,020
(c) Loans	5,475	4,620	3,544	4,257
2 Contributions to multilateral institutions	2,163	2,848	3,310	3,788
3 As a percentage of GNP	0.32	0.31	0.27	0.29
II Other official flows	2,699	3,585	3,962	3,300
1 Export credits (over 1 year)	510	61	43	616
2 Direct investment and others	3,155	2,461	3,287	614
3 Finances to multilateral institutions	54	1,063	631	2,070
III Private flows	11,142	838	1,517	11,531
1 Export credits (over 1 year)	602	1,005	1,975	1,701
2 Direct investment	5,003	2,811	2,355	7,437
3 Other bilateral securities and claims	6,227	2,076	997	5,263
4 Finances to multilateral institutions	690	3,045	3,809	2,870
IV Total official and private flows as a percentage of GNP	0.74	0.44	0.40	0.62

Source: Japanese Foreign Ministry

Table 3.2   Japanese direct investment and total net ODA to four Asian countries in 1993 ($ million)

Country	Direct investment	Total net ODA
China	1,691	1,351
Indonesia	813	1,149
The Philippines	207	758
Thailand	578	350

Source: Direct investment figures on accumulated approval basis from Keizai Kōhō Center; total net ODA figures from DAC

1993 they amounted to less than $40 billion they increased to well over $50 billion in 1994. This is also the case with Japanese private flows to developing countries. Their direct investment is heavily concentrated in certain Asian countries.

An examination of the four countries which are the subjects of the case studies in this book reveals the pattern shown in Table 3.2.

Direct investment in Thailand by Japanese companies has been much greater than ODA for the last few years. Japanese direct investment in Indonesia since 1980 has also generally been greater than ODA, with a few exceptions, one such being 1993. In China, direct investment by Japanese companies has been greater than ODA since 1992. The Philippines is the sole exception. In this country ODA consistently exceeded direct investment throughout the 1980s.

JAPANESE TRADE WITH THE COUNTRIES IN ASIA

Since 1991, Japan's largest trading partner by region has been South East Asia.[8] The largest export markets in the region have been Hong Kong, Taiwan and Korea. The largest export markets for Japan among those countries with a lower level of development include China, which gets 4.8 per cent of Japanese exports, Thailand with 3.4 per cent, Malaysia with 2.7 per cent, Indonesia with 1.7 per cent and the Philippines with 1.3 per cent. Japanese imports from the developing countries are primarily from China with 8.5 per cent of Japan's total imports, Indonesia with 5.2 per cent, Malaysia with 3.2 per cent, Thailand with 2.7 per cent and the Philippines with 1.0 per cent.

Japanese trade with China is significant but it cannot be said that Japanese trade is particualarly dependent on any one Asian country, although the region as a whole is of great importance. It is obvious from the Table 3.3 that trade dependence on Japan by the developing

Table 3.3   Japan's share of imports and exports as a percentage of the 1994 total

	Exports to Japan	Imports from Japan
Indonesia	30	22
Thailand	17	30
China	17	22
Philippines	17	21

Source: Economist Intelligence Unit, London

countries included in the case studies is much greater than the converse situation.

THE IMPORTANCE OF INDUSTRIAL PROMOTION IN THE DEVELOPING WORLD

The Japanese government regards the promotion of private industry in Asian countries as important to their economic development. There are a number of programmes to promote industrialization. One of them, provided by ODA, is the so called 'two-step loans' in which private companies in the developing world are provided with capital at a subsidized cost. Another programme is OECF equity investment in companies in developing countries.

OECF also supports the Japanese International Development Organization (JAIDO), a body established by Keidanren, the Japanese Federation of Economic Organizations, and a number of private companies. JAIDO's aim is to promote foreign currency earning projects in which Japanese companies and local enterprises jointly invest. Japanese industry is in favour of ODA and Keidanren has a special department to deal with 'economic co-operation'. It formulates programmes on ways economic co-operation should be implemented and submits policy proposals to the ministries and the Government of Japan.

KEIDANREN'S VIEW OF ODA

Keidanren would like ODA to be increased to 0.7 per cent of GNP. It is also seeking to raise the proportion of grants above current levels and improve co-operation between loans, grants and technical assistance.[9]

According to Keidanren there is a decreasing interest in ODA among Japanese corporations.[10] This trend has become particularly evident during the last five or six years, and is to a large extent connected with two important factors. The first is the general untying of Japanese aid which has been official government policy since April 1978. Since 97 per cent of the loans now are untied there is no longer any guarantee that Japanese industry will profit from them. The second factor is the appreciation of the yen during the last few years, which has made it increasingly difficult for Japanese companies to win contracts for loan aid projects where procurement is undertaken by international competitive bidding. Recently, Japanese companies have increasingly found themselves beaten in the bidding process, primarily by companies from NICs, such as South Korea, Hong Kong and Taiwan, where, with weaker currencies and lower labour costs, they have a clear advantage over companies from Japan. Japanese companies' share of ODA contracts has dropped from 67 per cent in 1986 to 29 per cent in 1993. This will be highlighted in the Indonesian case study where Japanese aid money helped a Korean company to establish itself in the hydroelectric electricity market. LDCs in general increased their share from 24 to 53 per cent and European companies from 9 to 18 per cent (see Table 2.3).

The high untied ratio of Japanese ODA is seen by Japanese companies as being extremely unfair, allowing companies from other countries to bid on their aid projects while they are not allowed to bid on projects from other OECD countries that usually have a much higher percentage of tied aid.[11] What the Japanese companies fail to consider is that other OECD countries do not have ODA loans to the same extent as Japan but have a much higher percentage of grants. In principle, Japanese grant assistance and technical assistance is tied and this amounted to more than $4.6 billion in 1993 (see Chapter 1). This is one part of aid where Japanese industry interests have not diminished.

Improved co-operation of the different parts within the concept of economic co-operation, that is, between ODA and private flows is also seen as vital to Keidanren: 'A better system is needed to effectively organize governmental and private activities, so that ODA and private activities may go like two wheels of a cart.'[12] It also considers that the shortage of personnel at OECF and JICA should be solved by commissioning private concerns to undertake aid projects: 'When it comes to ODA, what the government has is the money, but it is the private sector that has the best technological and financial know-how and expertise.'[13] This know-how in the private sector is also used in

Japan to create and plan for new projects that may be eligible for ODA. This is part of the work of Japanese engineering consultant companies.

ENGINEERING CONSULTING FIRMS

A survey was carried out by the Engineering Consulting Firms Association (ECFA), of overseas projects undertaken by its 53 regular members in 1992. This showed that these projects amounted to ¥55,290 million ($437 million) and 77 per cent of them were undertaken in Asia.

About half the clients of Japanese engineering consulting firms were governments of developing countries, although in most cases projects were financed through OECF loans. Other major clients were the Japanese government in JICA-related projects. About 9 per cent of the projects were carried out on behalf of private companies and 11 per cent for international organizations, such as the UN or World Bank (see Figure 3.1).

The role of development consultants is to identify projects, carry out field surveys and conduct feasibility studies. They can be engaged in design of the project and preparation of tender documents, tender assistance and inspection, as well as selection of construction companies and suppliers. They can supervise construction and, upon completion, supervise operation of the implemented project and provide on-site training.

Although ECFA has 53 companies as members, there are a few large engineering consulting companies that dominate the market.

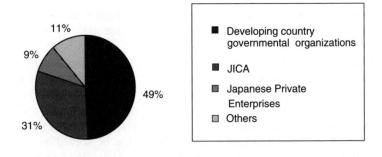

Figure 3.1   Clients of Japanese engineering consulting firms working on overseas projects
Source: ECFA

Two in particular have a dominant position: Nippon Koei (founded in 1946) and Pacific Consultants (founded in 1969). Each company has more than 300 employees engaged in overseas consulting work. Their overseas business turnover for 1992 is ¥11 billion ($87 million) and ¥11.7 billion ($92 million) respectively. Both companies have much experience and well-established contacts in Asia.

One of the main purposes of ECFA's research department is to find potential new projects and develop proposals in various areas. ECFA does not have specialists in all areas but uses experts seconded from member companies who then carry out the work under ECFA guidance. MITI provides grants for studying new areas of co-operation. ECFA, on occasions, performs different kinds of research for OECF. It also lobbies politicians (particularly those who are former MITI employees) in its endeavours to interest the government in various proposals.[14]

ECFA has 45 associate members, these are mainly banks and manufacturing companies. It also maintains contact with trading houses and they sometimes carry out so-called 'upstream project preparation' together.

TRADING HOUSES AND THEIR ROLE

As a representative of a Japanese trading house in Indonesia in 1989 I had to go out to the airport and collect the different government delegates connected with ODA when they arrived. It is also the trading companies who have to arrange these visits and set up meetings with people with whom they can meet and inspect sites which might be of interest to them. We even had to pay for their entertainment and host different kinds of parties for them.

In the case of Indonesia this is no small task as in 1989 there were more than 1,100 delegates who visited and most of them did not stay in the capital but travelled extensively in the countryside. Trading house representatives used to meet and decide who had to do what for each delegation and then decide the time and place when one person took over from another. Recently trading houses have become very tired of this business as they are not paid for it at all.[15]

JICA and OECF differ in this respect. JICA projects are mostly tied and the money-making potential of projects is still good and, consequently, the interest of the trading houses remains strong.[16] With

OECF projects, which are now mostly untied, the trading houses can never be sure of receiving anything in return.

This does not mean that the trading houses are not interested in ODA loan aid related projects, which still have certain advantages, including a low level of risk. They know that they will receive payment because money is set aside for the project by the Japanese government. Another important aspect of ODA loans is the access they give, to people in prominent positions within developing countries. Rather than being interested solely in ODA projects, many of the trading houses regard these projects as a useful asset in their general 'networking' in recipient countries. ODA then, is just one of the services offered by the trading houses.

Trading houses can also play a role in ODA with the good relationships their employees form with government officials in developing countries. They know many officials well and may, for instance, play golf with them or be invited to their parties.

The governments of recipient countries are usually wary of acting against the policy recommendations of the donor. There may also be competition between government agencies resulting in a long list of proposed projects, which is far too long to be handled easily so there is a need for someone who can select a few projects suitable for the Japanese ODA policy programme. This selection role can be performed by representatives of the trading houses in the recipient countries.

In Tokyo representatives from the six biggest trading houses meet monthly with officials from MITI, MOF and MOFA to exchange ideas; they form a small group of people who know each other well. The trading houses also have their own economic co-operation departments, similar to Mitsui's which is examined below, and they are generally well informed about ODA business.

Traditionally, the trading houses have largely co-operated with Japanese companies but with the high value of the yen their competitiveness has been considerably weakened. This makes it difficult for them to win orders through international competitive bidding and a new trend has emerged of the trading houses being more open to co-operation with foreign companies, a necessity if they are not to lose business. This will be highlighted in our Philippine case study where all the Japanese trading houses involved worked with foreign suppliers.

INDUSTRY IN THE RECIPIENT COUNTRIES

Staff of the executing agency in the recipient country are in charge of the tendering process and contracting for OECF loans. They are the ones who decide the number of contracts a project should be divided into as well as what should be included in each of them. This could be a competitive advantage for local companies, which are often well-connected in their own country. However, often they do not have the competence nor the technologies needed for advanced economic infrastructure. The degree of competence and technological know-how required is dependent, of course, on the project factor. Companies in the recipient countries can manage some projects extremely well by themselves, as will be shown in our Thai case, while in others their share of the work is limited to sub-contracting.

One way for them to overcome this problem is by forming joint ventures with foreign companies that have the technological know-how. The advantage for a foreign company with a joint venture is that they obtain knowledge of local conditions and can, in some countries, be more favourably considered during the contract process. It is no coincidence that most of the foreign companies tendering for projects in Indonesia have local partners. They know that this makes the process easier. Different regulations and practices in recipient countries can work in favour of different constellations of companies in the bidding process, as will become clear from the case studies.

INDUSTRY IN OECD COUNTRIES

The interest of DAC countries in participation in projects in the 'emerging markets' of Asia has grown considerably, demonstrated by, among other things, the substantial increase of private flows to the region. The reasons for this interest are obvious: whereas many European countries have struggled with recession and have had sluggish economic growth in recent years, the situation in East Asia has been the reverse. Economic growth in most of the countries has been very high (the Philippines being one of the exceptions). One bottleneck to further economic progress is a lack of infrastructure. There is a great need for many items and plans are ambitious. The problem is how to finance it all.

One method that has recently been used more often is the so called BOT (Build–Operate–Transfer) or BOO (Build–Operate–Own). Private companies invest in infrastructure projects and then recoup their investment with the profit earned from operating a power plant or from charging a toll for a road for a certain number of years. The companies are often involved in a high level of risk since it is not certain what regulations may be imposed by governments or whether the political and economic situation will remain stable.

Another means of financing infrastructure projects has been through different types of ODA loans. The most predominant, apart from perhaps the World Bank, are OECF loans. Foreign company interest in participation in such projects has grown considerably as the loans have become increasingly untied. The profits involved may be smaller than in the private sector, but the risk is extremely low and the companies are paid in cash.

Several European embassies in Tokyo actively inform companies in their home country of these business opportunities. Larger companies, established in the Asian market, are already well informed and bid extensively when an opportunity arises.

THE MITSUI CASE – A STUDY OF HOW ONE COMPANY APPROACHES ODA
by Magnus Berg

Mitsui & Co. Ltd (Mitsui Bussan in Japanese) is one of Japan's largest trading houses, or *sōgō shōsha*. It was founded in 1876, and quickly became one of the leading companies behind Japan's stunning transformation from an isolated country to a modern industrialized nation. The company prides itself on being instrumental in developing such areas as rice and coal exports, and also playing a key role in Japan's early spinning industry.[17]

Until the end of World War II, Mitsui was one of Japan's leading *zaibatsu* (family-controlled industrial and financial groups). In 1947, following Japan's defeat in the war, the company was dissolved by the Allied occupation powers, to become a dispersed group of about 220 companies. In 1959, most of these companies were reunited to form today's Mitsui & Co. The company, one of the largest in the world, ranks second or third among Japanese companies, with trading turnover for fiscal 1994 of $173 billion. This constituted a small increase over 1993, but the gross trading profit dropped by 60.3 per cent, reflecting the continuing recession in Japan's domestic market.

Mitsui operates all over the world, and in almost every conceivable industrial sector. Its largest business segment are, in order of importance, non-ferrous metals, machinery, energy, iron and steel, foodstuffs, and chemicals. These six segments comprise around 89 per cent of Mitsui's total trading turnover. In 1992, a major restructuring took place. Previously the organization had been very fragmented with approximately 100 different business areas, but for practical reasons these were combined into 11 larger areas. These operate as independent companies, in that they have their own budgets, although they are supported by an administrative area whose operations are included within the parent company's budget. One of the administrative divisions is the Overseas Co-ordination and Administration Division (OCAD), which handles all matters concerning overseas business. The OCAD employs some 40 people and presides over even smaller units. One of these units is the Economic Co-operation Department, the Mitsui department responsible for ODA matters.

Mitsui's Economic Co-operation Department

The Economic Co-operation Department (ECD) was established in 1987 as a means of co-ordinating ODA-related information within the company. Prior to this, the different business areas undertook their own research on ODA, which was time-consuming and led to a lot of unnecessary duplication. One of the reasons for setting up ECD was that Mitsui considers ODA to be of growing importance. The work of ECD is very long term, and it can investigate suitable projects for up to two years before ODA is actually given by the Japanese government. This was another reason for setting up ECD, each business area could not afford such long-term planning by itself.

At first, ECD employed only a few people and their activities were rather small-scale. In the beginning of the 1990s, however, as Mitsui started placing greater emphasis on ODA work, staffing was increased and the department became more active, travelling abroad far more. Today, ECD employs nine people, plus three who are stationed outside the main office. Apart from the divisional manager, all employees of ECD have their own fields or areas of research. Usually these areas are geographical regions, such as China, South-East Asia, Africa, ASEAN, South America, etc. ECD also has one person working full-time at Keidanren's ODA organization, JAIDO. It has two overseas offices, one in Mexico, responsible for all of the Americas, and one in Johannesburg, South Africa, responsible for Southern Africa. There are no overseas offices in Asia, allegedly because it is so close to Japan that the Tokyo staff can travel frequently themselves. The background of ECD staff is almost exclusively in economic studies, which means that they have no previous work experience in ODA business (for example with JICA, OECF, etc.).

The purpose of ECD's work is to find suitable and profitable ODA projects for the Mitsui branches. This is achieved mainly by travelling to foreign countries and by visiting the relevant agencies and ministries in Tokyo. When going abroad to developing countries, ECD staff will visit the Japanese embassy in the country to obtain information about what projects might be in the planning process and which ministries to visit. To a certain extent it is possible for the ambassador or other embassy personnel to steer the company in a direction that suits their preferences or those of the recipient country. ECD staff will then visit, at the higher levels of the country's administration, the ministries who handle transportation, energy, communications (telephone systems, etc.), agriculture, water (irrigation projects, etc.) and other areas where Mitsui operates. They will obtain information about planned projects, budgets, yearly reports, etc., as well as searching for construction and business partners, that is, everything needed to make a decision about which projects to bid for.

Although foreign travel is the main task of ECD staff, a lot of research is also done in Tokyo. The ministries involved in the ODA process are visited, MITI, MOFA, JICA, OECF, and to a lesser extent MOF, to obtain information about projects. When discussing projects in the planning stages, advice can be given such as, for example, that for the government to consider extending ODA, more data on one aspect or another is needed. Mitsui will then return and obtain additional information about the project. According to ECD personnel, the contacts between Mitsui and these government agencies are strictly limited to formal visits. Allegedly, no working groups or contact networks between the political and business worlds exist in this area, either official or unofficial. 'Japan Inc.' obviously does not operate in foreign aid, at least not where Mitsui is involved.

The philosophy, if there is such a thing, behind Mitsui's ODA activities is fairly simple. For Japan, a non-military power with enormous economic importance in the world, aid to developing countries is one of the most important parts of the country's foreign policy. In line with Japan's increasing importance in ODA, the business opportunities linked to foreign aid will also increase and grow more profitable. Therefore, Mitsui must seek out ODA projects, or risk the loss of business opportunities and competitiveness. This could seem to be contradictory to Keidanren's worries that Japanese companies are losing interest in ODA, but according to officials at ECD, this loss of interest applies to smaller companies only. For large corporations like Mitsui, there are still profits to be made from ODA business. Large companies can afford to have a non-profit-making, long-term research department because of the range of industry sectors covered. For example, if a company in the iron and steel business goes abroad to search for projects, but finds them only in areas where it does not operate, it will have wasted the effort. If Mitsui's ECD does the same thing, there will almost certainly be a Mitsui division operating in that field. Accordingly, it is only for the really large companies that ODA will remain profitable. And it is of course profit that constitutes the foundation of Mitsui's ODA policy. It is a profit-making company and it makes no pretence of having any 'humanitarian' motives behind its ODA activities. However, it is trying to increase participation in projects concerning such relatively newly targeted areas as environment protection, overpopulation and AIDS. This is because Mitsui considers it important that the quality of ODA is improved. With all the know-how it and other Japanese companies have in areas like the environment and hospital building, Mitsui believes companies should support developing countries in these areas.

A further reason for Mitsui becoming involved in ODA projects is that, compared to other overseas business projects or investments, ODA is considered less risky, since payment is guaranteed. This is of course because the client, that is, the recipient country, receives money as loan or grant from the Japanese government. With money earmarked for a particular project, companies know that payment is certain.

When it comes to concentrating on particular countries and regions this is mainly determined by two factors. First, to a large extent it naturally follows the pattern of overall Japanese aid. Since Asia is by far the biggest receiver of Japanese ODA, it is natural for Mitsui to concentrate most of its efforts there. The second selection principle is to focus on countries where Mitsui traditionally has a strong business influence. An example of such a country is the recently independent Uzbekistan in Central Asia, where Mitsui has been operating for many years and has built up a strong network of business contacts. With many of the newly liberalized countries of the former Soviet Union now increasingly targeted as recipients of Japanese ODA, and this is a very interesting area watched closely by Mitsui. The opposite would be true for Mongolia, where Mitsui's business has always been very small-scale, but where other large Japanese companies have built a strong base. Although Mitsui does not disregard a country like Mongolia, it is not one of its prime targets. Instead, it is in countries like China, the Philippines, Indonesia, Myanmar (Burma), and Bangladesh that Mitsui most often engages in ODA projects. New targets in Asia are also Cambodia and, in particular, Vietnam, whose transition to a market economy makes it an interesting prospect for the future.

However, perhaps the most interesting new target for Mitsui at the moment is South Africa, which is illustrated by the fact that from 1994 ECD has had someone stationed there permanently. The ECD expect a large increase in Japanese ODA to the recently democratized former apartheid country in the near future, as well as strong business opportunities in the future. The government's future policies on certain countries is again something that Mitsui is aware of, thanks to thorough research by ECD. It closely follows and tries to anticipate government policy.

The largest business segment involved in Mitsui's ODA projects is machinery, where the company has some of its strongest business areas, such as road building, dams, ports and other construction projects. The total amount of ODA money involved in Mitsui's projects has been increasing steadily in the last few years to a level of about ¥85,200 million ($665 million) in fiscal 1992, but took a sharp drop in 1993 to ¥65,400 million ($540 million). Almost the entire drop was accounted for in the machinery area, where the company lost two big contracts that would otherwise have raised the figures to about the same level as the previous year. On the positive side, though, Mitsui noted that most other areas increased slightly, and also that some new business areas became involved. Grants constituted the largest part of ODA money, about three times as much as the income earned from loans. Mitsui's share of the Japanese 'ODA market' lies around 7 per cent, placing them fourth among Japanese companies in 1992.[18] The company's target over the five-year period 1992–97 is to double the 1992 profit by 1997. One means of doing this is an increase in manpower and funds for overseas travel for ECD.

Many observers would consider that the question of tied or untied aid is the biggest problem for Japanese companies in dealing with ODA, but in Mitsui's opinion that is not the case. Instead, Mitsui cites appreciation of the yen during the last couple of years as the biggest problem. The skyrocketing value of the yen has led Japanese companies to lose competitiveness, mainly to companies from NICs and ASEAN, and lately also from China. In Mitsui's view, obtaining more tied loans should not be a target, since an increase in Japanese exports is not necessary or even desirable, considering the severe criticism Japan has received for its huge trade surplus.

The slow decision-making process in Japanese ODA is also a matter of concern for Mitsui. Sometimes it takes as much as a year to 18 months from request to approval. Such long waiting periods are, of course, costly to companies who have spent time and money preparing for projects. It is Mitsui's goal to try and speed up the process. An additional problem with Japan's aid administration is that it is extremely understaffed, compared to the big donors in North America and Western Europe. This is one reason why Mitsui would like to see an increased role for NGOs in the ODA process.

Mitsui always uses outside consultants for overseas ODA projects, and invariably Japanese companies. The two largest consulting firms presently used by Mitsui are Pacific Consultant International (PCI) and Nippon Koei. At the moment, PCI are engaged in a project in South Africa, trying to find suitable water projects for Mitsui. This includes construction of a piping system supplying the people in the former South African homelands with drinking water. PCI is also investigating the possibility of building railroads that would connect the homelands with Johannesburg.

There are cases when feasibility studies made for Mitsui by, for example, PCI, will be used directly in the country's application for ODA. This is especially true for poorer countries that cannot afford to make their own investigations. Then only a letter asking for a loan or grant will be added and sent with the report. In such a case, Mitsui will in fact have paid for the country's application, but this is something the company does not object to. (Although Mitsui does of course expect eventually to be awarded the contract.) Sometimes, a report may need to be supplemented, which is then done by JICA or OECF, before the final decision about ODA is taken by the decision-making authorities in Tokyo. Mitsui's and other companies' role in ODA project finding is something that is much appreciated by government ODA organizations, according to officials of ECD. When a suitable project has been found by ECD and investigated by a consulting firm, the responsibility then shifts to the Mitsui business area involved. It does all the planning and the budgeting for the project, and eventually submits a bid for the contract. However, it keeps ECD informed throughout, enabling ECD to evaluate the project afterwards.

88   *Marie Söderberg*

NOTES

1 Masamichi Hanabusa, 'A Japanese perspective on aid and development', in Shafique Islam (ed.), *Yen for Development*, Council of Foreign Relations Press, New York, 1991.
2 Interview with an official of Economic Co-operation Co-ordination Office, MITI.
3 David Arase, *Buying Power: The Political Economy of Japan's Foreign Aid*, Lynne Rienner Publishers, Boulder, CO, 1995.
4 MITI interview, op. cit.
5 DAC figures (net flows).
6 DAC *Annual Report 1994*.
7 Ibid.
8 Merchandised trade on a custom clearance basis; figures from Keizai Koho Center, *Japan 1995: An International Comparison*, Keizai Koho Centre, Tokyo, 1995.
9 Keidanren, *Economic Cooperation for International Causes, A Proposal for Formulation of Basic Rules of Official Development Assistance*, 24 March 1992 (This is Keidaren's main policy document on ODA which was to have been revised in the summer of 1994 but as there was no change in circumstances the revision did not occur.)
10 Interview with an official from Keidanren's Economic Cooperation Department.
11 Ibid.
12 Keidanren, *Economic Cooperation for International Causes*, op. cit.
13 Keidanren interview, op. cit.
14 Interview with an official at ECFA.
15 Interview with an official of a Japanese trading house in April 1994. This section is primarily based on interviews with a number of representatives from different Japanese trading houses.
16 In September 1994 the Fair Trade Commission of Japan on the order of the Foreign Ministry started an investigation (or 'raid' as it was dubbed by the media) of 37 major companies suspected of bid-rigging (*dango* in Japanese) on ODA contracts for technical assistance which are open only to Japanese companies. As a result of the investigation a year later, 37 companies were fined ¥165.5 million for forming a number of illicit cartels.
17 Mitsui & Co., Ltd, *Annual Report 1994*.
18 Mitsubishi, Nissho Iwai and Itochu are the three companies ahead of Mitsui.

4 Road to development in Thailand

Marie Söderberg

INTRODUCTION

Everyone who has visited Bangkok is aware of it. Travelling from the airport into the city gives you a preview of what to expect. It is not the friendliness of the Thai people that I am referring to. Even if your taxi driver is very friendly you are likely to become rather weary after, in the worst case, spending three or four hours sitting in the taxi with him.

What I am referring to is the traffic. It rules the lives of the city's eight million inhabitants, making it impossible for people to organize more than a few meetings each day even within the city centre. Travelling around is time-consuming, unless you are willing to risk your life on a motorbike cruising between the cars. Some people do, but most play it safe and spend long hours in cars and buses every day. I have not seen any estimates of the number of productive hours lost each day to traffic congestion in the whole of Bangkok, but it must be an astonishing amount of wasted time. It is not that Bangkok is lacking in roads; it has plenty and new ones are being built all the time. The problem is that there are three million cars in the city, which is far too many for the existing roads. The car is a status symbol of the new Thai middle class.

Road building, especially highways and expressways, is expensive and there is a limit on how much the Thai government is able to spend on it. This is not something peculiar to Thailand but rather a result of its status as a developing country. There is an urgent need for a number of infrastructure projects but a constant lack of money to finance them. This is where foreigners enter the picture. Outside my hotel window there is a huge expressway high up in the sky with a multitude of roads underneath it disappearing in different directions. The expressway has a sign 'Rama IV flyover for Thai–Japanese friendship'. A little further away there is another sign 'for Thai–Belgian friendship'.

This case study examines a road project, the Chonburi–Pattaya New Highway, on which construction of the last intersections was still underway in June 1994. At that time contracting was also taking place for the next stage, a new highway from Chonburi all the way into Bangkok. Both projects were mainly financed by ODA in the form of Japanese OECF loans. In this study, emphasis is on the first project.

Why choose a road for a case study? Because road projects or, at least, highway building, cost a great deal of money which makes them into 'major' infrastructure projects. Transportation is also the main sector for aid from Japan to Thailand, measured by volume. The Department of Highways (DOH) has been the largest single Thai recipient of ODA from Japan over the years.

OECF has financed several new roads in Thailand. The loan for the Chonburi–Pattaya New Highway, totalling ¥9,787 million ($88 million), has not been the largest. The extension of this highway, the Bangkok–Chonburi Highway, received two loan agreements totalling ¥37,124 million ($334 million). Contracting for this project was still in progress when this case study was undertaken. It was, therefore, considered premature to study it and thus it was deleted from the list of possible projects. However, as it is an extension of the Chonburi–Pattaya New Highway, some information concerning it can be used as a reference and for comparison with the case study project.

The road improvement programme of three major routes is another recent project that received OECF loans, amounting to ¥22,959 million ($170 million), although this was co-financed with IBRD and the Asian Development Bank (ADB). As it involved three different organizations and three different roads it was considered too complicated to be suitable as a case study.

The Ramindra–Atnarong Expressway Construction Project received a total of ¥36,654 million ($330 million). This was administered by the Expressway and Rapid Transit Authority of Thailand[1] and not the Department of Highways. Since the Department of Highways has been the largest overall recipient of aid, it was deemed more appropriate to choose one of its projects as well as a recent major road project financed by Japanese money. This narrowed it down to the Chonburi–Pattaya New Highway.

The chapter commences with a short introduction on Thai–Japanese relations with special emphasis on economics. It is followed by an examination of Japanese ODA to Thailand in general, as well as ODA loans and OECF-specific factors. It also includes a discussion of relevant Thai regulations and country-specific factors that can affect the aid process. The case study itself begins with an analysis of the Thai motives for requesting loans for the highway and OECF motives for providing them. The Eastern Seaboard Development area will be discussed in this context.

This is followed by a discussion of the process from the request for a Master Plan of Road Development for the central area to contracting for the Chonburi–Pattaya New Highway. Finally, some conclusions are drawn from the Thai case, taking into account factors that are project- and country-specific, are related to developing countries in general, and are ODA loan- or OECF-specific.

THAI–JAPANESE RELATIONS

The Japanese are not newcomers to Thailand. As early as in 1898 the first commercial treaty between the two countries was signed. In this, the Japanese were given the same extraterritorial rights as Western nations.[2] Initially, no great importance was placed on this relationship as the countries were not particularly interested in each other and trade with Siam was totally dominated by Britain. At that time 80 per cent of Siam's import and export trade was with Britain and her colonies.

During World War I there was a shortage of Western goods, a gap that the Japanese were quick to fill. This changed the previous trading situation. Due to the cheap price of their goods, the Japanese managed to maintain their market presence and by 1932 the Japanese had captured by far the single largest share of the market.[3] Political changes in Siam in that year put an end to the absolute monarchy. The new elite that emerged tried to strengthen their power, among other ways, by strengthening their relationship with Japan. In World War II they co-operated with the Japanese who, as a result, never invaded Thailand. By the end of the war the Thais had cleverly managed to end up on the winning side.

In the 1950s, Japanese interest in trade and investment in Thailand was reawakened. Little trade was expected with China and, in addition to economic benefits for Japanese companies, the industrial development and strengthening of Thailand was also viewed as a security measure. Anti-communism was a strong reason for Thai leaders to try to strengthen and develop their nation, and Japan was regarded as another country besides the USA which could provide what was needed for their economic development.[4]

For the next two decades Japan vigorously pursued a policy of trade promotion in the area and by the early 1970s it had become the leading investor. By then it seemed obvious to the Thai people that Japanese economic diplomacy (*keizai gaiko*),was mainly dictated by commercial motives and concerned with profits. The trade imbalance that had been chronic since 1957 progressively worsened and a lot of anti-Japanese sentiment and criticism began to surface. The National Students Centre (NSC) in Thailand organized an anti-Japanese goods movement in 1972 and boycotted Japanese products at various department stores in Bangkok. When Prime Minister Tanaka arrived in Thailand on his regional goodwill trip in 1974 he was met by anti-Japanese demonstrations.

Japanese businessmen were criticized for arrogance and ruthless behaviour and some companies, afraid of repercussions, removed their business signs.[5] Since that time Japanese businessmen have tried to keep a lower and more friendly profile. They have started to donate money to different Thai charity funds and mingle more with Thai people.[6] The Japanese government also realized that something had to be done to improve the situation and the academic and culture exchange programme was greatly expanded. When Prime Minister Fukuda embarked on his trip to ASEAN countries in 1977 he was well prepared, promising large aid packages as well as declaring an equal partnership and a 'heart to heart' relationship with the people.[7]

Today, the Japanese maintain a lower profile and are more sensitive to Thai feelings, but the trade surplus and Japanese business interests in Thailand still remain. The dominance of Japanese industry is apparent to anyone entering the country. The first traffic jam you are caught in brings the realization that almost all the cars are Japanese (they control 85 per cent of the market). According to foreign investment statistics,[8] the value of Japanese investment amounted to around 50 per cent of total foreign investment (measured by start-ups) during 1991–93 (see Table 4.1). Furthermore, it amounted to over 30 per cent of the total investment in Thailand for the same period.

The Thai–Japanese Chamber of Commerce with 994 members is the largest such chamber of commerce in the world.[9] In reality there are probably twice as many Japanese companies in the country although they have not bothered to become members. Approximately 30,000 Japanese live in Thailand and an estimated 300,000 to 400,000 Thai people are employed by Japanese companies. For example, Minibear (producing bearings) employs 20,000 people in Thailand, which is more than it employs in Japan. Most of the Thais

Table 4.1 Foreign investment to Thailand, start-ups (value $ million; number)

Country	1991	1992	1993
Total investment	2,932 (433)	3,764 (438)	5,089 (374)
Total foreign investment	2,332 (292)	2,533 (265)	3,354 (22)
Japan	1,058 (122)	1,561 (107)	1,697 (86)
USA	535 (34)	361 (34)	382 (25)
Taiwan	254 (70)	226 (51)	341 (39)
Hong Kong	122 (24)	315 (22)	447 (23)
Korea	85 (7)	118 (9)	137 (13)
Singapore	214 (24)	521 (32)	205 (19)
Europe	390 (23)	647 (55)	837 (50)

Source: Thailand's Board of Investment, February 1994
Note: The total of individual countries exceeds total foreign investment as firms with investment from more than one country are counted more than once

working for Japanese companies are employed in manufacturing. These Thais comprise the new middle class, a growing consumer group who want a new home and a car of their own.

The Japanese car industry is firmly established in Thailand. In 1993 Toyota's production jumped 35 per cent to 114,700 units, Isuzu's rose 40 per cent to 87,000 units, and Nissan's climbed 2 per cent to 61,000 units.[10] Altogether Japanese car production in Thailand is expected to reach 500,000 cars per year in the near future.[11]

The trade imbalance has been consistent. The Japanese export more than twice as much as they import from Thailand[12] and it continues to be a source of complaint to the Thais. However, the general sentiment about the Japanese and Japanese investment appears to have changed. Thais are not pleased with too great a Japanese presence but they accept it. Further foreign investment is wanted and, therefore, campaigns are launched to entice more foreign companies to Thailand. Thais welcome investment from any country, but it is only Japanese companies that respond. For example, over 1994–97 the Thai Board of Investment is launching a National Supplier Development Programme and expects more than 5,000 foreign supporting industries to relocate their operations to Thailand within three years. Companies from all countries are welcome and, depending on their category, will be given certain promotional privileges. The Thais expect the response to be primarily Japanese.[13]

The field of ODA is similar. Thailand would gladly except aid from most foreign countries or multilateral organizations. The fact is that it is only Japan that is willing to offer any substantial loan packages on really favourable terms.

JAPANESE ODA TO THAILAND

The origins of Japanese ODA to Thailand were in the settlement of war-related claims. In 1955 an agreement was reached on a special yen repayment of money borrowed during 1942–45. Thailand was to receive ¥5.4 billion in cash and ¥9.6 billion in capital goods and services.[14] In 1968 Thailand received its first OECF loan of ¥10 billion and in 1972 another one of ¥17 billion. During this early period until the beginning of the 1970s Japanese aid was closely related with business interests and with promoting an export market for Japanese companies.

Strong criticism from many South East Asian countries led to some readjustments and Japanese grant aid began addressing rural and agricultural development.[15] Loan aid continued to emphasize infrastructure projects, especially in the transportation and power generation sectors.

After the Vietnam War and the decline of American influence in the region, there was an expectation that Japan, as an economic power, would play a greater role in the region. Japanese aid came to be used for political and diplomatic purposes beyond the earlier commercial objectives. With the Fukuda Doctrine there followed an increasing recognition of the importance of the ASEAN countries for Japan. It was also in the late 1970s that Japan rapidly increased its ODA all over the world, and Thailand received its share of this expansion. Annual aid packages have been steadily increasing since this time.

The Thai government has partly viewed Japanese aid as a compensation for the deficit in bilateral trade. In the middle of the 1980s it requested more Japanese aid to support the expansion of Thai manufactured exports to Japan in order to help reduce the imbalance. It also requested that ODA should be extended to the private sector. To some extent this coincided with Japanese interests. After the Plaza Accord and the revaluation of the yen, many Japanese manufacturers wanted to locate part of their production abroad. In 1986 the 'New Asian Development Plan' proposed by MITI called for a division of labour in the region and local export-oriented companies were promoted through so-called 'two-step loans'. However, this never became more than a minor part of Japanese ODA, and infrastructure projects have dominated throughout the years.

In the 1980s, opposition was raised against both a cultural centre and a historical museum built with Japanese grant aid (all tied). The Thai government subsequently requested that more Thai consultants be involved in engineering consulting services and the procurement of equipment and material for Japanese ODA business.[16] Since the Thai economy has continued to expand, this problem is now partially resolving itself. In fiscal year 1993 Japan decided to stop giving new grant aid to Thailand because the country's economic growth had been so successful that the per capita income level was well over $1,840 per year,[17] a level at which it is no longer considered appropriate to give grant aid. That means that no more Japanese projects will be tied.

Minor grant projects in the environmental field may still occur. Technical assistance and development studies will also be permitted. As of June 1994 there were 165 technical experts and 46 Japanese volunteers in Thailand under the auspices of JICA who were working on a total of 29 projects. More than 500 Thai people were also sent to Japan under different assistance programmes.

Recently there has been a trend for closer links between JICA development studies and actual projects or OECF loans. The reason for this closer link, according to JICA, is that there have been a lot of JICA studies that were never realized but 'just ended up in the trash can'.[18] Plans 'ending up in the trash can' may be considered a typical Thai problem, but it is one which is also common in other developing countries. Governments change rather often and the old plans are scrapped when new ones are brought forward. Thai bureaucrats also tend to make overly ambitious plans without considering the financial realities.[19]

Closer links between JICA development studies, which are tied to Japanese consultants, and OECF loans are something that Japanese industry favours. It is often mentioned as one way of directing a higher percentage of OECF loan-related business contracts to Japanese companies, since the studies can be written in such a way that Japanese companies gain certain competitive advantages.

Procurement for construction has been generally untied for many years, but since 1992 companies from all countries have also been invited to submit consulting proposals in connection with OECF-financed projects. This was allowed after criticism that a policy of 'only Japanese consultants' was unfair and favoured Japanese companies. OECF officials at the Bangkok office, as well as other Japanese involved in OECF-financed aid projects, have voiced considerable concern over the reduced number of contracts Japanese companies have received recently.

Compared to the percentage of contract values that the Japanese companies are getting in general on OECF loans, they get considerably less in Thailand, and so do companies from other OECD countries.[20] Contractors from LDC countries get more than in other countries. Joint ventures are usually listed in this category and since only the main contractors are listed and many of them use subcontractors, it is very difficult to determine the real origins of the companies receiving the orders.[21]

Thailand signed its eighteenth loan package with Japan in September 1993. For the first time the annual agreement exceeded ¥100 billion ($901 million). That made Thailand the third-largest Japanese loan aid recipient on a cumulative basis, after Indonesia and China, accounting for around 9 per cent of the total sum. Considering that the population of Thailand is only 56 million as compared with Indonesia's 181 million and China's 1,150 million,[22] the Thai people received considerably more per capita.

Aid has been extended to 28 different implementing agencies and transportation is the sector that has received the largest amount of funding (see Figure 4.1). The agency which has received the greatest share has been the Department of Highways.[23] Together with the Expressway and Rapid Transit Authority, the two agencies have received almost 20 per cent of the total OECF loans. The sector that has received the second-largest funding has been electricity, followed by telephone and railway construction.

The Thai government not only borrows from OECF but also from multilateral agencies such as IBRD, and ADB as well as from private capital markets at home[24] and abroad. It also issue its own bonds. OECF is still, however, by far the largest supplier of capital. In July 1993 the Thai government had an outstanding debt of $4,783 million to OECF, which is 37 per cent of its total outstanding debt.[25] Almost 50 per cent of the Thai debt is in yen which, with the rising value of the yen, is a major problem for the Ministry of Finance, which is now studying ways of trying to swap some of it. There is a country-specific factor that effects Thai borrowing as well, namely, that there is a limit to how much the government of Thailand is allowed to borrow as in 1985 it adopted 'the Regulation of the National Debt Policy' according to which a ceiling must be set every year. This is done by the National Debt Policy Committee which bases its decision on the demands and the financial position of the country. In no case may the debt be more than 10 per cent of the national budget.[26]

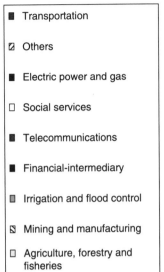

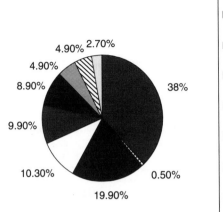

Figure 4.1 OECF loan commitment by sector
Source: OECF
Note: Airport construction and port construction as well as railway cars and
locomotive procurement are included in the figures for transportation

For fiscal 1994[27] the National Debt Policy Committee set the
ceiling at $3.2 billion, or roughly the same amount as the previous
year.[28] The debt service ratio of government loans is not allowed to
exceed 10 per cent of the national budget. In reality it is not currently
more than 3.9 per cent and Thai finances must, therefore, be considered rather good.

All government agencies or state companies have to request permission for loans from the National Debt Policy Committee. The
Committee, after considering the return of projects, not only decides
if they will be allowed to borrow or not, but also selects the appropriate source from which to borrow.

The Ministry of Finance is the centre of the National Debt Policy
Committee, but its members are from other ministries and institutions
as well (see Table 4.2). Once a year the Committee sends a ques-
tionnaire to government agencies and state companies to find out
what projects and funding level they would like to have. The agencies are also allowed to indicate from whom they would prefer to
borrow, but it is the Committee that decides this and on many
occasions it has decided to use other sources.[29]

Table 4.2 Members of the National Debt Policy Committee

1 The Finance Minister (who chairs the committee)
2 A deputy Finance Minister
3 Another deputy Finance Minister
4 A high-ranking official from the Ministry of Finance (who is the permanent secretary)
5 The Secretary General of the National Economic and Social Development Board
6 The Governor of Bank of Thailand
7 The Director of the Budget Bureau (under the Prime Minister's Office)
8 The Director-General of the General Controllers Department
9 The Director-General of the Department of Technical and Economic Co-operation (under the Prime Minister's Office)
10 The Director-General of the Fiscal General Policy Office
11 The Director-General of the Economic Department, Ministry of Foreign Affairs

About 50 per cent of all loan applications to the National Debt Policy Committee are accepted. The remainder are put on a list for further investigation or are rejected outright.

The Committee is offered far more money than it needs from the World Bank and the ADB but conditions are tighter now that Thailand's per capita income has become too high to make them eligible for the softest conditions. Loans from these banks are still taken for technical assistance, evaluation or follow-up purposes. In no way can the loans from private or multilateral sources be compared with those offered by OECF.

In fact, OECF loans are the only ones with really favourable conditions that Thailand has access to now.[30] Consequently, Thailand takes all loans offered which means that it is actually OECF that sets the debt ceiling, depending on how much it is willing to lend to Thailand. The loan package that was signed in September 1993 had an interest rate of 3 per cent, and a repayment period of 25 years including a seven-year grace period.

MOTIVES FOR THE NEW CHONBURI–PATTAYA HIGHWAY

Considering the severe traffic congestion in Bangkok it would seem logical to concentrate road construction efforts there. Why would anyone then want to build a new highway between Chonburi, a town of 800,000 people located south-east of Bangkok, and the tourist resort of Pattaya, famous for its beaches, bars and prostitution (see Map 4.1).

Tourism is one of the key economic areas that Thailand is trying to promote, but this is certainly not the only motive for building the highway. The main motivation is that Pattaya happens to be situated in the so-called 'Eastern Seaboard Area', a zone which the Thai government decided to give highest priority during the sixth National Economic and Social Development Plan (1986–91). In this plan, Chonburi was designated as a growth centre and the whole area was to be the spearhead in a systematic transformation

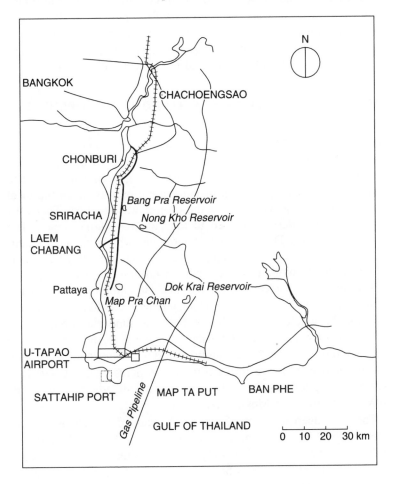

Map 4.1 The Chonburi–Pattaya New Highway

of the country from an agrarian society to a newly industrialized economy. In order to achieve this, infrastructure, including roads, was needed. In addition, another motive was to encourage decentralization from Bangkok in an effort to reduce traffic congestion, deteriorating environmental conditions and haphazard growth.

The Eastern Seaboard Development Programme, was one of the major undertakings of the Thai Government during the 1980s.[31] Japan had committed itself to provide overall support. A little further north of Pattaya, construction was in progress for a deep-sea port, Laem Chabang and, in connection with the port, an industrial estate. Both these projects were financed by OECF money. Without good road access they were unlikely to be successful. Something had to be done about it. The solution to this problem was the Chonburi–Pattaya Highway, designed with a spur road to connect both facilities.

THAILAND'S EASTERN SEABOARD DEVELOPMENT PROGRAMME

During the late 1970s the ASEAN countries, following promises from Japan of loans totalling $1 billion, had decided to undertake one industrial project each. At the time the Thai government wanted to build a soda ash project north of Pattaya but protests from the local inhabitants were so violent that the project was stopped. Thai officials, however, were awakened to the potential of the area.[32] The Eastern Seaboard Development Programme which includes Chonburi, Chachoengsao and Rayong, covers a total area of 13,215 km^2 and has a total population of around 1.8 million people.

The plans and aspirations for the area are ambitious. Laem Chabang will not only be a port for Thailand but it should also become a port for the whole region. This includes neighbouring countries in whose development Thailand wants to play a leading role,[33] one which should become increasingly important when industrialization and investment improve in the former communist state of Vietnam. Roads leading to Laos should be upgraded and already the new bridge to Vietnam, over the Mekong river,[34] is in use.

The new deep-sea port of Laem Chabang, designed mainly for container traffic, was completed in December 1991 and the adjacent industrial estate is now also completed. This area is reserved for so-called labour-intensive non-polluting industries, such as agriculture and food, consumer goods and equipment and parts. It is divided into two zones: one is for general production and the other for export.

Contracts have been signed with 39 companies for the first zone and 14 for the second. A second industrial estate is already being planned.

Further south in the Eastern Seaboard Area, west of Rayong City, is the industrial port of Map Ta Put, which was completed in 1992. Nearby is an industrial estate designed for so-called polluting, heavy industry where contracts have been signed with 46 companies. This was also financed by OECF money. Map Ta Put is located where the world's longest submarine gas pipeline comes ashore to meet the gas separation plant constructed by the Petroleum Authority of Thailand in 1985. The plant is connected by pipelines to distribution facilities in Laem Chabang. Map Ta Put harbour is already considered too small and drawings are now being made for a phase II expansion.

A new high-speed train is planned from Bangkok to Rayong. A study for this, paid for by the US Trade and Development Agency, was finished in April 1994. Some further investigations are still needed, but the line is expected to be completed around the year 2003.

Bangkok airport is considered too small and land has been secured for a second international airport that is to be built before the year 2000. This is not within the Eastern Seaboard Area but a very large project north of it. The Eastern Seaboard Area already has an airport about five times the size of Bangkok airport but it is on a military base. Some of it is used for civilian purposes, however, and there are plans to build a maintenance base for civil aircraft there.

Water pipes have been constructed to serve the area and Thailand's most modern telecommunication centre is located in the Eastern Seaboard. Many countries have contributed to the development of the area but the Japanese have easily contributed the most. JICA has provided 12 packages of technical assistance and feasibility studies for the respective projects under the Eastern Seaboard Development Programme. OECF has financed more than 15 projects in the area to a total amount of ¥173 billion ($1.5 billion).

Nevertheless, the Eastern Seaboard Development Programme has not been as successful as anticipated. There might be several reasons for this: one is the general slowdown in economic growth after the Kuwait crisis, another is the *coup d'état* in Thailand in 1991 and ensuing demonstrations in the streets of Bangkok in 1992 which may have frightened foreign investors. Another reason is that the area is still lacking in infrastructure, such as hospitals, schools and universities. This makes, for example, Thai managers reluctant to move from Bangkok to the area with their families. They either have to maintain two homes or commute, which is time-consuming although the distance from Bangkok to Laem Chabang is no more than 130 kilometres.[35]

The Chonburi–Pattaya Highway was completed in the summer of 1994. Construction has begun on the next part of the road system, Chonburi–Bangkok, which the Japanese had originally suggested as the project to start with, but which Thai officials did not give priority because they thought it would only bring more people into Bangkok.[36] This new road will take about two years to build. At the moment, congested roads are also an effective way of preventing people from entering the area.

Things are slowly starting to improve in the Eastern Seaboard Area. Although the land in the industrial estates around Laem Chabang and Map Ta Put is all contracted, companies are only gradually building facilities there. Instead, many companies have leased sites in preparation for future growth. Since rents have been very low, there has been no urgency to commence construction.[37]

A number of industries have also built plants in the surrounding area. Laem Chabang port, which was considered a joke among Thai people when it was opened without the necessary infrastructure and equipment, such as good roads and terminal cranes, is now finally starting to take off. In 1993 total container throughput was 169,052 TEUs,[38] which is 13 per cent of Bangkok's throughput, but is growing rapidly.[39]

Nearby Pattaya is already a well-established tourist resort, and there are now plans to make it a centre of tourism and trade in the region. The problem is that the water in Pattaya is no longer clean. In 1989 JICA carried out a study of the rehabilitation of Pattaya and proposed a programme that, if implemented, would cost around $141 million. This is money that the Office of the Eastern Seaboard Development Committee considers it cannot afford at the moment, and instead small increment steps will be taken to rehabilitate the environment.[40]

In essence, the main priority in the Eastern Seaboard area is on industrial production and attracting companies to build factories in the area.

ROAD BUILDING IN THAILAND

During the sixth National Economic and Social Development Plan the economy grew at a much faster rate than expected and although the government decided (in June 1989) to expand the road programme, it usually takes a long time before new capacity comes into service. Many of the projects had to be rescheduled indefinitely, due to lack of financing, or carried over to the seventh National Economic and Social Development Plan (1992–96). In this plan transport is identified as a key problem area. The government proposes to improve matters by mobilizing necessary funds, accelerating investment and fostering private sector participation.

Funding is the key problem. Although government appropriations are expected to increase by almost 100 per cent from the sixth to the seventh plan this is far from being sufficient.[41] The government decision not to allow tolls on any of the Department of Highways' roads does not improve the situation. Privatization as a means of funding may not be as easy as anticipated. This was discovered recently by the Expressway and Rapid Transit Authority of Thailand (ETA) which operates the expressways and is allowed to charge tolls on them. Acting on ETA's behalf, a consortium of companies led by Japanese Kumagai-gumi built part of the Second Stage Expressway in Bangkok.[42] When it was completed, the politicians, prompted by public opinion, would not at first allow the fee on the road to be, by Thai standards, the huge amount of 30 baht ($1.20), as stipulated in the contract. Finally the authorities had to concede this point and the fee was set at 30 baht but another dispute erupted about who should collect the money, ETA or the construction consortium. Throughout the dispute Kumagai-gumi refused to open the road, claiming all kinds of safety precautions that, according to ETA, did not exist. Finally ETA turned to the district court to force the road open by legal means. A few months later Kumagai-gumi sold their shares in the project.

Construction of the Third Stage Expressway in Bangkok was also to be financed by private money. A tender for its construction was called but only one bid was submitted, by a Japanese–Thai consortium.[43] With only one bid and the recent experience with Kumagai-gumi, ETA decided to establish its own construction subsidiary (NTT) which will now build the road. When the road is completed the company will be listed on the stock market and sold to the public. ETA policy is still to obtain as much private participation as possible to cover the cost and speed up the pace of construction.

Other problems with road construction in Thailand are land acquisition and resettlement of citizens and other costs that now amount to about two-thirds of the sum required for new roads. These are costs that have to be paid by the government and for which it does not receive foreign loans.[44]

ETA is the sixth-largest recipient of OECF loans. According to ETA, the Department of Highways receives a greater share of these loans because the Thai National Debt Policy Committee tries to direct as many soft loans as possible to it since it does not possess rights to charge tolls and, as a result, has difficulties in recouping its investments.[45]

MASTER PLAN FOR ROAD DEVELOPMENT IN THE CENTRAL REGION

One of the country-specific factors for Thailand is its process of receiving foreign aid. All grant aid projects are dealt with by the Department of Technical and Economical Co-operation (DTEC). It is responsible for classifying projects submitted by all the implementing agencies and preparing priority lists. Consequently, the Department of Highways (DOH) had to first consult DTEC about the preparation of a master plan of road development for the Central Region. After DTEC's approval, the government of Thailand formally asked the Government of Japan for a master plan and the Government of Japan (that is in this case the Foreign Ministry) directed its implementing agency, JICA, to prepare one.

The 'Road Development Study in the Central Region' was the last in a series of road master plans covering the southern, northern and north-eastern regions that JICA undertook on behalf of the Thai government which, for a period of 20 years, had given priority to road development to improve the nation-wide transportation network system. The Central Region covers an area of 104,000 km^2 and includes Bangkok. It was the most populous region of all those studied and in 1986 it had a population of 17 million people.

Rapid industrial development resulted in the manufacturing sector exceeding the agriculture sector in gross regional product (GRP). However, the road situation was poor. The road length per GRP was the lowest among all regions, with no more than half or less than half that of other regions.[46] With the promotion of industrial development, including the Eastern Seaboard area, the situation was likely to grow worse. This prompted the Thai government to request a road development study.

The Government of Japan, which had a preference for funding economic infrastructure and had promised overall support for the Eastern Seaboard Development Programme, considered this well in line with its ODA policy. Development studies are generally undertaken by grant, including this one, which was entrusted to JICA, whose counterpart on the Thai side was the Department of Highways (DOH).

As is always the case with development studies by JICA, this was done in the form of tied aid and only Japanese consultants were permitted. A number of these were invited to participate and submitted proposals for the study.[47] A joint venture team consisting of experts from Katahira & Engineers Inc. and Nippon Koei Co. Ltd were awarded the job, with Katahira & Engineers acting as team leader. These companies were two major Japanese consulting firms which both had almost 20 years of experience working with and for DOH.[48]

The study lasted for a period of 20 months (August 1987–March 1989).[49] The objectives of the study were:

- To identify the needs of road development from the viewpoint of national and regional development and to establish a master plan.
- To select priority projects and carry out associated feasibility studies. Feasibility studies were to be divided into two groups.
  - Phase I projects: included those which required urgent implementation from the viewpoint of road congestion and the present road situation. Studies for these were finished by the end of September 1988.
  - Phase II projects: included other proposed projects.

The Bangkok Metropolitan Area was not to be included in the study.

At the end of March 1988 a first interim report, which described the results of the study up to the preliminary evaluation step, was submitted. The Master Plan Study was also completed at this time.

Forecasts of traffic volume had been calculated primarily on population and gross provincial product (GPP)[50] and estimates of these were done for the years 1993, 2000 and 2008. The study noted that it had not incorporated the recent acceleration in economic growth because of the lack of concrete data and therefore the traffic projections were to be considered conservative. Additional calculations were also performed about reduced journey length and timesaving as a result of the road projects and these were all incorporated into cost and benefit statements for the different roads.

The conclusion was clear. The Chonburi–Pattaya New Highway was given the highest ranking and was chosen for a feasibility study during Phase I. The study team also recommended that it should be extended all the way to Bangkok for effective operation of the Eastern Seaboard Area. DOH also requested that such a feasibility study should be included, although the Bangkok metropolitan area in general was not included. This feasibility study was to be dealt with in Phase II.

On the subject of the development and social impact of the Chonburi–Pattaya New Highway, the Master Plan concluded that:

> The projected road, if implemented, will have characteristics of an
> expressway. Impact on adjoining communities would be generally
> more negative than positive. However, it will greatly boost the
> accessibility of the Eastern Seaboard, thus helping its develop-
> ment, which in turn should benefit residents in the area.

THE PROCESS OF SEEKING OECF FINANCING

Thai internal processes – country-specific factors

Before requesting money from the Japanese government, the Department of Highways needed permission from the Thai government
which is the official borrower. First the DOH consulted with DTEC
and received advice and support for the project. Then it had to
approach the Ministry of Transport and Communication to receive
permission for construction of the Chonburi–Pattaya New Highway
and to request funding or instructions on where to seek funding. If the
Ministry of Transport and Communication has money in its own
budget for construction a project can proceed. This is not usually
the case and, indeed, was not the case for the Chonburi–Pattaya New
Highway. It needed to borrow the money for the project which meant
that it had to be approved by the National Debt Policy Committee. As
part of this process the National Economic and Social Development
Board (NESDB) as well as the Ministry of Finance also give their
opinions.

The fiscal year in Thailand is from the first of October, at which
time the ceiling of borrowing from abroad is decided by the National
Debt Policy Committee. From that point applications for loans are
examined and projects are chosen as well as their source of funding.

Approval to proceed with the Chonburi–Pattaya New Highway was
given by the National Debt Policy Committee in October 1987.[51] This
was long before the Master Plan for road development of the Central
Region (begun two months earlier) was completed. The Interim
Report was not published until March of the following year, when
the Master Plan studies were considered finished. This meant that any
plans for the road existing at the time must have been rough drafts
only. The estimates on which the National Debt Policy Committee
based its decision to proceed could not have been particularly
detailed. The lack of sufficient drawings and concrete plans for the

road was probably also the reason why the Chonburi–Pattaya New Highway was not included in the customary list of projects that the Thai government presented to the Japanese government six months before their annual consultation. However, DOH must have had some indications that it had a chance to obtain OECF financing since it submitted a request for approval to the National Debt Policy Committee.

Japanese internal process – OECF-specific factors

The formal request to the Japanese government for money to build the Chonburi–Pattaya New Highway was submitted in June 1988, although no feasibility study existed. That a request could still be made seems to confirm that regulations at the time were relatively lax and that there was a range of assessment manuals in use, but no basic guidelines available for the Four Ministries in their joint decision-making. Such operational guidelines were not prepared until 1991.[52]

At the time of the formal request to the Japanese government for the Highway, all that existed was an Interim Report to the Master Plan for the Road Development Study in the Central Region. Compared to a feasibility study, which can take up to a year to complete, an Interim Report is a very rough document. In the Final Report of the Master Plan, the Route Report for the Chonburi–Pattaya New Highway occupies only seven pages and there is no detailed information provided about the different sections of the roads nor about technical problems that have to be solved for local conditions. Consequently, cost estimates for the road must have been distinctly rough.

OECF claims that although no detailed description was included in the Master Plan itself, sufficient information from JICA was collected to enable it to estimate the necessary cost for the Highway. The fact remains, however, that there was no feasibility study from which to calculate costs.

The Thai request for money for the new road was not submitted six months in advance, as is the usual procedure, but given directly to the government mission at the time when annual consultations were held. This does not mean that the OECF was unaware of such a request before it was formally submitted. A number of informal contacts had already occurred between DOH and OECF in Bangkok. Contacts had also been made between OECF and the JICA study team working with the Master Plan.

Government missions are part of the process which is specific for OECF loans. They are dispatched each year to Thailand to convene annual consultations on loan aid. On the Japanese side there are representatives from MOFA, MOF, MITI, EPA and OECF officials as well as representatives from other ministries or agencies that might be concerned.

On the Thai side there are representatives from the Fiscal Policy Office as well as the Budget Bureau of the Finance Ministry. There is also a representative from NESDB and representatives from agencies that will be executing the works concerned (in the case of the Chonburi–Pattaya New Highway, the Department of Highways).

These meetings last two days: one day is spent on general discussions and the other on discussing requested projects. The limited amount of time allocated to these discussions demonstrates that they are more or less a formality and that most of the work has been done beforehand, even though the government formally decides on the need for an appraisal mission after these meetings. The government mission subsequently decided to send an appraisal mission for the Chonburi–Pattaya New Highway project. The mission was dispatched the same month together with all other appraisal missions.

Each proposed OECF project is allocated its own appraisal mission, although all missions are sent out simultaneously. Not surprisingly, the OECF office is crowded, every June, with people working on appraisals which are carried out by staff from OECF, sometimes in co-operation with officials from the other ministries concerned. Each mission usually consists of two people, one OECF economist and one engineer. In the case of Chonburi–Pattaya New Highway there were two engineers, one from OECF itself and the other external to OECF, most probably from the Ministry of Construction. The work of the appraisal mission usually takes around two to three weeks. Discussions are held with the borrower, that is, representatives from the Government of Thailand, as well as representatives of the executing agency, in this case the Department of Highways, on most aspects of implementation including time schedule and cost estimates. Field surveys are also conducted to collect as much detailed information as possible. In the case of the New Highway this must have been a rather difficult exercise since no feasibility study existed.

The appraisal mission finally writes a report (an internal document that is not made public). Based on this, OECF decides whether or not it considers the project suitable for OECF financing and what the appropriate level of funding should be. The final decision is then made by the Government[53] although it is often more of a formality and it rarely rejects OECF recommendations.

In general, OECF does not finance 100 per cent of a project. Japanese policy is that aid should be 'help to self-help' and so the recipient country's government is also expected to contribute. This is often the case for other aid agencies as well. The amount contributed depends on each agreement. For example, under the sixteenth loan agreement (of September 1991), for the Road Improvement Programme of Three Major Routes which OECF co-financed with ADB and the World Bank, DOH financed 20 per cent of the cost. In the case of the Chonburi–Pattaya New Highway, DOH financed 27 per cent and OECF 73 per cent – a fairly standard formula for OECF road financing.[54]

Prior notification is given when agreements have been reached on various key points (amounts, terms and conditions). This occurred in the beginning of September.

The formal Exchange of Notes for the fourteenth loan package took place on the 22 September between the Japanese Ambassador in Bangkok and a representative of the Thai Government. The total sum of the package was ¥75,818 million ($592 million). The interest rate was 2.90 per cent with a repayment period of 30 years and grace period of 10 years. Of this money, ¥4,117 million ($32 million) was allocated to the Chonburi–Pattaya New Highway Project.

Conditions for construction procurement were general untied. The provision of consulting services (including supervision of the project) was so-called LDC-untied. That meant it was open to Japanese and Thai companies as well as companies from LDCs but not to companies from other OECD countries.

Two months later, contracts for the loan agreement were signed in Tokyo (22 November 1988) by a representative of the Thai government and the OECF. This contract set out the legal terms and conditions, rights and obligations as well as the purpose, scope and content of the project. Following signing of this loan agreement the project could theoretically have commenced but more time was required for completing paperwork. First of all, a detailed design for the road was needed. The lack of this prevented DOH from proceeding immediately. It was not until April of the following year (1989) that DOH announced the procurement for the first parts of the project through ICB.

The results of the feasibility studies for the Phase I projects of the JICA Master Plan (which included the Chonburi–Pattaya New Highway) were submitted in October 1988, after an Exchange of Notes for the loan agreement had already taken place. From this point the detailed design study usually takes another six months. In the case of DOH, detailed design studies are carried out internally or by a local consultant at the expense of the department.[55] The task of DOH or the consultant is to perform an in-depth analysis of technical details so that the tendering and construction can be successfully completed. Often these consultants have discussions with the individuals who prepared the feasibility study, particularly if the consultants propose alternative technical solutions.

The detailed design study for the Chonburi–Pattaya New Highway was partly prepared by DOH and partly by the local consultant company, Asian Engineering Consultants Corp. Ltd. Subsequently this consultant company formed a joint venture with Katahira & Engineers International to bid successfully for the supervision of construction of the new highway. At this time, bidding for consultants was LDC-untied. General untying for consultant services was not introduced until the sixteenth loan package and, in practice, from 1992.

THE BIDDING PROCESS

The detailed design study divided the construction of the Chonburi–Pattaya New Highway construction into eight different parts, four parts dealt with the road and the other four with intersections. This kind of division is a common practice in Thai road building and it is supposed to accelerate construction and increase competition. The Bangkok–Chonburi Highway which was contracted in 1994 was divided into 22 different sections. DOH endeavours to have the tender value of each section set at around $20 million and never to exceed $60 million. The tender for the first and second sections was announced in April 1989 and closed in August of the same year.[56] Separate tenders are held for each section.

To be able to bid a company must first pre-qualify. Pre-qualification is conducted annually or bi-annually by DOH. Invitations to apply for pre-qualification are extended by sending letters directly to Thai companies, foreign companies working in Thailand, and to all foreign embassies in Thailand. Advertisements are also placed in various Thai newspapers, including the English language newspaper, the *Bangkok Post*. The last time such an invitation was extended, about 200 companies applied. Approximately 50 failed to qualify, and the remaining 150 companies were added to the list of pre-qualified companies. This list is divided into sub-groups depending on the type of work for which the companies are considered qualified. To be able to bid on special large projects such as the construction of new highways or sections of highways, a company must belong to group 1A. At the time of the tendering for Chonburi–Pattaya this group consisted of 23 companies of which the majority were Thai companies. There were only five companies that were not 100 per cent Thai-owned, of which four were joint ventures (of which one was Thai-Japanese) and the fifth was a German company.

DOH tries to limit the number of companies bidding to a maximum of ten per section. If more than ten pre-qualified companies wish to bid, a shortlist of companies is prepared by a consultant. This situation of too many companies wishing to tender rarely occurs. Most often it is the other way around and DOH often must encourage companies to bid for different sections.

Once the tenders are submitted, evaluation commences in accordance to Thai country-specific procedures. In recent years, DOH has had a foreign consultant carry out an initial evaluation of tenders.[57] After this initial evaluation the results are presented to a DOH committee, consisting of five engineers, created for each section. Different engineers are selected for each section, although some members may sit on more than one committee. Around 20 engineers at DOH are eligible for committee membership. The Director-General of DOH appoints them and each committee should be chaired by either one of the Deputy Director-Generals or a Chief Engineer. The committee generally meets about three times before it can agree on selection of the best tenders, having obtained any necessary additional information or clarification. Once agreement is reached, a recommendation is given to the Director-General, who takes the final decision, although he usually follows the recommendation of the committee. (The committee is not required to select the lowest tender but this usually happens.)

The process of bidding for road construction in Thailand is marked by a general lack of competition.[58] The companies consult each other before submitting a tender and tend to divide the work amongst themselves, although this is not openly admitted. It is not unusual for all the tenders DOH receives to be unreasonably high, which is why it always prepares its own cost estimate. This so-called 'government medium estimate'[59] is calculated by analysing the cost of similar road construction undertaken in the past or in progress. If the lowest tender or the preferred tender has a considerably higher price than the government medium estimate, DOH negotiates the tender price with the company concerned. On such occasions prices are often reduced considerably. Hence procurement for road construction although complying, in principle, with the international bidding process differs, in practice, from 'Western' standards and is influenced by Thai country-specific factors.

Sections 1–4

After DOH had selected a contractor – which occurred in October 1989 for sections 1 and 2 of the Chonburi–Pattaya New Highway[60] – OECF had to concur with the contract. It had to be certain that nothing was included in the tender documents that favoured any particular company. It also checked on the membership of the evaluation committee and that the lowest satisfactorily conforming bid was selected.

After this, DOH proceeded with the awarding of contracts, which was completed on 7 March 1990 for the first two sections. This was followed in April by a concurrence from OECF in Bangkok. With this completed, the DOH could issue a notice to proceed to the contractors in June 1990.

Tendering was announced on 22 November 1989 for section 3 with a closing date of 5 January 1990, although the signing of the contract did not occur until ten months later, on 25 October 1990, when the contract for section 4 was also signed (tendering for that had been announced on 4 September 1989 and closed on 19 October 1989). A year later, on 25 October 1990, contracts were signed between DOH and the contractors. OECF gave final clearance for both contracts in January 1991 and in that month notice to proceed was also given.

The companies who submitted tenders as well as those who won for the first four sections were all Thai companies (see Appendix 4.2). Why were there no foreign companies? To begin with it should be noted that of the 23 pre-qualified companies that were able to tender only five were foreign, and four of these were joint ventures. The most common reason given for the lack of foreign bids by people interviewed for this study was lack of competitiveness. A factor specific to this project is that there were a fair number of local companies with considerable skill in road construction with whom it is difficult to compete. Another plausible reason was that there was a construction boom in Thailand at the time. The 'Government Medium Estimate' limited the profits that could be made from road building; private construction was probably more lucrative.

After these first four sections the project encountered problems. All the allocated money had been spent although only four of eight sections had been built. OECF had granted a loan of ¥4,117 million but the contract sum requiring payment was already ¥4,604 million.

In fact it was obvious at the time the contracts for sections 3 and 4 were signed that there was insufficient money remaining to complete the whole road or, indeed, any of the four remaining sections. It must have been obvious to DOH at a much earlier date because the same month as contracts for section 3 and 4 were signed (October 1990) approval was also received from the National Debt Policy Committee to request more money from Japan. This request for additional funds from the Government of Thailand to Japan was submitted the following month in November 1990.

A new government mission was dispatched to Bangkok in January 1991 and after consultations with representatives of the Thai government, the decision was made to send a new appraisal mission to perform a second evaluation of the Chonburi–Pattaya New Highway. This mission arrived in the same month. It did not have to make a second technical appraisal but concentrated instead on reasons for the cost having become so much higher than budgeted. The conclusion was that it was due to the construction boom in Thailand leading to increasing prices for materials as well as higher labour costs.[61] Negotiations were held with Thai counterparts and a new appraisal report was written. Based on this, the Japanese Government made a decision to give additional OECF loans. In July 1991 prior notification of the loan agreement was given.

Sections 5–8

Several months previously, tendering had already begun for the four remaining sections of the Chonburi–Pattaya New Highway. This suggests that DOH must have reached some kind of prior agreement with OECF to proceed with the tender prior to the loan agreement.

Sections 5 and 6 were announced on 4 and 5 February 1991 respectively and tenders closed on the 21 and 22 of March 1991. Sections 7 and 8 were announced on 29 January and 25 February and tenders closed on 15 March and 11 April 1991.

On 6 September in the same year the Exchange of Notes were completed for the sixteenth loan package to Thailand. This entitled Thailand to another ¥84,687 million ($627 million) in loans from OECF and ¥5,670 million ($42 million) of these loans were allocated for the Chonburi–Pattaya New Highway. This was more than the original cost estimate for the whole project. The interest rate this time was 3 per cent, with a repayment period of 25 years and grace period of seven years. On 18 September 1991 loan agreements were signed between representatives of the Government of Thailand and representatives of the OECF. Exactly one month later contracts were signed for two of the remaining sections. The last two contracts were also signed that month, on 22 October 1991. (See Appendix 4.3 for details of contractors.)

In June 1994 construction work on the last sections was almost complete. Whereas the project had run out of money mid-term there was now money left over from OECF's second loan. Total contract sums for construction of the last four sections only amounted to ¥3,305 million (not counting the fee of the Japanese consultants supervising construction) and the loan approved for the second phase of the project was ¥5,670 million. There was also excess money from DOH's own budget for the road. These sums will be combined to build six overpasses to separate local traffic from highway traffic.[62]

The fact that there was money remaining indicates that prices did not increase as much as was anticipated in 1990 when estimates were prepared. This is probably due to the fact that the construction boom slowed down during the early 1990s. The slowdown, which was most obvious in the private sector, could explain why foreign companies have begun to show a somewhat greater interest in road construction.

In the case of the Chonburi–Pattaya New Highway there were no foreign contractors at all, apart from the Japanese consultants supervising construction. In the extension of this road, the Bangkok–Chonburi Highway, for which the awarding of contracts was in progress in 1994, six of the 21 sections were won by companies that were not 100 per cent Thai-owned. Two sections were won by a Japanese company called Nippon Road, two by a joint venture between the Japanese Tokyu Construction and their Thai partners, one by Korean Daewoo and their Thai partners and one by Italian Vianini and their Thai partners.

For another recent road project, the Bangkok Outer Ring Road, which was divided into 16 sections, 15 were won by Thai companies and one by a German company.

As at June 1994 there are 36 companies belonging to the so-called 1A group which are pre-qualified by the DOH to bid for construction of highways. Eleven of these companies are not 100 per cent Thai with one Japanese, one German and one Italian company in addition to two Japanese–Thai joint ventures, one Korean–Thai, one Taiwanese–Thai, two Italian–Thai, one Spanish–Thai and one German–Thai company.

CONCLUSION

Thailand's, economic growth rate has slowed in the last few years from double digit figures and now appears relatively stable at slightly more than 8 per cent of GNP.[63] The nation's goal to develop by industrialization remains firm. To achieve this aim, improved infrastructure is badly needed and priority is given to this in the seventh National Economic and Social Development Plan. Such infrastructure development will require huge amounts of capital.

With a per capita GNP of more than $1,800, Thailand has reached a relatively advanced level of development and cannot expect to receive as much foreign aid as in the past. Loans extended to Thailand by the World Bank and ADB do not carry such favourable conditions as those for countries with lower incomes. OECF loans are the only substantial loans with really soft conditions available at the moment. Since there is such a great need for capital, Thailand seeks aid from Japan and willingly accepts as much of it as it can get. Consequently, OECF loans are now dominant.

Japan views Thailand an important country. It is an Asian neighbour that does not harbour many grudges from World War II and Japanese companies have made considerable investment in various production facilities. Although Thailand is economically better off than many other developing countries, there remain a lot of infrastructure projects that still need financing. This helps explain why Japan, unlike other countries, continues to give loan aid on a significant scale and with soft conditions.

OECF surely considers Thailand to be a reliable recipient of loan aid. It has a very low debt ratio and its economy is moving in a positive direction which means that it is likely that it will be able to repay loans as they fall due. Aid loans are required as there are still a number of badly needed infrastructure projects for which regular commercial credits would not be viable.

The Chonburi–Pattaya New Highway project fails to comply with all the procedures that, according to OECF in Tokyo, are necessary for such projects. No actual feasibility study existed at the time of the appraisal mission but in spite of this the project was accepted. Information received from DOH and JICA on an unofficial basis was sufficient for the appraisal mission to recommend approval for the project. When it became apparent that the OECF loan was insufficient to cover the cost of the project, a second loan which exceeded the first, was extended. Further, when the Exchange of Notes for this loan was signed the international bidding process had already closed.

To a certain extent the acceptance of the project without a feasibility study and with deviation from the regular procedure may be attributed to the urgent need for the road to support another OECF project, a new deep-sea port under construction in Laem Chabang without a road of sufficient capacity to move the goods from the harbour. There was, therefore, a pressing need to solve the problem caused, it would appear, by a lack of co-ordination in the planning of infrastructure development.

The Laem Chabang port was also financed through Japanese loan aid and there must have been a mutual Thai–Japanese interest in accelerating the process of road construction so that traffic congestion could be relieved and Laem Chabang could have a reasonable chance of operating efficiently. Neither Thai nor Japanese officials would have received any positive publicity by having work stopped on an incomplete road while proper procedures were complied with. Another important factor was that the loan agreement was signed in 1988 before OECF operational guidelines had been issued. According to a report by the Administrative Management Bureau there was a range of different assessment manuals available at the time and a lack of clarity in the loan approval procedure existed.

The second loan was much larger than necessary and when construction was nearing completion in 1994 a lot of money remained which OECF agreed could be used to build six overpasses to separate traffic on the highway from the local traffic.

The OECF loan process, portrayed in Tokyo as rigid, instead showed a considerable amount of flexibility.

It is apparent that informal consultations took place at various stages. It would be difficult for DOH to go to the National Debt Policy Committee and request approval for borrowing money from abroad for a new highway unless it had some indication that a funding source was available. If DOH had not done that and had not had any prior understanding the Japanese were interested in financing the project, the process would have been considerably prolonged.

Thailand has its own country-specific regulations on how aid is to be received and the OECF has its ODA-specific regulation on the process of giving aid. These regulations do not give attention to each other on paper but in the implementation phase a more flexible and pragmatic view is adopted in order to get the operation working. The OECF loan condition was 'general untied' and in the case of Chonburi–Pattaya New Highway, nothing was discovered to suggest aid was tied to any Japanese companies, at least not within the construction phase. Tendering took place in accordance with the rules of international bidding and was monitored as far as possible by the Japanese. That there is a lack of competition among Thai companies bidding and that they sometimes prefer to distribute the work among themselves on the basis of secret negotiations is clear, but this is, of course, difficult to prove. These factors can be considered country-specific. Thai business has its own way of functioning and knowledge of how the process works is probably essential for any foreign company that wants to be 'part of the game'. The Thai Government has taken measures to protect itself against tender price manipulating by introducing the 'Government Medium Estimate'. This has limited the potential for companies to earn an excessive profit from tenders on road construction projects.

The division of road construction into sections each of a smaller value may make the projects of less interest to large foreign companies and hence favour local companies. Indeed, with the Chonburi–Pattaya New Highway no Japanese or other foreign company was awarded a construction contract. In fact, no foreign company even bothered to bid. This was probably because there were larger and easier profits to be earned with other projects at the time.

Another reason why there were no foreign companies may be project-specific factors, namely, the characteristics of the highway itself. It was a fairly uncomplicated construction and did not include any complexities in the form of bridges or tunnels where foreign constructors are generally considered to have a competitive advantage. For regular road construction there are many Thai companies with considerable experience.

Foreign companies are not excluded from road building, as demonstrated by the winning of contracts for some sections of the Bangkok–Chonburi Highway. It is debatable, however, whether examining the country of origin of the companies awarded the contracts would reveal foreign influence in the process. A large amount of the work is sub-contracted to Thai construction firms. Road building is not an area where foreign construction companies perform a large part of work themselves. If construction of a power plant had been chosen as a case study instead, the results might have been different.

Consultancy work was given to a Japanese–Thai joint venture because the rules, with effect from 1988, stated that consultants from OECD countries other than Japan were not allowed to bid. The Japanese consultant company selected was well acquainted with the project as it had participated in the preparation of the Master Plan for Road Development in the Central Region, a JICA project where consultancy services were tied. For the next part of the highway (Bangkok–Chonburi) consultant contracts were awarded to four foreign consultant companies of which only one is Japanese.

This case study found no proof of any Japanese company gaining special treatment or favour from OECF aid loans, except for the limited fees paid to the Japanese consultant company. Indeed, if it can be claimed that one or more parties profited from the project, it would be the Thai construction companies involved.

Indirectly Japanese companies, as well as other foreign companies (although the Japanese are in the majority), will profit as the road extends to the Eastern Seaboard Area, where many companies have already established production facilities and more are expected to do so. Producers of equipment for road building, of which many are Japanese, are also bound to profit from infrastructure development.

NOTES

1 A state enterprise under the Ministry of Interior and separate from Department of Highways, which is under the Transport and Communication Ministry, it is one of the major road builders. Other major road builders are the Public Works Department and, in the Bangkok area, the Bangkok Metropolis.
2 Supaporn Jarunpattana, 'Siam–Japan relations, 1920–1940', *Thai–Japanese Studies*, December 1989, Thammasat University, Thailand.
3 William Swan, *Japanese economic relations with Siam: aspects of their historical development 1884–1942*, doctoral dissertation, at Australian National University, Canberra, 1986.
4 Chulacheeb Chinwanno, 'Japan as a Regional Power', in *Thai–Japanese Studies*, August 1988, Thammasat University, Thailand.
5 Interview with Dr Surachai Sirikrai, Director of the Institute of East Asian Studies, Thammasat University in June 1994.
6 There is still a small street in Bangkok with a lot of clubs catering only for the Japanese.
7 This was declared by the Prime Minister in Manila in August 1977 and afterwards known as the Fukuda Doctrine.
8 Figures from Thailand's Board of Investment statistics.
9 Information from JETRO Bangkok. The next largest Japanese Chambers of Commerce are those in Singapore and Los Angeles with around 750 members each.
10 *Bangkok Post*, 3 June 1994.
11 Interview with officials at JETRO Bangkok.
12 According to Bank of Thailand's figures Thai exports to Japan in 1993 amounted to 159,500 million baht whereas imports amounted to 353,500 million baht. Thailand had a total trade deficit of 235,700 million baht.
13 *Bangkok Times*, 25 May 1994.
14 Prasert Chittiwatanapong 'Japan's ODA relation with Thailand' in Bruce M. Koppel and Robert M. Orr (eds) *Japan's Foreign Aid, Power and Policy in a New Era*, Westview Press, Boulder, CO, 1993.

15 Pranee Tinakorn and Patcharee Siroros, 'Japan's ODA and Thai development: a successful story?', in Chulacheeb Chinwanno and Wilaiwan Wannitikul (eds) *Japan's Official Development Assistance and Asian Developing Economies*,Thammasat University, Bangkok, 1991.

16 Prasert Chittiwatanpong, *Japanese Official Development Assistance to Thailand: A Study of the Construction Industry*, USJP Occasional Paper 92–04, Harvard University.

17 Figures for 1993, The Japanese Foreign Ministry, *Waga Kuni no Seifu Kaihatsu Enjo*, Tokyo, 1994.

18 Interview with an official at the JICA office in Bangkok.

19 One such area is roads where many have to be placed on hold for future consideration. See the Asian Development Bank, *Preparation of an Investment Programme for the Department of Highways*, Final Report, Vol. I, Main Text, Bangkok, April 1992.

20 There are Japanese statistics on how high a percentage of the contracted value of loans Japanese companies, companies from other OECD countries and from LDC countries are getting in Thailand. We have not been allowed to publish these. Recently the Thai Finance Ministry started its own records which might in the future be compared with the Japanese statisics.

21 For a further discussion of this, see Chapter 2.

22 Figures for 1991 from the *World Bank Atlas*, 1993.

23 Figures according to OECF statistics.

24 According to existing regulations local borrowing is not to exceed one-third of debt amount allowed.

25 OECF figures.

26 This section is based on an interview with officials at the Loan Policy and Planning Sector, Fiscal Policy Bureau, Thai Ministry of Finance.

27 October 1993 to September 1994.

28 The official figure then was $2.5 billion but that did not include Thai International airline's borrowings which are roughly $700 million a year. They were included from 1994 which makes the figures for the ceiling approximately equal.

29 Interview with an official at Fiscal Policy Bureau, Thai Ministry of Finance.

30 Ibid. (They still consider this to be true even if one takes the high value of the yen into consideration.)

31 Since then the Southern Seaboard Development Programme and other development programmes have been adopted. None of them is on as large a scale as the Eastern Seaboard Development Programme.

32 Interview with officials at the Eastern Seaboard Development Committee.

33 Office of the Eastern Seaboard Development Committee, *Thailand's Eastern Seaboard Development Programme*, February 1994.

34 Financed by funds from Australia.

35 Interview with Suruchai Sirikrai, op. cit.

36 Interview with representative of the Japanese consultant involved.

37 According to OECF 41 out of 43 leases in Map Ta Phut and 62 out of 71 leases in Laem Chanbang are in operation or construction has started.

38 TEU – 20-foot equivalent unit, a measurement for container goods.

39 Peter Janssen 'Thailand port gets its chance', *Asian Business*, May 1994.

The fact that the harbour of Bangkok is not a deep sea one and that it has long waiting times because it is totally overcrowded helps the prospect of Laem Chabang.

40 Eastern Seaboard Development Committee interview, op. cit.

41 Asian Development Bank, op. cit.

42 This was done under a so-called 'Build–Operate–Transfer' (BOT) system. According to this a private company wins the right to build, for example a road, and then to operate it and collect fees on it for a certain number of years (in this case 30 years) after which it is required to transfer all rights to the project to the state (in this case ETA).

43 Obayashi and Italia-Thai, the latter company although having 'Italia' in its name is one of the major Thai construction companies with negligible if any, Italian influence.

44 Interview with officials at Expressway and Rapid Transit Authority of Thailand in June 1994.

45 According to OECF the difference in amount of money received is due to the fact that DOH has a nation-wide road network to deal with and needs more money, whereas ETA so far only has the expressway network within the Bangkok area.

46 JICA, *Road Development Study in the Central Region*, Master Plan Study, Final Report-Main Text (Volume I–1) References of the traffic situation in the area at that time are all taken from this study.

47 When presenting their proposals the consultants are, in the initial stage, requested to refrain from mentioning price. JICA instead examines the people involved and how they propose to execute the job. After having selected a winner price negotiations commence.

48 Interview with a Japanese consultant involved who also was one of the participants of the Master Plan Study.

49 Information in this part is taken from JICA, Master Plan Study, op. cit.

50 For an explanation of the rather complicated methodology, see JICA, Master Plan Study, op. cit.

51 According to information from the Finance Ministry.

52 See Chapter 2 on the lack of standards for assessment at the time and how a report from the Administrative Management Bureau of the Management and Co-ordination Agency in 1991 led to the adoption of 'Operational Guidelines on OECF Loans'.

53 In this case by officials from the MOF, MOFA, MITI and the EPA acting on behalf of the government.

54 Interview with officials at the Planning Division, Department of Highways.

55 Interview with Japanese consultant involved, with the project (but not the detailed design study).

56 Information of the dates for opening and closing of tendering for the different sections were for the first four sections recieved from OECF and then counterchecked with information from DOH. There were no differences. For sections five to eight information was given by DOH but no countercheck was done as the information was not easily available at the OECF.

57 Interview with consultant for DOH involved with such evaluation.

58 Ibid.

59 Government Medium Estimates are calculated for other government procurement as well.
60 Information on dates for contract signing as well as notice to proceed from DOH to contractor (that is, commencement of contracts) was for the first four sections obtained from *Chonburi–Pattaya New Highway Project Monthly Progress Report No. 19* submitted to Kingdom of Thailand, Ministry of Transport and Communication, Department of Highways, in January 1992 by Katahira & Engineers International Inc. in Association with Asian Engineering Consultant Corp. Information has been counter-checked with OECF. For the last four sections dates have been taken from *Chonburi–Pattaya New Highway Project Monthly Progress Report No.46*, submitted in April 1994.
61 Interview with OECF representatives in Bangkok.
62 Source: DOH.
63 Estimates and predictions by the Economist Intelligence Unit, UK.

APPENDIX 4.1

Time schedule for the Chonburi–Pattaya New Highway

	1987	1988	1989	1990	1991	1992
Jan.				Tender closing for section 3	1 OECF agree contracts 3, 4 2 DOH notice to proceed for sections 3 and 4 3 New Japanese Government mission 4 New appraisal mission 5 Announcement of tender for section 8	Notice to contractor to proceed with section 8
Febr.					Tender announcement, sections 5, 6 and 7	
Mar.		First Interim Report of Master Plan completed	End of 'Road Development Study in the Central Region'	DOH sign contract for sections 1 and 2	Closing of bidding for sections 5, 6 and 7	
Apr.			Tenders announced for sections 1 and 2	OECF agrees sections 1 and 2	Tenders close for section 8	

	1987	1988	1989	1990	1991	1992
May						
June		1 Formal request for money 2 Japanese Government mission 3 Appraisal mission		DOH gives notice to proceed to contractor for sections 1 and 2		
July					Prior notice of second loan	
Aug.	Master Plan 'Road Development Study in the Central Region' starts		Tender closing for sections 1 and 2			
Sep.		Exchange of Notes on Loan Agreement	Tender announced for section 4		1 Exchange of Notes for second loan 2 Signing of loan contract	

APPENDIX 4.1 *continued*

	1987	1988	1989	1990	1991	1992
Oct.	National Debt Policy Committee gives go-ahead to borrow money	Feasibility study completed	1 Closing of tenders for section 4 2 DOH chooses contractor for sections 1 and 2	1 DOH signs contracts for sections 3 and 4 2 DOH gets go-ahead from National Debt Policy Committee to request more money	DOH signs contract for sections 5, 6, 7 and 8	
Nov.		Loan agreement signed	1 OECF agrees sections 1 and 2 2 Tender announced for section 3	Thai government requests more money		
Dec.		Detailed design study started			DOH notice to proceed for sections 5, 6 and 7	

Note: Construction was completed by June 1994. Surplus money from the project was to be used for building six overpasses.

APPENDIX 4.2

Companies submitting tenders for the first four sections,[a] contractors and contract sums[b] of the Chonburi–Pattaya New Highway

Section 1

1 Namprasert Construction Co. Ltd contracted at an amount of ¥1,190 million[c] ($8 million)
2 See Sang Karn Yotha
3 Thai Phi Phat
4 Pra Yoon Vis Karn Chang
5 Kam Pang Phet Wi Wat
6 LCC Lim Charoen

Section 2

1 Thaipipatana Limited Partnership, contracted at an amount of ¥3,118 million ($21 million)
2 Thaiwat Wis Sa Wa Karn Thang
3 See Sang Karn Yo Tha
4 Pra Yoon Wis Karn Chang
5 Namprasert Kor Sang
6 Italian–Thai Development

Section 3

1 Thaiwat Engineering Co. Ltd/J/V Vanichai Construction Co. Ltd, contracted at an amount of ¥1,093 million ($8 million)
2 Rojsin Construction Ltd
3 Krungthon Engineer Ltd

Section 4

1 Thaiwat Engineering Co. Ltd/Vanitchai Construction Co. Ltd, contracted at an amount of ¥911 million ($6.7 million)
2 See-Sang Karn Yo Tha Co. Ltd
3 Thai Phi Phat
4 Pra Yoon Vis Karn Cang
5 Rojsin Kor Sang

Notes:
(a) Source: DOH
(b) Source: *Chonburi–Pattaya New Highway Project Montly Progress Report No. 19* (see note 60)
(c) The contract was actually 216,686,815 baht but is here converted into yen according to the rates specified in the contract. The yen rate is then converted into dollars to make it easier for the reader to comprehend the figures. The fact that the figures in dollar terms for the first four sections greatly exceed the first loan amount is due to fluctuations in the exchange rate between the yen and dollar. OECF financing was for 73 per cent of this sum

APPENDIX 4.3

Companies submitting tenders for the sections 5–8,[a] contractors and contract sums[b] of the Chonburi–Pattaya New Highway

Section 5

1 Kampangphetviwat Construction Co. Ltd. Contracted at an amount of ¥1,404 million ($11 million)
2 Namprasert Construction Co. Ltd

Section 6

1 Thaiwat Engineering Co. Ltd. /Vanitchai Construction Co. Ltd. Contracted at an amount of ¥594 million ($4.7 million)
2 Thaiphiphat

Section 7

1 Thaipipatana Limited Partnership. Contracted at and amount of ¥896 million ($7 million)
2 Thaiwat

Section 8

1 Kampangphetviwat Construction Co. Ltd. Contracted at an amount of ¥1,646 million ($12 million)
2 Siam Civil Engineering / Sahawis Construction/Vanitchai Construction

Notes:
(a) Source: DOH
(b) Source for contract amounts: *Chonburi–Pattaya New Highway Project Monthly Progress Report No. 46*, Katahira & Engineers

5 Power and development in Indonesia

Åsa Malmström

In 1942, a Japanese engineer named Kubota surveyed Lake Toba and the Asahan river in Northern Sumatra for possible hydroelectric development. Mr Kubota's two companies, the Korea Power Company and the Yalu river Hydro-Electric Power Company, had previously been involved in several development projects in Korea, Manchuria and Vietnam. Development of the Asahan area was suspended due to the war, but in 1958 his new company, Nippon Koei, was back in Indonesia, and under the war reparations agreement the company 'gained nearly an exclusive hold over Indonesia's infrastructure projects'.[1] In 1972, in a report on a hydro station in the Asahan River, the possibility of developing the Renun river was first proposed by Nippon Koei.[2] Ten years later, JICA granted development assistance for a feasibility study, and finally in 1995 construction began on the 82 MW Renun power plant, financed with OECF loans. This study will follow the Renun plant from project idea to construction, and the Renun case will be used to illustrate Japanese ODA to infrastructure in Indonesia and particularly the development of the power sector.

INDONESIA – STEADY GROWTH AND INDUSTRIAL CHANGE

Indonesia is the country in South East Asia which has had the most steady economic development over the past quarter of a century. And it has also been relatively stable politically under President Suharto's rule. The country is vast, spread over 13,000 islands, and covers a geographical area as large as Europe. With a population of close on 190 million people, it is the world's fourth most populous country. Since 1969 the annual GDP growth has averaged 6 per cent, and annual inflation has been kept around or below 10 per cent. The level of absolute poverty has been reduced from 60 per cent of the population to 14 per cent.[3] But the country has also accumulated an enormous debt, amounting to $90 billion in 1994, and this is likely to increase over the coming years. The first Twenty-five-Year Development Plan, which was launched in 1969, aimed at developing industries, improving infrastructure and achieving self-sufficiency in food production. During the 1970s, economic growth was fuelled by oil revenues and access to credits and ODA. Agriculture made up the bulk of GDP, while export earnings and the government's revenue came from oil and natural gas. The dependence on oil and gas exports made the economy extremely vulnerable to external shocks, and contributed to structural imbalances. The drastic drop in oil prices in the mid-1980s significantly reduced revenues and contributed to doubling the current account deficit. The government's revenues dropped, while debt service payments rose, and the situation led to structural adjustment loans from multilateral agencies, and also from Japan. The crisis also led to a restructuring of the economy which aimed at reducing the dependence on oil and gas. Comprehensive liberalization of trade and investments was initiated, and the rupiah was devalued twice. The measures have helped diversify the economy, reduce the dependence on oil revenues and develop other industries. In the early 1990s, manufacturing industries took over as the most important export, and non-oil and gas exports accounted for 73 per cent of total exports in 1993.[4] Foreign investments skyrocketed in 1994, during the first seven months alone $15.4 billion were approved, which was more than the total for 1993.[5]

The business scene is dominated by the Chinese who, although they make up only 3 per cent of the population, control 75 per cent of private businesses in Indonesia. President Suharto's family has become increasingly involved in business and, for example, alliances with companies controlled by any of Suharto's children are a must in order to obtain major government contracts.

In April 1994, the second Twenty-five-Year Development Plan, and the sixth Five-Year Plan, Repelita VI, began. Both aim at continued macroeconomic stability, high growth and poverty reduction. Measures include reduced external borrowing, privatization of public companies and increased private participation in public sector projects. Continued growth of non-oil exports is especially important as that will drive growth in employment and gross domestic product (GDP), and ease the debt burden. Total external debt stands at $90 billion, and the debt service ratio at 30 per cent.[6] The goal is to decrease the debt service ratio to around 20 per cent over the next five years. The rapid development of industries and the influx of foreign direct investment since the mid-1980s have increased the demand for infrastructure, especially power. The power sector is the sector in the economy that has received most project aid from abroad, and it will soon be opened for private ventures.

JAPANESE–INDONESIAN RELATIONS

Indonesia and Japan have enjoyed overall good relations since the end of World War II, in spite of the Japanese occupation of the country. Some claim that the occupation, though brutal, helped Indonesia achieve independence. During the first years after the war, there was little contact. But in 1951, it was decided that Japan should pay war reparations to Indonesia and other South East Asian countries. Indonesia received ¥288 billion, and promises of economic co-operation amounting to ¥144 billion.[7] Economic co-operation continued with more loans and then sums of ODA, and relations developed rather well. Indonesia became very important to Japan, as the country had all the resources which Japan lacked and needed. Furthermore, stable relations are very important given Indonesia's strategic, geographical location by the Malacca and Lombok Straits, which are vital for sea transport to and from Japan.

In the early 1970s, relations between Japan and South East Asia became frosty, as Japanese companies were perceived as ruthlessly exploiting developing countries. During a trip to the region in 1974, then Prime Minister Tanaka was met with demonstrations in every country, and protests were very intense in Indonesia. Japanese authorities subsequently advised Japanese companies to keep a low profile, but there was no reduction of Japanese investment. In 1977, then Prime Minister Fukuda announced the so-called 'Fukuda Doctrine'. This announcement and assurance that Japan did not aspire to become a military power, meant significantly improved official relations. And they have remained favourable since that time. Unlike many Western countries, Japan has refrained from harsh criticism of Indonesian domestic affairs. The incident in East Timor in November 1991 drew much international criticism. Japan criticized it also, but with a more moderate voice than Western countries, and viewed the incident as just an incident. Tokyo has also kept a low profile when it comes to discussions of the human rights situation in Indonesia.

Although political relations have not always been smooth, economic relations are strong. Japan is Indonesia's main economic

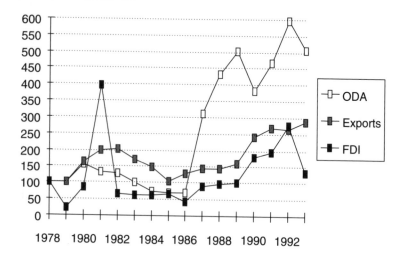

Figure 5.1 Relative growth of Japan's Indonesian ODA, exports and investments (base year 1978 = 100)
Source: Ministry of Finance, Tokyo

partner when it comes to foreign investments, trade and ODA. Figure 5.1 illustrates the trend since 1978.

Between 1967 and July 1994, Japanese investments totalled $15.2 billion, close to 18 per cent of total foreign investments (see Table 5.1).[8] Most investments are related to resources, but investment in manufacturing, especially export-oriented, and tourism are rising.

Table 5.1 Cumulative foreign direct investments (1967–July 1994)

Country	Cases	Amount ($ million)
Japan	625	15,203
Hong Kong	286	11,551
Taiwan	292	8,514
Singapore	296	4,567
United Kingdom	143	4,401
USA	165	3,790
Korea	306	3,666
The Netherlands	117	2,700
Germany	62	1,973
Other	685	28,926
Total	2,977	85,291

Source: BKPM, Jakarta

There was a slowdown of investments in the early 1990s due to the recession in Japan, but the trend turned upwards again in 1993, and this is likely to continue. Several sub-contractors to the large Japanese multinationals are setting up operations in Indonesia in order to keep costs down.

Japan is also Indonesia's main trading partner. In 1993, 30 per cent of Indonesia's exports were destined for Japan, and 22 per cent of imports originated there.[9] The composition of exports and imports is typical for trade relations between a developing and an industrialized country. Oil, gas and minerals accounted for 57 per cent of Indonesia's $12.5 billion exports to Japan in fiscal 1993, and manufactured goods, mainly textiles, comprised 26 per cent. General machinery formed 65 per cent of the $6 billion imports. Indonesia is one of the few countries that enjoys a trade surplus with Japan.

The relationship between Japan and Indonesia would seem to be one of dependence, given Japan's position as main financier and investor. The impact on Indonesia's economic development is undoubtedly considerable, although it is difficult to estimate how large the impact is. Even so, many analysts refrain from saying that Indonesia is dependent on Japan. Instead, they claim that the relationship is rather one of interdependence, and refer to Indonesia's abundance of natural resources and strategic geographical location, which are important to Japan. Furthermore, Indonesia has a very strong government, determined to pursue the goals set for development, and will not give way to foreign pressure easily. The very strong government and political stability are country-specific factors that influence international relations and also ODA.

ODA AND DEVELOPMENT

Most economists agree that ODA has been absolutely essential to Indonesia's economic development. Since Repelita I was launched in 1969, the principle has been to have a balanced budget and deficits funded by foreign borrowing, primarily ODA. Until the mid-1980s, ODA contributed on average 15 per cent of the budget.[10] During the crisis years the ratio increased to 25 per cent, and then fell to about one-fifth of revenues.

The administration of ODA is centralized within the National Development Planning Agency, BAPPENAS, which is responsible for contacts with donors and allocates ODA funds to various governmental bodies. As the English name indicates, BAPPENAS is responsible for development plans. These build on development plans made for each sector of the economy by the regional planning board, BAPPEDA. The development plans and projects are published in the so-called Bluebook each year, which is one source of information for donors. BAPPENAS has the administrative responsibility for ODA, but the budget is set by the Ministry of Finance, which sets the ceiling for foreign borrowing including ODA loans. The centralized planning is another country-specific factor. By keeping the administrative power centralized the Indonesian Government maintains control over both finances and projects.

ODA to Indonesia is channelled through the Consultative Group on Indonesia (CGI). All formal ODA pledges are made at annual CGI meetings. CGI was formed in 1992 to replace the Intergovernmental-Group on Indonesia (IGGI), which had been the forum for ODA to Indonesia since 1967. IGGI, an international consortium, was set up at the request of the Indonesian Government with the objective of discussing Indonesia's economic situation and need for development assistance. In 1966, Indonesia faced an inflation of 600 per cent, an external debt of $2.4 billion and debt service payments of $530 million, which was more than total foreign earnings.[11] Indonesia had mainly borrowed from the communist bloc – nearly $1 billion from the Soviet Union alone. Those loans were mostly for military procurement. At the time, Japan was the largest non-communist lender, and had extended $231 million. The situation called for acute debt re-scheduling, and new aid pledges. At a meeting in Tokyo in 1966 with twelve non-communist countries, new credits were promised. Further discussion led to the formation of IGGI at a meeting in February 1967.[12]

The group was dissolved in 1992 – the incidents on East Timor in 1991 triggered strong international protests, and the Government of The Netherlands was particularly harsh in its criticism. As a result, the Indonesian Government decided that it no longer either wanted or needed Dutch aid. IGGI was then replaced by CGI, which has the same function, but is chaired by the World Bank. The group meets annually in June or July, and the formal pledges for ODA allocations for the coming year are made. However, additional pledges are made at other times, with each donor having its own procedures for discussing ODA with the Indonesian Government. CGI is another country-specific factor. Although the group wields little power, it has an administrative function.

At the meeting in July 1994, $5.2 billion was pledged. Although this was an increase from $5.1 billion the previous year, most analysts doubt that funds will continue to grow. One reason is the

Government's goal to reduce foreign borrowing, including concessional ODA loans. Another reason is that the Government disap-
proves of conditionalities attached to ODA, such as human rights
issues, as they are perceived as interference in domestic affairs. As
the bulk of ODA consist of concessional loans, it is likely to remain
stable or decrease. The largest single donor is Japan who pledged
$1.67 billion, which is more than the International Bank for Recon-
struction and Development (IBRD) with $1.5 billion and ADB with
$1.1 billion.[13] These three contribute more than 80 per cent of total
funds. Of the three, Japan offers the most concessional loans, with
an interest rate of about 2.6 per cent and a repayment period of 30
years including a 10-year grace period. IBRD and ADB have
fluctuating interest rates slightly below the market rate, and shorter
repayment and grace periods. The second largest bilateral donor is
Germany, who pledged $157 million, followed by the United King-
dom, $150 million, and France, $140 million. Japan and European
donor countries pledge both loan and grant aid, whereas Australia,
Canada, and the United States only give grant aid.

JAPAN'S ODA – FROM PAST TO PRESENT

Japan's economic co-operation with Indonesia began with the war
reparations. Foreign aid, as defined today, began in 1968. With the
exception of a few years in the mid-1980s, Indonesia was the main
recipient of economic assistance until China became the main
recipient in 1993. On a cumulative basis, it is the number one
recipient of yen loans, and technical assistance, and the fourth or
fifth largest recipient of grant aid. Japan overtook the United States'
position as the main donor in the early 1970s. Between 1969 and
1973, Japan's share in IGGI commitments was 24 per cent, until
1980 the share was below 20 per cent, but from 1980, it increased
significantly to reach almost 40 per cent in 1982. In 1988, Japan
became the single largest donor when its pledges surpassed those of
the multilateral agencies as well as bilateral donors. Today, Japan's
share is 32 per cent.[14] Japanese ODA to date has financed, among
other things, 45 per cent of hydroelectricity and 17 per cent of
railroads in Indonesia, and 76 per cent of telecommunications in
Jakarta.[15]

As 1994 marked the beginning of a new Twenty-five-Year Development Plan, a special government mission from Japan visited Indonesia in February of 1994, and discussed mid- and long-term policies

for economic co-operation. The outcome was that the target areas for Japan's assistance to Indonesia include:

1 To further the achievement of equality, Japan will support poverty alleviation efforts, basic human needs and the development of Eastern Indonesia.
2 Human resources development support will include the strengthening of elementary and secondary education, and the education of engineers.
3 Assistance will be extended to protect natural resources, improve the environmental conditions of human settlements, and incorporate pollution control measures.
4 Japan will support the re-organization of industrial infrastructure, advise Indonesia on macroeconomic management, and help promote key industries and agricultural development.   ·
5 Support for Indonesia's economic infrastructure will include electric power development, and transportation and communication facilities.[16]

At the CGI meeting in July 1994, Japan pledged $1.67 billion in ODA to Indonesia. Of this, $170 million, or 10 per cent, is grant aid and technical assistance handled by JICA, and $1.5 billion is yen loans, of which $200 million is sector programme loans and the bulk, project loans.

ASSISTANCE BY JICA

JICA administers 10 per cent of total Japanese ODA to Indonesia.[17] Since 1989 the amount of grant aid and technical assistance has slowly increased, but the increase is unlikely to continue due to Indonesia's development and also the increasing number of grant aid recipients. JICA's activities in Indonesia include project-type technical co-operation, development studies, assignment of experts and 'junior experts', grant aid projects, disaster relief and acceptance of participants for training in Japan.

There are currently 563 Japanese experts stationed in Indonesia, and 206 of them are assigned to different governmental bodies, mostly to the planning divisions of various ministries.[18] These experts are familiar with the development plans and the priority projects, and often make preliminary assessments of projects. Several development studies JICA has carried out later became ODA projects financed by OECF.

OECF – MAJOR FINANCIER OF DEVELOPMENT

OECF started giving loan assistance to Indonesia in 1968, with ¥27 billion ($75 million) for ten specific projects. Since then OECF has granted loans to Indonesia annually. As of December 1993, a cumulative total of ¥2,382 billion ($21.5 billion) had been committed and ¥1,850 billion ($16.7 billion) disbursed, equalling one-fifth of total OECF loans. The loans to Indonesia are comprised of loans pledged at the IGGI/CGI meetings and loans on a non-IGGI/CGI basis. The latter are given on an *ad hoc* basis for specific projects after consultation between the two governments. These loans are extended for large-scale projects such as industrial development which do not fit under the framework of IGGI/CGI loans. However, infrastructure projects such as power and transportation projects are financed through IGGI/CGI project loans.

As indicated in Table 5.2, most loans are extended on IGGI/CGI basis. The sectoral division for the *project loans* are as follows: power 24.7 per cent, transportation 37.8 per cent, telecommunications and broadcasting 8 per cent, irrigation, flood control, agriculture, forestry, and fisheries 19.7 per cent, industry 0.9 per cent and social development 8.9 per cent.[19] Non-project IGGI/CGI loans amount to ¥628.52 billion ($5.7 billion) in programme loans and local cost financing. The programme loans are either commodity loans, or sector programme loans. Both types are given to ease balance of payments problems, with the difference that for the latter type, the equivalent sum in rupiah has to be set aside and allocated to specific development projects approved by OECF. As the economic situation improves, it is unlikely that commodity loans will be extended during the coming years. The loans for local cost financing are intended to cover the local currency cost for OECF-financed projects.

Table 5.2 OECF loan commitments to Indonesia (cumulative total, 31 December 1993)

Type	Amount (¥ billion)	Share (%)
Total IGGI/CGI loans	2,092.79	87.9
of which project loans	1,464.27	61.5
non-project loans	628.52	26.4
Non-IGGI/CGI loans	289.44	12.1
Total OECF loans	2,382.23	100.00

Source: OECF, Jakarta

In 1993, 90 per cent of the loans were general untied, and the remaining 10 per cent LDC untied, and the latter were only loans for consulting/engineering services. In effect, this means that consulting and engineering services are usually provided by Japanese companies or through joint ventures with Indonesian consulting firms.[20]

The figures for nationalities of contractors are confidential, but the share of contract value awarded to Japanese companies is higher than in general for OECF loans. However, the figures are somewhat misleading for two reasons. First of all, they only reflect the nationality of the main contractor, and not the nationality of sub-contractors. With large infrastructure projects there are usually quite a large number of sub-contractors involved, and these companies are not necessarily connected to the main contractor. Secondly, the figures do not reveal in which category joint ventures are recorded. In Indonesia most foreign companies have a local partner, and there are also a number of short-term alliances formed for specific projects. Such company alliances and regular joint ventures are not recorded in available statistics.

Each year between October and January, OECF sends sector service missions to Indonesia. About 20 teams arrive and meet with officials at BAPPENAS and concerned line ministries, to study sectoral developments and identify priority projects. The teams present their findings/results of studies of projects that OECF could extend loans to, both to BAPPENAS and to the responsible ministries in Tokyo. In January, BAPPENAS makes its final choice of candidate projects, and this is followed by a formal request for loans given to the Japanese Government via the Japanese Embassy. Meanwhile, the Four Ministries dealing with ODA in Tokyo (MOFA, MITI, MOF, EPA) meet and decide on ODA amounts and specific projects to lend to during the coming fiscal year. In March or April a government mission from Japan with delegates from concerned ministries travels to Indonesia, with the objective of discussing projects and making final decisions on which projects will be subject to OECF loans. Usually a few projects are taken off the list that OECF could consider financing. The government mission should then be followed by OECF's appraisal mission. Two persons per project, usually an economist and an engineer, analyse details for proposed projects and prepare the proposals for the CGI meeting. However, in practice, the loan package is already decided when the government mission is in Indonesia, and the mission is thus more of a formality, and the appraisal mission often takes place parallel to the government mission. The formal pledges, or prior notification, are made at the annual CGI meeting in June or July. Then in September/ October the Exchange of Notes between the governments is made, followed by the actual signing of loan agreements. The annual process is for loans given in that particular fiscal year.

POWER IN DEMAND

The power sector has received a quarter of all OECF loans to Indonesia, and it is a sector that has grown tremendously since 1970, and demand is estimated to continue to grow. Construction of power plants is also costly, and considerable sums are needed to cope with the planned expansion. The Government has thus decided to open the power sector to the private sector to build and operate power plants as one way of coping with the demand increase and shortage of funds.

The consumption of electricity produced by the state electricity company, Persahaan Listrik Negara (PLN), grew by an average of 15.5 per cent annually between 1970 and 1991, and by 1992 the total electricity consumption had reached 49.5 TWh. The total installed capacity reached 19,138 MW by April 1993. Of this 8,265 MW was captive power mainly for industrial use and 10,873 MW was for public use.[21] Growth forecasts indicate an average annual demand increase of between 9 and 12 per cent until 2004, according to estimates by ADB and PLN. There has been a shortage of electricity since the late 1980s, which has hampered industrial development and, if the economic growth and industrial development is to continue, it is necessary to expand power capacity. During Repelita VI (1994–99) power capacity will increase by 13,000 MW. The government estimates that about 4,960 MW of the planned expansion will be plants constructed by private companies.[22] The total cost including the private plants is estimated to be $13.1 billion (Rp 27.7 trillion).[23] Of PLN's total installed capacity the bulk, or 36.2 per cent, is steam, 20 per cent is hydroelectric, 19 per cent is diesel, 12.23 per cent combined cycle, 11.25 per cent gas turbine, and the remaining 1.29 per cent is geo-thermal.[24] Hydroelectric power is the cheapest source of energy but these plants require a great deal of land. Java is the site of 70 per cent of PLN's installed capacity.

PLN

PLN, Persahaan Listrik Negara, or State Electricity Company, is the implementing agency for power projects. Up until now it has been responsible for construction and operation of all publicly owned power plants, and sales of electricity to the end-users. PLN is placed under the Ministry of Mines and Energy. The regional planning boards, BAPPEDA, identify the needs for electricity in their development plans and make suggestions to PLN's regional offices. These offices in turn create system plans, demand forecasts and identify potential power projects for each region. The regional plans are assembled at PLN's national office. Feasibility studies are made for potential power projects and these studies are often financed by ODA. Projects which are deemed feasible are put on priority lists and submitted to the Directorate-General of Electricity and New Energy and the Ministry of Mines and Energy. The plans are also submitted to BAPPENAS and the Ministry of Finance. The Directorate-General decides which projects are to be implemented given the financial situation, and PLN's role is to plan and execute. PLN's sources of finance are government funds, self-generated funds and external borrowing. External funds comprise ODA loans, export credits and commercial loans, and together comprise 40 per cent of PLN's total funds.[25]

In the future, it is proposed that PLN becomes a company, PT PLN, 100 per cent owned by the Government and as such it will be responsible for the construction and operation of power plants outside Java, and will also sell all electricity to end-users. PT PLN will have two subsidiaries, PT KJB, and PT KJT. The former will be responsible for construction and operation of plants on West Java, and the latter for East Java. The two subsidiaries will be free to form joint ventures with private companies for individual plants.

In addition to this, the Government has started build–own–operate (BOO) schemes for private companies. Seven private plants are planned on Java. Four of these are coal-fired plants, two gas, and one geothermal.[26] No hydroelectric plants are planned for operation by the private sector, as it is perceived to be too difficult to raise external financing due to the high percentage of civil works, with an accompanying high degree of local content. The first contracts for privately built plants were awarded to an international consortium in early 1994 after long negotiations. The Paiton Swasta 1 power project on Java consists of one 1,200 MW coal-fired units and is estimated to cost $2.5 billion. Sceptics claimed that this was too large a project for a private venture, and pointed to the difficulties of raising finance. However, international banks responded positively, and $1.8 billion has now been secured from American, Japanese and European banks. The remaining $700 million will be provided by the Paiton group.[27]

The contract for Paiton Swasta 2, another 1,200 MW, has also been nominally awarded but funding has not been secured.

THE PROJECT CYCLE

When power projects are to be implemented, PLN, as the executing agency, divides the projects into different lots. As most projects are large in scale this means that there will usually be a number of different contractors. The reasons for dividing projects are several. The different parts of power plants require different technology and know-how, and the plants are divided according to that. Also, by having several contractors, PLN has more control over quality. For preparatory work, PLN and the government wish to promote local companies, but the type of financing determines whether or not that is possible. Competitive bidding is the normal practice for awarding contracts for projects financed by the government or self-generated funds. For projects financed by international lending institutions, procurement is subject to international competitive bidding (ICB), according to the lending agency's rules and guidelines. Procurement is usually tied to the donor country for projects financed by aid or export credits, except the OECF loans which are untied.

There are, however, exceptions to these policies. In 1994, export-credit allocations for three projects worth approximately $1.2 billion were awarded on a repeat-order basis to companies which had previously provided similar plants to PLN.[28] The contracts encompassed three gas and steam plants on Java and they were all awarded to international consortia. The 900 MW Muara Tawar plant was awarded to ABB and Marubeni, the 500 MW Tambak Lorok II was awarded to Sumitomo and General Electric, and the 500 MW Grati plant was awarded to Mitsubishi and Siemens. This repeat-order caused some debate because another bidder, GEC Alsthom, offered lower prices. PLN claimed that through direct negotiations with the contractors, lower prices were achieved than GEC Alsthom could offer. Furthermore, the repeat-order would speed up implementation. The repeat-order was later approved by the President.

OECF loans are usually untied and procurement should be carried out according to OECF's 'Guidelines for Procurement under OECF Loans'.[29] Consultants can be employed for feasibility studies, detailed engineering studies, supervision of construction work, and other advisory services. If consultants are to be employed, PLN and OECF decide the terms of reference that the consultant must follow. This describes the project and the consulting services to be performed, in detail. PLN assembles a shortlist of three to five qualified consultants. Those consultants are invited to submit proposals through a *Letter of Invitation*. The *Terms of Reference* and the *Letter of Invitation* are submitted to the OECF for review and approval. Proposals are then evaluated by PLN, and the evaluations are given to the OECF for review and approval. When the contract has been awarded, it is submitted to BAPPENAS and then to OECF for review and approval. However, consultants can also be selected through direct appointment, in which case the procedure is the same except for review of proposals.

Procurement of goods and services should, in general, be subject to international competitive bidding. There are a few exceptions to this rule. If equipment must be compatible with existing equipment, if the amount involved is so small that foreign firms would not be interested or if administrative costs are too high to make international bidding worthwhile, then procurement may be done differently. OECF can agree to local competitive bidding (LCB), and if that is the case then it is stipulated in the loan agreement. For LCB contracts worth less than ¥500 million, PLN is responsible for the whole process, and only needs to submit the contract to BAPPENAS and OECF's Jakarta office for reference. For LCB and ICB contracts worth more than ¥500 million, OECF is involved in each step. If pre-qualification takes place, PLN evaluates the interested companies. The results of the pre-qualification are then sent to OECF for review and approval. Pre-qualified companies are then invited to bid, and the bids are evaluated by PLN who also ranks the bids. OECF reviews the evaluation and suggestion, and may concur, or make another suggestion. The proposed contract is then submitted to BAPPENAS and then to the OECF for review and approval. If contracts amount to more than Rp3 billion (approximately $1.5 million), they must be cleared by EKUIN (the co-ordination ministry for economy, finance, industry and development supervision) in Indonesia before they are signed.

Tenders are announced in the local press, but trading houses and companies involved in the power sector usually have close contacts with PLN and know of the long-term plans well ahead. Supervision of projects is normally done by PLN staff and the consulting company, but OECF supervises at distance, that is, it is informed and updated on how projects proceed.

RENUN AND ASAHAN – A HISTORY OF
HYDROELECTRIC POWER

The Renun hydroelectric plant is closely connected to the Asahan hydroelectric plant and aluminium smelter plant located along the Asahan river west of Lake Toba in North Sumatra (see Map 5.1). When Mr Kubota's team arrived in 1942, they were far from the first to discover the possibilities of the Lake Toba area. The area was investigated by a Dutch survey team as early as 1908,[30] and the Asahan river was eyed for power development in 1919. In 1939, MEWA Enterprise, a joint venture between Dutch companies and The Netherland Indies Government, contemplated generating power on the Asahan river for aluminium production and in 1941 the company acquired the water right to start such a project, but it was suspended due to World War II. Mr Kubota's team pursued further investigations and resumed construction of the power station and aluminium smelting plant. The construction was discontinued when the war stopped. After the war, several international teams made further studies and submitted reports – among them, French, Japanese, American, and Swedish companies. In 1960, under the Indonesia–USSR 'Economic and Technical Mutual Agreement', a Soviet investigation team made a detailed survey of hydroelectric power development and the possibility of using cheap energy for aluminium smelting.[31] And as relations with the USSR were good, there was a significant possibility that the project would have been implemented. However, due to the attempted coup in Jakarta, the team left on 30 September 1965.

In January 1967, a Japanese consulting company, Nippon Koei Co. Ltd submitted a proposal to the Indonesian Government to undertake the Asahan overall study, the development project and to promote its realization. The company specializes in water systems, hydroelectricity and dam building and had considerable experience with such projects in other developing countries. The preliminary investigation was done in 1967 and 1968. The interim report was presented in February 1968, and the feasibility report in May 1969. In April 1972, a financial agreement was made between the governments of Japan and Indonesia on detailed investigation and design of the hydroelectric plant called Asahan No. 2. Nippon Koei Co. Ltd conducted a detailed engineering study which was not financed by Japanese ODA. The Asahan project started formally in 1975.[32] The hydroelectric plant was to be combined with the construction of an aluminium smelter to be implemented by a joint venture between the Indonesian

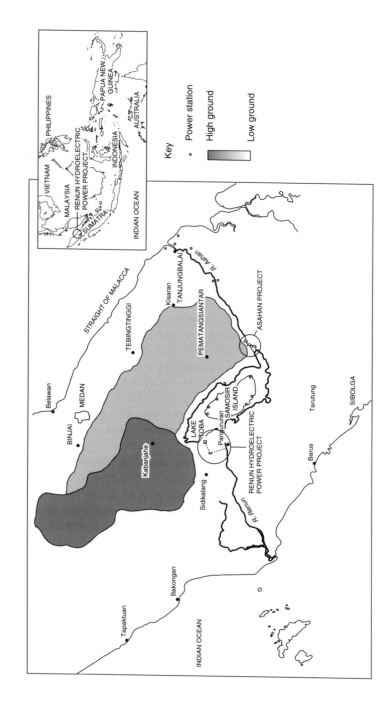

Map 5.1 Renun Hydroelectric Power Project

Government, Japanese Government and Japanese private industry.[33] The company, PT Indonesia Asahan Aluminium (PT Inalum), was established in 1976. In 1977, construction of Siguragura and Tangga power stations including a regulation dam, river channel improvement and 275 kV transmission line started. The Siguragura and Tannga power stations were completed in 1981 and 1983 respectively. ¥61.5 billion ($295 million) in OECF loans plus another ¥34 billion ($128 million) in OECF investment was extended to Asahan No. 2 and the aluminium smelter. That is equvalent to 25 per cent of total cost. The Export-Import Bank of Japan is the single largest financier, contributing around 50 per cent.

Following the construction of Asahan No. 2, Asahan No. 1 and No. 3 have been suggested on the up- and downstream sides of Asahan No. 2. The Government of Indonesia requested technical assistance for the feasibility studies of these plants. The request was approved, and JICA, in co-operation with PLN, carried out the study in 1981 and 1982. However, as yet, no loans have been extended for the construction.

THE RENUN PROJECT

The Renun plant was first proposed in April 1972, in a report entitled 'The No 2 Hydro Power Station Project of the Asahan Overall Development Scheme' prepared by Nippon Koei Co. Ltd.[34] According to PLN, Renun was also envisaged in their system planning of projects in North Sumatra to cope with the increased power demand. The plant is designed to harness the hydroelectric power potential between the Renun river and Lake Toba by diverting water from the river to the lake through a 20 km tunnel. It is to utilize water head of about 500 m between the Renun river and Lake Toba. The power generated will be transmitted to the greater Medan area, about 100 km north of the project area.

In 1982, the government of Indonesia asked JICA to undertake a feasibility study on the Renun plant. The request was accepted and a contract with JICA for the feasibility study was concluded on 1 January 1983. Nippon Koei was appointed by JICA in Tokyo to carry out the feasibility study, and it was conducted between July 1983 and October 1984. The study, which was presented in March 1985, concluded that the Renun project was technically feasible, economically and financially viable, as well as socio-environmentally acceptable.

The Renun plant will consist of one main intake and 11 tributary intakes which will divert water from the Renun river to Lake Toba.[35] The water will go through tunnels and a regulating pond. The main dam will be located at Pangiringan, and the power station at Silalahi on the shore of Lake Toba. The power capacity and annual energy production will be 82 MW and 313.5 GWh. In addition to generating energy at the Renun power station, the flow of water to Lake Toba will increase, and it is estimated that the power generation at power stations along the Asahan river will also increase. During the past 12 years the water level in Lake Toba has dropped by 5 m, and as a result of the reduced water flow into the Asahan river, Asahan No. 2 is currently running below capacity. With the Renun plant, the incremental energy at Asahan No. 2 will be 304.5 GWh, thus the combined production will be 618.2 GWh. The project cost, including indirect costs such as compensation costs, was estimated at $175.48 million in 1985 non-inflated prices. The financial internal rate of return was estimated at 13.3 per cent and the economic rate of return at 28.3 per cent. The rates of return are calculated on the combined return from the Renun and Asahan plants. The Renun plant alone was estimated to generate a return of just 4.4 per cent. According to a report by Nippon Koei, the project was estimated to cost $252.2 million (¥17,988 million and Rp188,979 million) in 1988 prices. The economic rate of return, with a net benefit of $48.8 million, is 17.7 per cent, and the financial internal rate of return is estimated at 16.2 per cent.[36] Again the rates of return are for the combined effect of Renun and Asahan 2. The feasibility study concluded that there would be no negative social effects, the local government has not opposed the construction, and the positive contributions to the standard of living, for example electrification and improved roads, have been emphasized. Furthermore, there will be no serious influence on water use and water quality along the main stream and tributaries of Renun river and Lake Toba. The Renun plant is linked to the Asahan complex. If the latter did not exist, it is highly unlikely that Renun would have been constructed ODA financing is also crucial.

To date, four loans have been extended to the Renun hydroelectric power plant, one for engineering services and three for construction. The request for OECF loans for engineering services was made in 1985, by the time the feasibility study was near completion. In spring 1985, OECF's appraisal mission for the Engineering Services Loan took place, and in December the same year, the first loan of ¥910 million ($3.8 million) was signed for the engineering design study. The fact that a request was made for a loan for engineering services in

1985 when the feasibility study was not yet finished indicates that informal discussions do occur, and that OECF staff are well aware of which projects are being studied. A shortlist of Japanese consultants was prepared by PLN, based on consultants' experience, methodology, and staff. The shortlist and letter of invitation were then approved by OECF. PLN evaluated and ranked the proposals from consultants, and submitted their evaluations to OECF, which in turn approved PLN's choice. Nippon Koei Co. Ltd won the contract, and the engineering design study was carried out between 1987 and 1989. Since Nippon Koei had already done the overall Asahan studies, and hydroelectric plants is one of its areas of expertise, it was the obvious choice of consultant, according to PLN and OECF officials in Jakarta. Nippon Koei refused to discuss its role.

In February 1990, a loan request for Phase I of the construction to cover access roads, base camps and electricity for the base camps, was made.[37] After the request, the appraisal mission took place, and in September 1991, the loan agreement for Phase I was signed. The loan amounted to ¥5,460 million ($38 million), with 2.6 per cent interest, and a 30-year repayment period including a 10-year grace period. Phase I was divided into seven lots (see Table 5.3) and these were subject to local competitive bidding. Lot 6 will not be realized until Phase III.

In November 1993, the loan agreement was signed for the third loan amounting to ¥15,668 million ($141 million). The terms were

Table 5.3 Construction – Renun project, Phase I

Lot 1	Access road to main intake and inspection road. PT Prima Sarana Usaha Mandiri was awarded the contract worth $2.1734 million (Rp 4,535,552,106.94). OECF concurred in November 1992.
Lot 2	Surge tank and access road. PT Lampiri Jaya Abadi was awarded the contract worth $3.108 million (Rp6,485,597,872.43). OECF concurred in February 1993.
Lot 3	Power house access road. PT Karya Jasa Mandiri was awarded the contract worth $3.541 million (Rp7,390,516,000.00). OECF concurred in April 1993.
Lot 4	Base camp and
Lot 5	electrical works in base camp. PT Perkutut was awarded the contract worth $1.696 million (Rp3,539,971,159.00). OECF concurred in May 1993.
Lot 7	Supply and erection for distribution line. PT Dhana Julaga Ekada was awarded the contract on 30 November 1994. The contract amounted to $534 846 (Rp1,153,643,800).

Source: PLN

the same as for the second loan. This loan will cover civil works and hydro-mechanical works (that is, lots 1, 2 and 4) of Phase II of the construction (see Table 5.4). The construction in Phases II and III is divided into nine lots, and will be subject to international competitive bidding, in accordance with 'Guidelines for Procurement under OECF Loans'. As of September 1994, contracts for lots 1 and 2 had been awarded.

Lot 1 of civil works includes the main intake, tributary intakes numbers 1 to 8, upstream headrace tunnel and the regulating pond. Lot 2 of civil works includes tributary intakes numbers 9 to 11, downstream headrace tunnel, branch tunnel, surge tank, penstock line and power station. Pre-qualification for lots 1 and 2 opened in August 1993, and closed on 14 September 1993. In all, 23 companies participated, and after PLN's evaluation 13 companies were qualified to submit bids. The list of pre-qualified companies based on PLN's evaluation was agreed by OECF in February 1994. The tender for lots 1 and 2 opened in January 1994, and closed in April. The following nine companies submitted bids. With one exception, the companies have formed joint ventures or some sort of alliance with Indonesian companies.[38]

1 Bilfinger & Berger – PT Washita Karya Jaeger J.O. (German/Indonesian)
2 Hazama Bruntas – Adhi J.O (Japanese/Indonesian)
3 Spie Batignolles – PT Hutama Karya J.O (French/Indonesian)
4 Torno SrL (Italian)
5 Taisei – PT Pembangunan Perumahan (Japanese/Indonesian)
6 Maeda – PT Wijaya Karya – PT Yala Perkasalnt J.O (Japanese/Indonesian)

Table 5.4 Construction – Renun project, Phase II

Lot I	Civil works; main intake, tributary intakes numbers 1 to 8; regulating pond and intake.
Lot II	Civil works; waterway, tributary intakes numbers 9 to 11; power station and substations. Hyundai–MBRC–JINRO was awarded the contract worth *c*. \$82.197 million.
Lot III	Hydromechanical works including gates, stoplogs, and trash racks. PT Boma Bisma Indrqa/PT Indra Karya/PT Brantas Abipraya were contracted on 14 March 1995. The amount was \$3.4 m (¥88,001,647 + Rp 4,970,702,378).

Source: PLN

7 Hyundai – MBRC – Jinro J.O (Korean/Indonesian)
8 Kajima – Kumagai – Teguh J.O (Japanese/Indonesian)
9 Damez – Impregillo SpA – PT Istaka Karya J.O (French/Italian/
  Indonesian)

PLN evaluated the bids and ranked them. Hyundai's bid was perceived to be the best technically, and it also had the lowest price. The
preferred bid was approved by PLN's board on 15 July 1994. The bid
was approved by the Government on 6 August. Then, on 18 August,
the ranking with PLN's suggestion, was submitted to OECF for
approval, which took place on 30 August. In September, OECF and
PLN commenced detailed contract negotiations with the winner about
time-schedule, equipment, etc. Before the final contract was to be
signed in October 1994, it had to be approved by EKUIN. Then the
signed contract would be agreed by BAPPENAS and OECF.

On 29 November 1994, the loan agreement for a fourth loan was
signed. The loan amounted to ¥5,479 million ($54 million), and will
cover the remaining lots as indicated in Table 5.5. Pre-qualification
will only be done for lot 3, as the other lots are more basic. All lots,
except lot 6 (phase I), will be subject to international competitive
bidding. The construction of the actual plant is scheduled to start in
early 1995.

The consulting company, Nippon Koei Co. Ltd, and a project
manager from PLN will be supervising the construction. Nippon
Koei seemingly exercises considerable influence, but as it refused
to grant an interview it is difficult to assess its role. Renun is one of
approximately 30 projects that Nippon Koei is involved with in
Indonesia at the moment. Nippon Koei has worked with PLN and

Table 5.5 Construction – Renun project, Phase III

Lot III	Hydromechanical works including penstock, and drain tunnel facilities. The pre-qualification finished in February 1995 and the tender closed in July 1995.
Lot V	Turbines and auxiliaries. The tender opened in January 1995.
Lot VI	Generators and auxiliaries. The tender opened in January 1995.
Lot VII	Main transformer, switch gear, and power line carriers communication system. The tender opened in July 1995.
Lot VIII	Transmission line materials. The tender opened in June 1995.
Lot IX	Inflow monitoring system. The tender is scheduled to open in July 1997.
Lot 6	Erection for transmission line. The tender is scheduled to open in January 1997. LCB

Source: PLN

OECF on several other power projects, most notably the Asahan project, and consequently is very familiar with the project process.

CONCLUDING REMARKS

The Renun plant is clearly a Japanese project, as it is more or less part of the Asahan complex, and Asahan is forecast to generate higher returns once Renun is operating. This assumption is supported by the fact that the loan for engineering services was, in principle, approved by the time the feasibility study was concluded. The Renun plant becomes even more important when the financial difficulties and recent bail-outs for PT Inalum are considered. Furthermore, the fact that appraisal missions took place more or less parallel to the Government mission clearly shows that plans were known to OECF staff before the formal decisions were made, and that also supports the conclusion that it is a Japanese project.

There is of course a strong Indonesian interest as the Asahan complex is a joint venture, but the issue of financing tilts the scale towards the Japanese side. As Renun is not commercially viable, ODA financing is crucial for the realization of the plant. Thus, the ODA factor is very strong. And it is doubtful whether any other ODA agency than OECF would have been prepared to finance a plant the main purpose of which is to support the Asahan complex. A multilateral agency might have considered it in order to support the government of Indonesia and northern Sumatra, but multilateral credits are not as soft as OECF loans. So, from the Indonesian government's point of view, OECF financing was undoubtedly the best alternative. Hence, the OECF factor is also very strong.

In the Renun case, the Indonesian authorities have clearly been the decision-makers in the procurement process, and OECF has acted as a financial intermediary. Although Renun is a Japanese project overall, there is a marked absence of Japanese companies at contract level. The major trading companies are all involved in PT Inalum, and it is clearly in their interest that Renun is realized. However, they have not been directly involved with Renun. Furthermore, the major contract to date has been awarded to a Korean company. Hyundai will, with this plant, build its first hydroelectric plant in Indonesia, and it is remarkable that a company that is relatively unknown in this regard was awarded the contract. Hyundai feels that this a major step, and that it will consolidate its position in Indonesia.

This case indicates that ODA is a two-way trade and that the Indonesian authorities clearly have the decision-making power in the bidding processes. Renun is only one of many power plants financed by OECF loans in Indonesia, and may therefore not be representative. But when one considers the nature of the Renun plant with the connection to Asahan, the Indonesian authorities' position come across as even stronger. They have evidently not been governed by OECF in the procurement process. Instead, the project process has been characterized by interaction, and a maximization of utility.

NOTES

1 Masashi Nishihara, *The Japanese and Sukarno's Indonesia–Tokyo–Jakarta Relations 1951–1966*, Center for Southeast Asian Studies, Kyoto, 1976, p. 103.
2 JICA, *Feasibility Report on Renun Hydroelectric Power Development Project*, JICA, Jakarta, 1985.
3 World Bank, *Indonesia – Stability, Growth and Equity in Repelita VI*, Jakarta, 1994.
4 JETRO Jakarta Office.
5 *South East Asia Monitor*, Business Monitor International, London, September 1994.
6 Asian Development Bank, *ADB Asian Development Outlook 1994*, Manila, 1994.
7 Nishihara, op. cit.
8 Investment figures from BKPM, the investment co-ordinating board of Indonesia.
9 Trade figures from JETRO's Jakarta office.
10 Central Bureau of Statistics, *Nota Keuangan*, Jakarta, various years.
11 Jeff Kingston, 'Bolstering the new order: Japan's ODA relations with Indonesia', in Bruce Koppel and Robert Orr (eds), *Japan's Foreign Aid Power*, Westview Press, Boulder, CO, 1993.
12 The meeting was attended by representatives from Australia, Belgium, France, Germany, Italy, Japan, the Netherlands, UK, USA, IMF, IBRD, ADB, UNDP and OECD, and observers from Switzerland, Norway, and New Zealand.
13 BAPPENAS document.
14 OECF, Jakarta.
15 Embassy of Japan, *Indonesia ni okeru keizai gijutsu kyōryoku*, Jakarta, 1994.
16 OECF, *Annual Report 1994*, Tokyo, 1994, p.41.
17 JICA, *JICA di Indonesia*, Jakarta Office, 1993.
18 JICA, *Technical Co-operation and Grant Assistance for Indonesia FY 93/94*, Jakarta Office, 1994.
19 OECF, *Japan's Contribution to Economic Development in Indonesia through OECF Loan*, Jakarta Office, 1994.
20 In some cases other LDC firms have been contracted.
21 PLN, *PLN Statistics 92/93*, Jakarta, 1993.
22 PLN and *Jakarta Post*, 13 September 1994.

23 *Far Eastern Economic Review*, 28 October 1993.
24 PLN, *PLN Statistics 92/93*, op. cit.
25 PLN, *PLN Financial Statistics 92/93*, Jakarta, 1993.
26 *Far Eastern Economic Review*, 28 October 1993.
27 *Indonesia Business Weekly*, 5 August 1994. (The Paiton group's partners are General Electric, Mission Energy, Mitsui and PT Hitam Perkasa.
28 *Jakarta Post*, 4 September 1994, and PT InterMatrix, *Study of the Power Sector Market in Indonesia*, Jakarta, September 1994.
29 The standard procurement procedures are taken from the OECF Loan Handbook, Jakarta Representative Office, March 1993.
30 JICA, *Feasibility Report on the Asahan No.1 and No.3 Hydroelectric Power Development Project*, December 1982.
31 *Far Eastern Economic Review*, 9 April 1976.
32 JICA, *Feasibility Report* op. cit.
33 Twelve Japanese companies are involved: Sumitomo Chemical plus, Mistsubishi Chemical, seven trading companies – Sumitomo Shoji, C. Itoh, Nissho-Iwai, Nichimen, Marubeni, Mitsubishi Corporation, and Mitsui – and three smelting companies – Nippon Light Metal, Showa Denko, and Mistui, *Far Eastern Economic Review*, 9 April 1976.
34 Cited in the JICA, *Feasibility Report on Renun Hydroelectric Power Development Project*, March 1985. The actual report belongs to Nippon Koei, it is confidential and no details were released.
35 The technical details are from JICA, *Feasibility Report on Renun*, op. cit.
36 Nippon Koei, *Renun Hydroelectric Power and Associated Transmission Line Project – Project Description*, December 1993.
37 Lot 1 to 7, except lot 6 in Phase I.
38 Source: PLN.

6 Power and democracy in the Philippines[1]

Ben Warkentin

WHY CALACA?

Things take time in the Philippines. Bearing this in mind I left the guest house at 6.30 a.m. My appointment had been arranged for 9.00 a.m. in central Manila, less than 13 km away from the University of the Philippines' campus in Quezon City. Since the address stated 'Office of the President', I wanted to be sure that I arrived in time and I deemed that two and a half hours was reasonable. But the taxi driver was sceptical as it had been raining during the night. He was proved right – I never made it to my appointment. By 7.30 a.m. all traffic to downtown Manila had slowed to a halt. After wading through knee-deep water and waiting in front of a public telephone for some 30 minutes, I finally received the news that the person I was to interview had not made it either. Central Manila would not be working today!

It took another three hours to reach the location of my appointment scheduled for the afternoon, the Japanese Embassy in the uptown Makati district. The official only nodded without surprise when I tried to explain my sad appearance. But later when he called the Manila office of JICA without success – located just around the corner – he remarked in a mixture of frustration and confirmation: 'That's why we have to build up infrastructure over here.' Not yet convinced, I returned to my office at the university in the late afternoon. There I met one of the secretaries standing in the hallway next to the atrium trying to read something, with the door to her dark office wide open. 'Brown out all day', she replied when she saw my puzzled face: no lights, no air conditioning, no computer – another day wasted.

More than just a traveller's tale, the term 'brown out' captures the frustrations associated with the Philippines' capital region's infrastructure. These power failures form the agonizing background against which the topic of this chapter is considered, namely, the events surrounding the planned construction of a second unit of a coal-fired thermal power plant, in the small coastal city of Calaca some 100 km south of Manila. 'Brown out' is the Philippine phrase for a black out in the middle of the day caused by an insufficient supply of electrical energy. To make ends meet, NPC (the National Power Corporation) or the distributor in the central capital region, MER-ALCO, switch off parts of the electrical grid on a rotating basis.

Brown outs came to symbolize the policy failures that haunted the late Aquino administration even more than the armed communist opposition or the military uprisings. After the Aquino Cabinet decided not to operate the ill-fated 600 MW Philippine Nuclear Power Plant in Bataan,[2] a prestige project that contributed to the downfall of Marcos, the mounting energy crisis drained the optimism that had spread after the 'EDSA-Revolution'.[3] A count of articles in Manila's main papers related to this subject during the crisis years may indicate the socio-political dimensions. While in 1991 more than 300 articles were published, in 1992 the number jumped to over 900, and to well over 1,000 in 1993.[4] Indeed, in spite of various measures, such as energy saving campaigns, the import of small generators and the 'crash' construction of small-sized power plants, the situation on the main island of Luzon grew worse in 1993, with electrical supply about one-third short of demand. That amounted to rotating brown outs of between 8 and 12 hours daily in the central capital region during the summer. One must experience such a brown out in a metropolitan city to under-stand its full meaning, beyond the economic implications.

The problem was consequently addressed by President Ramos' action plan 'Philippines 2000!!!' and the subsequent high-priority 'flagship projects' intended to lead the Philippines into parity with its more advanced neighbours.[5] However, during the winter of 1994/95, only the abundance of rain that allowed the hydro power stations to maintain operations throughout the dry season of 1994 saved Manila from a return to the 1993 daily disruption of electrical supply. The recent economic growth of 5.1 per cent in 1994, the 20 per cent surge in exports, the explosion of new foreign investments[6] and the new overall confidence still rest on a shaky foundation. If the predicted 6 per cent growth for 1995 is realized, the energy situation will remain delicate. This explains some of the continued reluctance to select the Philippines for foreign investment, expressed by mid-sized and smaller Japanese companies that have been pushed abroad by the appreciation of the yen.[7] Only the larger sized base-load power plants that were expected to begin operating in 1995 can improve the long-term situation. Calaca II is one of them.

Energy and infrastructure will continue to be key issues of Philippine industrialization, a fact on which even the most outspoken leaders of the nationalist (socialist) opposition agree. The critical issues are quality and distribution of benefits,[8] questions for which Calaca became the 'classical case' in how they were addressed.

The Calaca project has many facets which are readily open to criticism. For instance, a report by a Japanese NGO that visited the site in 1991, described the noise, the freely combusting coal stacks and the unbearable foul smell and concluded: 'This is the reality created by the technology and the funds of a Japan that claims to be a technological superpower and one of the richest nations on earth . . . a power plant built by Japanese companies with Japanese funds.'[9] If an example is sought of a Japan Inc. expansionist conspiracy, tied aid, the 'Second Invasion', the 'gravy train' of Japan's aid business and similar interpretations, noting that these are even included in academic literature,[10] Calaca could be chosen as a case in point. Indeed, a glance at the list of projects in Table 6.1 suggests that the Philippine implementing agency was merely a small executing unit in an almost entirely Japanese controlled project.

The table suggests a Japanese and not a Philippine omnipresence which is further strengthened by the project's location in southern Batangas, part of the hinterland of metropolitan Manila that comprises to the south east, five provinces that together came to be called CALABARZON because of a regional JICA financed master plan. Today, the development of this whole region is widely identified as a Japanese project. It is here that recent Japanese and other foreign investments have accumulated, and Japanese grant aid has been concentrated. The Cavite Export Processing Zone, the Japanese–Philippine Friendship Highway (with the recent upgrading of the South Luzon Expressway) and the Batangas port development, all financed with Japanese ODA grants and loans, are all located near to Calaca (see Map 6.1).

The conclusion, however, that Calaca is a project of an expanding Japan Inc. implies a number of assumptions. One such assumption is that there is indeed a master plan or general scheme for collective Japanese action. A second would be the assumption that Japanese actors have the power to proceed according to these plans despite a complex political environment. A third is a 'rational story assumption' of a means–ends type (Weber, Habermas), that is, a direct connection is presumed between a general Japanese concept or

Table 6.1   Projects in or related to the Calaca Power Complex

---

1979–84   Calaca I (Batangas Coal-Fired Thermal Power Plant I)
   F/S: 1979, Kennedy & Donkins International (KDI), West Japan
   Engineering Consultants Inc. (WESTJEC), Engineering and
   Development Corporation Philippines (EDCOP)
   Financing: Japan, Exim Bank (approximately $238.5 million)
   Implementation: NPC with Mitsui (Foster Wheeler Energy
   Corporation, Toshiba and Ishijima Harima Heavy Industries, *et al.*)

1986–89   Calaca I (Performance) Upgrading Project
   F/S: 1986–88, JICA with group of specialists (JICA study group)
   Financing: NPC (approximately $8 million)
   Implementation: NPC with the consortium that built unit 1

1986–95   Calaca II (Batangas Coal-Fired Thermal Power Plant II)
   F/S: original 1979 study
   Financing: OECF (¥40.4 billion and ¥5.5 billion overrun costs,
   approximately $450 million in 1994 exchange rates, OECF loans
   No. PH-P76, PH-P141)
   Implementation: NPC with consultant NEWJEC (Japanese–
   Canadian–Philippine consortium with HOKUDEN, MONENCO,
   INTERNAFIL), GEC-Alsthom/Marubeni Corporation (French/
   Japanese; Schedule 1: electric generator), Mitsubishi Corporation/
   Combustion Engineering (Japanese/U.S.; Schedule 2: boiler),
   Marubeni Corporation (Japanese; Schedule 3: substations, etc.)

1991–95   Calaca Power Complex Environmental Upgrading Project
   '*supplementary study*': OECF's special 'emergency' facility with
   consultant Tōden Sekken in close co-operation with NPC and
   consultant NEWJEC
   Financing: OECF (¥6.1 billion, loan No. PH-P130) and NPC
   (altogether approximately $62 million by 1995)
   Implementation: NPC with NEWJEC (about 22 in-house projects)
   and NPC's direct negotiation of 26 smaller but more capital-
   intensive projects (financed by the OECF loan)

1991–95   Social Acceptance Projects
   Financing: NPC/GOP (approximately $1.5 million)
   Implementation: NPC and other GOJ line agencies

In Public Opinion Commonly Closely Associated Projects:

1989–91   CALABARZON Regional Master Plan Study
   Financing: JICA
   Implementation: BOI/DTI with consultant Nippon Koei

1990–92   M/P Rehabilitation of Power Facilities in Luzon Grid
   Financing: JICA
   Implementation: (group of specialists)

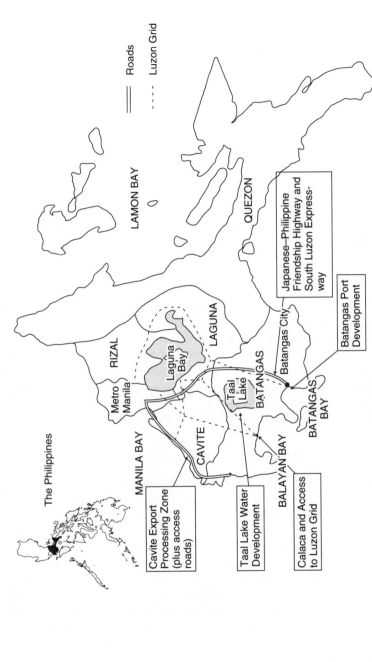

Map 6.1 The location of Calaca in the 'CALABARZON' region

action scheme, with detailed policies how to execute it, and implementation programmes, individual projects, and the realization of intended effects.

This case study initially accepts these three assumptions and analyses them within the framework of the book as the donor factor (ODA or OECF-loan factor). It will examine them – by arranging the material in chronological order and by focusing on the individual circumstances, rationales and perceptions of each actor at each step. The approach highlights the necessity to take other factors into account, especially the country factor and the project factor. Therefore, in an attempt to understand the actual decision-making process, the case study is divided into two parts. The 'Japanese side' is addressed first. Two overviews in the appendices provide a schematic guidance of the case study.

CALACA, A JAPANESE CASE

The widely shared perception of Calaca as a Japanese project, and its implications for the wave of Philippine and Japanese opposition against an NPC project financed by loans from Japan, must be understood within the context of the historical relationship between the two countries which still remains in the memories of both its peoples. The title *The Second Invasion*,[11] which captures the bitter sentiment and ever-present fear, might help to explain the sensitivity with which more technical matters were debated by all sides.

Overview of Philippine–Japanese relations

Japanese presence in the Philippines can be traced back to 1567 when the Spanish conquistadors reported regular trade expeditions from Nagasaki and subsequently established trading posts in Manila, Cagayan and Pangasinan (the Japanese port of Agō). Exporting wheat, salted meat, weapons and various crafts, the Japanese traders brought home Chinese raw silk and Spanish imports, as well as indigenous Philippine wares, such as, gold, deer skins, coral, etc. In 1623 the Japanese colony in Manila had a population of about 3,000. Despite the restrictions on trade during the Tokugawa period (1603–1867), by 1930 the Japanese presence in Manila and Davao had grown to be the largest overseas Japanese settlements apart from those in Brazil.[12]

The still-remembered cruelty and the hardships inflicted by the Japanese on the Filipino people, especially at the end of the military occupation and during the battle over Manila in early 1945, discouraged any Japanese presence in the Philippines prior to the 1960s, at which time investment slowly began again. It was only after the declaration of martial law in 1972 and the Treaty of Amity, Commerce and Navigation with Japan, ratified in 1973, that Japanese investments surged, reaching second position behind the United States by the end of the 1970s. It was mainly the large Japanese business groups represented at this time.

Japan topped the list of foreign equity investors in the Philippines between 1988–93 with $946.389 million, with the United States second with $578.969 million.[13] From 1989 to 1993 Japan was the largest investor, except in 1991 when it was surpassed by an exceptional amount of British investment. Japanese investment rose sharply until 1990 but then declined until 1992. In 1993 investment increased once more to P3,043 million ($112 million), but was only half of the 1990 figure as was overall foreign investment.[14] This decline was due to the power crisis which delayed projects of all foreign investors and frightened away small companies in particular. While overall foreign investments for 1994 were reported up more than fourfold, Japanese investment increased only 10.4 per cent in peso terms from the relatively low 1993 figure. With roughly $190 million in investment, Japan fell to fourth position. Since Japanese investment was now merely of smaller electrical and auto parts companies, the energy situation had a strong overall effect. It should be noted that Japanese ODA is more than five times the amount of investment.

More important than foreign investment may be trade relations. Japan remained the second largest trading partner overall but imports from Japan topped those from the United States from 1992 onwards, with a 30 per cent increase for two consecutive years leaving a trade deficit of $2.2 billion in 1993 (compared to a trade surplus with the United States of $849 million). With $1.8 billion in exports and $4.0 billion in imports, 1993 trade with Japan assumed an export share of 16 per cent, down from 20.3 per cent in 1989 but unchanged from 1986, and a growing import share of 22.9 per cent, up from 17.2 per cent in 1986. These figures can be contrasted with the Philippines' trade with the United States, where exports were up to a 38.4 per cent share and imports down to a 20.9 per cent share. For 1993, imports from Japan show 8.2 per cent light industrial goods and 87.5 per cent heavy industrial and chemical goods. The increased import share of machinery from 44.7 per cent in 1986 to 75.2 per cent in 1993 might reflect the impact of ODA. Exports to Japan are still dominated by agricultural and fishery products, with a share of 33.5 per cent and a raw materials share of 20.1 per cent, although both are declining. The share of manufactured exports to Japan has more than doubled to 41.2 per cent, with machinery (mostly auto parts and electrical equipment) up to 22.7 per cent from almost zero in 1986.[15]

History of Japanese ODA to the Philippines

Japanese ODA to the Philippines began with the reparation payments during the period 1956–76. With $550 million out of a total of $1.01 billion the Philippines received the largest amount, more than twice that of Indonesia.[16] Conceptualized as investment, rather than the provision of services, and including capital goods, more than 60 per cent was expended on infrastructure projects (public works, transportation, education and health facilities) and 15 per cent on industry (a cement mill, a steel mill, electrical machinery, communications equipment, household electrical goods, etc.). In addition, Japanese companies extended $250 million as economic development loans to their Philippine counterparts on commercial terms.

More genuine ODA commenced, as distinct from war reparations, with a $30 million loan for a highway project in 1969, the consequent establishment of loan packages in 1971 and the beginning of grant aid in 1972. Japan became a member of the donor Consultative Group for the Philippines in 1971. By the time the war reparations ended, the two-track system with grants and loans was fully established.

Until the 1980s approximately 50 per cent of all bilateral ODA (if US military-related assistance is discounted) came from Japan. By 1992 disbursements had reached 71.4 per cent of all bilateral and 65.2 per cent of combined bi- and multilateral ODA. From the 1980s until the present day the Philippines has usually ranked third in funding received from Japan. Following the EDSA-revolution in 1986, when commitments more than doubled, the Philippines briefly reached second place after China in terms of overall commitments, and maintained this position with respect to grant aid (after Bangladesh). While the increase in funds for the Aquino administration can be interpreted as a cumulative effect of political support and the appreciation of the yen, recent changes in disbursements appear more related to the GOP's capacity to absorb such amounts productively than to policy changes in Tokyo.[17] The overall majority of funds (about 80 per cent) has consisted of yen loans, and amounted to ¥1,054 billion ($10.3 billion) for 162 projects up until March 1994. Together with 16 rescheduling commitments, this totals ¥1,197 billion (almost $11 billion at 1994 exchange rates). The share of total

Japanese ODA disbursements amounted to 8.8 per cent of total Philippine capital formation in 1992, and has averaged about 6.7 per cent since 1986.[18] In 1991, Japanese ODA amounted to approximately 10 per cent of the national budget. (See Figure 6.1 for a breakdown of Japanese loan commitments by sector.)

Post-Marcos bilateral ODA policy[19] was determined in June 1987 by the High Level Policy Mission under former Foreign Secretary Saburo Okita while the USA initiated the 'mini-Marshall plan', labelled MAI/PAP.[20] It can be noted that 1994 was another turning point with the second High Level Policy Mission in February headed by the special assistant to MOFA, Ambassador Yasue Katori, an IMF agreement, and consequently the Consultative Group meeting in Paris in July.

By the end of 1986, the Government of Japan (GOJ) (through JICA's Institute for International Cooperation) set up a country study committee composed of scholars and professional ODA administrators to revise current ODA policy. Its comprehensive report *Basic Strategy for Development Assistance*, submitted in April 1987, was the first of its kind and formed the conceptual basis for the Okita mission that sought a bilateral understanding of its contents. Follow-

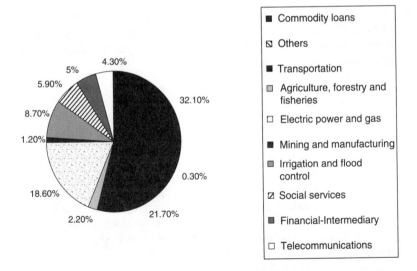

Figure 6.1   OECF loan commitments by sector
Source: OECF *Annual Report 1994*

ing this agreement, Japanese ODA was intended to support the rehabilitation of the Philippines' economic infrastructure and alleviate the balance of payment problems on a short-term basis. On a longer-term basis the core objectives of GOP's medium-term development plan up to 1992 were adopted. But the enhancement of GOP's absorptive capacity for ODA, support for export industries, increase of overall productivity and private sector mobilization remained critical targets.

Around the same time as the US Government began preparations for the MAI/PAP, it began negotiations for the extension beyond 1991 of the lease of its largest overseas military installations. With this initiative the United States attempted to retain its poilitical leadership by asking the other donors, especially Japan, to share the burden for the global security umbrella provided by it. Indeed, the main donors became – or remained – the multilateral institutions and Japan. Since they interpreted their continuing and unchanged programmes as compatible with the initiative and only re-labelled these funds, Philippine administrators complained about the missed chance of additionality, increased effectiveness and efficiency.[21] The diversity of and contradictions between donor programmes remained. Because the USA's initiative failed to meet the expectations it had created, the plan backfired and mobilized a nationalist opposition that ended the continuing US military presence. The MAI/PAP, therefore, marked the beginning of the US retreat from the Philippines altogether in terms of politics, military presence and ODA, and left Japan in an increasingly lonely ODA position.

Present ODA Policy

Today Japan, the World Bank and ADB remain the only macroeconomically significant donors. The Paris meeting of July 1994 not only witnessed the disappearance of the USA as a significant donor (pledge $67 million), but also as a political leader. Out of a total pledge of $2.8 billion for 1994, Japan promised the equivalent of $1.4 billion in loans and $156 million in grants, the ADB $300 million, and the World Bank $500 million in loans. These events have left Japan in a unique but not altogether welcomed position that underlines the significance of the above mentioned Katori mission, as far as the conceptualization of overall ODA and its (macro-)economic impact are concerned.

Current Japanese complaints in the field of Philippine development co-operation range from the absence of a clear separation of responsibilities between agencies, resistance of the bureaucracy and of the domestic industrial elite or the big landowners, to a serious lack of foreign assistance counterpart funds[22] limiting implementation and maintenance.

The agreement reached by the Katori mission and GOP included an endorsement of the new Philippine Medium Term Development Plan 1993–98 (PMTDP) and its basic goals: poverty alleviation, social justice and social equity, sustainable development or growth, generation of productive employment, and human development. The public investment programme for the PMTDP shows a strong focus on infrastructure projects, about 45 per cent of all projects of which the majority are scheduled for foreign assistance. Power generation, and roads and transportation easily account for the largest share. Overall, projects scheduled for foreign assistance are four times greater than the domestic portions measured in monetary terms.

The Katori mission reached an understanding of priority areas: economic infrastructure, support for restructuring of industries and the development of agriculture, poverty alleviation and the improvement of the basic living environment, and environmental conservation. At the opening of the press conference Mr Katori mentioned that 'Japan strongly expects an early agreement between the Government of the Philippines and the International Monetary Fund'. Given IMF's structural adjustment requirements, this statement carries severe policy implications for GOP.[23] An agreement between GOP and IMF was approved by the IMF board in June, just in time to make the Consultative Group pledging session in Paris possible.

A Japanese history of Calaca

Request and appraisal

In early October 1986, barely one month before President Corazon Aquino was to visit Japan for the first time, GOJ received an official request in advance of GOP's request for the fourteenth yen loan package. It consisted of one project, Calaca II. This separate request was not unexpected. It confirmed common ground between Manila and Tokyo with respect to Manila's focus on indigenous energy development to strenghten the balance of payments position and with respect to the abandonment of the nuclear experiment in Bataan. In addition, Prime Minister Yasuhiro Nakasone's pledge of the power plant on 10 November 1986 served as a generous, highly visible and desperately needed symbol of political support for the new government at a time of a complicated bilateral relationship. In fact, it would become the central and lasting symbol of the President's three-day state visit.

The breakdown of negotiations with creditor banks in New York and a strained relationship with the US Senate over a long-promised but not ratified increase of US assistance, together with domestic fears of an imminent military coup, a deadlock in negotiations with the communist New People's Army and fierce resistance against any liberal attitudes of President Aquino from within her own Cabinet made tangible support from Tokyo decisive in stabilizing the young democracy. But it was complicated by a GOP good governance investigation of illegal payments by Japanese trading houses to the former dictator, the continuing support that President Aquino's hard-line Cabinet opponents Laurel and Enrile enjoyed from the Tanaka faction (to which Prime Minister Nakasone belonged), and consequently Tokyo declining President Aquino's request to address the Japanese Diet as she had addressed Congress in Washington with much success.

In spite of these difficult circumstances both sides were able to claim success. President Aquino received a reasonable package of aid that was, as she emphasized by counting the actual amount of money as political support, much larger than that received by her predecessor, and a promise for much more in the future.[24] In turn, President Aquino's attitude towards Japan and Japanese investment changed. It was in Tokyo that she proclaimed a hardened stance against the New People's Army in a tone to convince Japanese leaders[25] and upon her return to the Philippines she dismissed the chief of the investigating committee on good governance who was now an embarrassment given that she was seeking new investments from business leaders in Tokyo.[26] However, a serious blow to the rudimentary process of confidence building, beyond the control of both governments, occurred only three days after President Aquino's return, with the kidnapping in the Philippines of the local general manager of Mitsui. In addition, no one could anticipate that when President Aquino left office in 1992 construction of the promised power plant would still remain a distant event leaving upsetting power shortages in Manila and the Tokyo visit consequently relegated to little more than a political gesture.

How Calaca II, which at that time formed $300 million of the total request of some $1,612.5 million, rose to such prominence requires another explanation beyond a purely political interpretation. The request, mainly for the fourteenth yen loan package,[27] had astonished GOJ by its sheer size[28] on top of requests from other Asian leaders visiting Tokyo in the same autumn. The Japanese Embassy and MOFA immediately rejected expectations that a 2.5-fold increase in assistance could be pledged during the Tokyo visit, on the basis of it being unreasonable due to the lack of time for budgeting and performing other administrative procedures. On the other hand, one single large project, Calaca – being a special request – which only required an appraisal mission and not a GOJ mission, appeared easy to deal with, and it was ready for rapid implementation. As a separate item from the fourteenth yen loan package, GOJ could proceed with it immediately.[29] Unlike the bulk of the package it was not impeded by GOP's struggle to expend the twelfth yen loan funds of 1984 before the disbursement for the thirteenth yen loan package could even begin.[30]

Finally, the Calaca project and, therein, that of unit 2 (Calaca II) was not an entirely new matter for the Japanese administration. This third interpretation relates to the history of the project. It is supported by the unusual swiftness with which the OECF appraisal mission concluded its task the same month as the request. Certainly, the feasibility study, written, in 1979, with the partial contribution of West-Japan Engineering Consultants but mainly by a British consultant, had envisaged a second plant from the beginning, and the construction of unit 1 (Calaca I) already included the basic facilities for both. The construction of a second unit had not been seen as a major event and the target date for the completion of the whole plant had initially been set for 1984, later postponed to 1986. Bearing this in mind the Mitsui-led consortium that had won the contract for unit 1 in 1981 almost immediately began lobbying both in Manila and in Tokyo, for the completion of the whole plant. Since unit 1 had been financed partly by the Japanese Exim Bank and the Bank of Tokyo, additional Japanese funding seemed reasonable.

However, for several reasons the Philippine and the Japanese administrations were reluctant to proceed, resulting in the extension of the plant not materializing in the way it was originally intended. One reason was that the losing bidder, Marubeni, continued to allege that the evaluation of the tender of unit 1 had been highly irregular. Accusations like that, among others, led to major investigations in the Philippines and then in Japan, focusing on ODA and other concessional loans during the Marcos period, and, in the case of Calaca, found direct confirmation of Mitsui's illegal payments to Marcos in the court testimonies (in 1988–89) of Marcos' former Minister of Public Highways.[31] Second, the breakdown of the 'crony' economy and the political instability of the final Marcos years made Japanese lending agencies cautious. Third, technical problems that appeared after unit 1 started operating in September 1984 had made NPC reluctant to push for a second plant with a similar design.

Nevertheless, given the larger political background of 1986 and the strong political will of both governments to complete the project and make Calaca II a symbol of their co-operation, the task of the appraisal mission of October 1986 was merely to update the old feasibility study regarding cost estimate, scope of work, implementation schedule and environmental impact assessment (EIA) which had been prepared for the Department of Environment and Natural Resources (DENR). Therefore, neither the feasibility of the whole plant with regard to its social environment nor the experiences with unit 1 appear to have been taken into consideration. In addition, a factor what would later become crucial: an environmental compliance certificate (ECC) issued by the Environmental Management Bureau (EMB) of DENR, which usually must be completed prior to the official request, was not made a requirement for the appraisal or a 'conditionality' before a binding Japanese commitment (such as an E/N or a L/A) was given. Since EMB maintains that the requirements concerning the ECC were in place at that time, this unexplained but decisive omission should be given some consideration. The appraisal mission only enquired about the EIA, which can be interpreted as an application for an ECC, but the ECC itself and any conditionalities that might be attached to it was simply not an issue.

Some interpretation must be allowed at this point, departing from the listing of confirmed facts, since there are several plausible reasons that could explain this apparent oversight:[32]

1 The predominance of political pressures aimed at producing a visible gesture of support for the state visit which would not allow entanglement with lesser issues that could be dealt with later;
2 The impression that an ECC would be merely a formality once the application (EIA) was filed – a reasonable conclusion since unit 1 had been exempted from an ECC requirement;
3 At that time an administrative manual might have been in place in which an ECC was required only at a later stage;[33] and
4 A period of non-governance in the years after the revolution, as perceived by some in the Japanese administration, during which legal requirements and administrative procedures that had seen

considerable erosion during martial law, had yet to be fully (re-)established.

Further, an observable difference in administrative attitude between Japan and the Philippines helps explain the sequence of events from this initial omission to the resulting crisis a few years later. Philippine administrative guidelines appeared to be understood more adequately as targets. There was little reinforcement, for example only an unclear identification of the enforcing agency and unknown deadlines for meeting the conditionality of the 'conditionally approved' projects in the Investment Coordination Committee process (see page 178). It was assumed that problems would be worked out in an informal consultative manner. As it could have been difficult to discover the exact status of requirements and given time constraints, the appraisal mission must have adopted a more tolerant interpretation of regulations as the only practicable solution at the time. This pragmatic spirit advanced the project but exposed OECF once the project was challenged. OECF had to respond to a different administrative rationality that interpreted guidelines and standards as rigid law, that are either violated or not. When Calaca later became controversial OECF belatedly carried out such an interpretation, and with this enforced reversal it broke open the conflict of the differences in administrative culture between the two countries. But at the time of appraisal, when OECF met an ambiguous situation, it obviously acted pragmatically, honouring the political circumstances in the Philippines and the spirit of the times in which it was operating.

Shortly after the Aquino visit, JICA also became involved. On 27 November 1986 JICA signed an implementing arrangement with NPC to finance a feasibility study, *The Study for Calaca Coal-Fired Thermal Plant (1) Upgrading Project.*[34] The study addressed technical problems that kept the utilization factor down to around 55 per cent in 1985 and the first half of 1986, namely, maintenance procedures, improvement of coal and ash handling, specification of equipment needed, analysis of the quality of the coal that was to be used (run-of-mine, washed, etc.), formulation of optimum blend with other coal, etc. It was carried out by a number of Japanese experts in co-operation with NPC and Unong Pit, the supplier of the coal from Semirara Island and was completed in January 1988.[35]

Although the preliminary feasibility study group which visited the Philippines in November 1986 included technical experts from MITI, it appears that there was little connection between this mission for unit 1 and the earlier OECF appraisal mission of October 1986 for unit 2. For OECF purposes Calaca II was a new project to be financed by ODA and, therefore, not related to the commercially financed project Calaca I, apart from its location. OECF did not have responsibility for Calaca I, nor was it OECF business. In addition, with the present feasibility study (F/S) progressing, it appeared that any technical problems of unit 1 were already addressed and did not require further action. Accordingly, for the E/N between the governments in June 1987 and the L/A between OECF and NPC in September 1987,[36] only the 1979 F/S was taken into consideration. The fact that it was written during a period of martial law when an ECC had not been required, the ensuing social effects resulting from this, the existing environmental situation around the plant and the poor performance of unit 1 all appear to have been given little attention.

Procurement

With the L/A settled, the highly politicized initial period came to a conclusion and OECF returned to business as usual, following standard procedure. Accordingly, in November 1987, the Terms of Reference and the shortlist of consultants (for PH-P76, at that time tied) were finalized. In July 1988 the evaluation of tenders[37] took place, and in July 1989 the contract for the consultant was approved. NEWJEC, a consortium of Japanese, Canadian, and Philippine companies, became the consultant.[38] From the point of view of OECF, except for the somewhat long and probably difficult negotiations between NPC and the prospective consultant, there was nothing exceptional about this period.

Similarly, the international bidding for PH-P76, prepared, announced and evaluated by NPC and NEWJEC, did not bear any surprises for OECF. Pre-qualification was approved in October 1989, NPC announced the tender in November 1989, tender opening followed in March 1990, and tender evaluation continued into the autumn of the same year.[39] The NPC board approved the bid evaluation report in October 1990 (resolution no. 90–427), and, after further inspection by the Congressional Energy Committee Chairman in November 1990, submitted it to OECF in December 1990. Approval from Tokyo came in March 1991. The first schedule (electric generator, $107 million estimated contract price) was won by a consortium of Marubeni and GEC Alsthom; the second schedule (boiler, $195 million) by Combustion Engineering/Mitsubishi Trading with Mitsubishi Heavy Industries; and the third schedule (transmission and substations, $8 million) by Marubeni.

The bid approval process of OECF is not a *de facto* criminal investigation into possible misconduct (which in any case would be the responsibility of sovereign Philippine jurisdiction) but rather a formal review on whether OECF guidelines and the procedure for international bidding have been properly followed.[40] This review mainly serves to protect the interests of OECF, for example, against MOFA, MOF or the Japanese Parliament. Institutional action follows institutional guidelines and in turn is protected by these same guide-lines – and OECF makes no exception in adhering to this practice. In the case of unit 2, this limited need of OECF for self-protection and mounting time pressures guided the decision-making. Having followed a proper, formal, procedure and given a reasonable evaluation outcome, the whole process was not to be halted because of purported irregularities that invariably surface. Except for cases of obvious misconduct, or in the event of a court decision, the cost of stopping the procedure, that is, the endangering of the project, the complications for bilateral relations, and, in a lucky case, the extra cost of a new tender, far outweigh any possible benefit. Although OECF was aware of several accusations against NPC, among them those of Senator Guingona (see the section 'Procurement' on page 182), it approved the bid evaluations for the reasons given: there was no infringement of formal procedure – and beyond that it did not care.[41]

Crisis years: approval of the contracts

In the meantime, reports on the environmental situation in Calaca and protests against the project had reached Japan. Position papers from Philippine NGOs from as early as 1987 were followed by reports from Japanese NGOs,[42] the Japanese media,[43] and finally carried into the crucial budget committee by Senator Akiko Domoto – pressing questions to which even Prime Minister Kaifu himself had to respond.[44] This occurred at the same time that the government was endeavouring to make Japan even more respectable as an ODA superpower by announcing the ODA Charter (in June 1991). Not surprisingly, accusations of promoting ecologically insensitive ODA projects did not suit such a desired image. Indeed, in the city of Calaca the first unit caused the 'worst violations of the environmental standard', in the wording of NPC and it mattered little that this project was *not* financed by Japanese ODA institutions because it was closely associated with it in the media.

For OECF, what had been a merely an unrelated project, suddenly became intensely relevant. In direct response to these developments it sent an intermediate supervisory mission for PH-P76 to collect information and set up a supplementary study mission to which the consultant Toden Sekken was invited. For this supplementary study of the technical and environmental problems of unit 1, OECF used a very limited fund reserved for emergencies, such as an immediate update for an existing F/S, for which other funds are not available or took too long to procure. In some ways this study took the earlier JICA financed F/S of 1988 as a point of departure but went beyond it by concentrating on extensive environmental measures that had not previously been taken into account. Ultimately this study would lead to an environmental upgrading project for the whole plant financed with an OECF loan (L/A in March 1993; No. PH-P 130).

Other events added to the attention Calaca was receiving. After a visit in April 1991 NGO representatives returned to Japan to spread information about the social and environmental conditions in Calaca.[45] Senator Domoto, who had made Calaca a case in the budget committee, turned to the Philippine public in several Manila papers with an open letter to the Japanese government asking it to take full responsibility for preventing any further pollution from the first plant.[46]

The growing opposition against a second plant in Calaca also awakened concerns in the Philippine Board of Investment/Department of Trade and Industry (BOI/DTI). At the same time as the issue of Calaca reached a peak of public awareness the BOI/DTI proceeded with a regional master plan study, financed by JICA and conducted by the consultant Nippon Koei. The M/P for the industrializing hinterlands of Manila (CALABARZON)[47] which include Calaca could be regarded, together with various other Japanese ODA projects, as the Japanese contribution to the Multilateral Assistance Initiative/Philippine Assistance Program (MAI/PAP) promoting foreign investments. At least it was presented in this way and as a concerted effort promoting foreign interests, so it remained in the public mind.[48] In fact, the project CALABARZON is, first of all, a BOI/DTI project administratively unrelated to other OECF projects which were conceptualized long before the M/P, and has little connection to other JICA activities in the region. However, because of this connotative link between Calaca and CALABARZON, BOI/DTI pressed for an immediate solution of the 'noisy' problems at Calaca. The good name of CALABARZON that BOI/DTI had been pursuing was endangered.

As with the Batangas port project, Calaca became a matter of concern at the time the M/P study was being prepared and given these circumstances a senior representative of the consultant Nippon

Koei met with OECF representatives in Manila and in Tokyo, with MOFA officials also present.

It is difficult to assess the impact of these activities outside the parliamentary supervision since 'government decision making cannot be influenced by any private individuals' – an assessment that was shared by the consultant and in OECF. On the other hand, the subsequent action taken by OECF strongly reflects all of these reproaches.

In August 1991 the conflict over the environmental situation reached crisis proportions when OECF decided to stop the procedure and actually sent back the request for approval for the contracts, quoting the missing ECC as the formal reason. Since the requirements for issuing an ECC were subject to negotiations between DENR/EMB and NPC, and the concerns that EMB wanted addressed had expanded into the domain of social acceptability, the conditions set out by OECF also reflected this:

1 NPC should obtain prior public acceptance of the project; and
2 NPC and DENR should reach prior agreement on the strings attached to an ECC.

This problem was expected to be resolved within a reasonable period of time since the supplementary study on the environmental upgrading of the whole plant provided a preliminary conclusion.The programme suggested in the report, *Environmental Improvements for BCFTPP (Calaca) Complex*, prepared by NPC with consultants Toden Sekken and NEWJEC, amounted to an estimated \$38.155 million plus a P47.5 million local portion (\$1.7 million).[49] It was subsequently approved by the National Power Board and the foreign portion was to be included into the eighteenth yen loan package, which GOP requested in September 1991.

This request, a package of 40 prospective projects, also included an additional loan for overrun costs for PH-P76.[50] Bidding prices higher than the appraisal estimation (and subsequently higher than the L/A) are not uncommon in international bidding, but they usually have to be borne by the implementing agency. Taking into consideration the overall circumstances and the reasons for the cost overrun,[51] OECF sent an intermediate supervising mission in October 1991 which subsequently approved the request (but not for inclusion in the eighteenth yen loan package). The mission also addressed the environmental issues in a shared meeting with DENR/EMB and NPC and discussed the NPC study in detail. The mission suggested further improvements (that NPC incorporated into its report) and pressed

DENR for approval. It also insisted on installation of flue gas desulphurization (FGD) equipment, which NPC strongly rejected. This
idea had apparently gained support within OECF because it suggested an easy resolution of the crisis, without realizing the price
tag attached to it. Irrespective of this aspect, the submission of the
final draft of the environmental upgrading report to DENR in November 1991, a critical step seen from the perspective of NPC, and the
issue of an ECC in April 1992 by EMB, can be regarded as a direct
outcome of this meeting.

Given these developments it could have been assumed that for
OECF the problem had been resolved, and it could recommence the
process and return to business as usual. Indeed, the government
mission for the eighteenth yen loan package in December 1991,
and subsequently the appraisal mission in January 1992, adopted
the foreign portion of the environmental upgrading project.

However, two events were to interrupt any such resolution. The
Pinatubo eruption required immediate disaster relief support, and the
Japanese media had once again raised the issue of the Calaca complex. The need for immediate funds for emergency relief commodity
loans led to a break-up of the eighteenth yen loan package. About one
quarter of the average annual amount of some ¥75–100 billion was
pledged in March 1992 (E/N July 1992, L/A September 1992) for this
purpose alone. Of the original eighteenth yen loan package only two
urgent projects that were ready for commencement were pledged in
July (E/N December 1992). One of these projects was the environmental upgrading of the Calaca complex (L/A No. PH-P130 in March
1993). The other projects, including the overrun costs, were delayed
due to problems of absorptive capacity, according to OECF.

The media attention that had once again raised the environmental
issue, presenting it now in the context of Japan's international standing in the forthcoming Rio conference,[52] created further worries. In
April 1992 Senator Domoto again raised the issue in Parliament.[53]
She tried to convince both governments to install desulphurization
plants and to take anti-pollution measures. The UN Conference on
Environment and Development in Rio de Janeiro brought into the
picture the larger context of global warming and exposed Japan's
responsibility as the world's biggest ODA donor – a connection
underlined in a NHK TV special on Calaca in July. Although the
NPC had finally received an ECC in April, and EMB had issued a
revised ECC in July in response to OECF requests, (and, in August, a
statement that a FGD was not necessary), these political circum-

stances made it clear that it would have been most difficult for MOFA and OECF to recommence the process at that time.

However, apart from a separate technical OECF mission that is reported to have visited NPC around September 1992,[54] the issue had reached higher administrative levels. In October 1992 a GOJ mission had visited the site and held discussions on the sulphur oxide (FGD) issue with NPC and GOP. Although it expressed its appreciation of NPC's self-financed in-house environmental upgrading programme, it tried to persuade GOP to install a desulphurization facility. To 'further strengthen its position with the Japanese Diet', and also hoping to speed up the conflict resolution process, the mission requested:

1 Formation of a multipartite monitoring team in which opposing NGOs were to be represented;
2 100 per cent support from Barangay (village) leaders through signature; and
3 DENR's acceptance of NPC's use of blended coal to meet the proposed revised air quality standard of DENR plus DENR's confirmation that Calaca could be operated without an FGD, even if air standards were revised afterwards.

Although the exact composition of the mission could not be ascertained, the requests suggest that it was somewhat balanced between MITI and MOFA. This is because – and contrary to Philippine suspicions (see below) – in contrast to MOFA, MITI had been opposing a FGD installation altogether since it would have had far-reaching consequences for the power plants at home and their future export.

Again, DENR complied with little delay and issued a letter in December 1992 stating that the coal-blending method would be sufficient to meet the environmental standards. But the GOJ mission for the delayed projects of the eighteenth yen loan package and the E/N for the first batch (which included the environmental upgrading portion) that arrived the same month verified the status of previous requests and conveyed additional demands regarding unit 2:

1 GOP should request from GOJ an expert in environmental monitoring for monitoring assistance on a grant basis; and
2 counterpart funds of ODA should be utilized in part for public acceptance programmes.

NPC complied with the first request and conveyed the second to NEDA and the Department of Finance for consideration. NPC noted a shift in the Japanese conditionalities. Since GOJ could not state a basis for its FGD requirement it turned to social issues, similar to those which some observers had noticed in the evolution of EMB's earlier requirements.

The mission also stressed that GOJ's approval of contracts would be expedited once the above requests had all been satisfied. Additional conditionalities for the GOJ's concurrence were:

1 Air monitoring, with results furnished to GOJ, and, if necessary, further consultations on the installation of an FGD and an understanding that in the worst case the GOJ might consider suspension of disbursements;
2 Space within the plant reserved for possible later instalment of an FGD; and
3 Consultation with GOJ if other than the specified coal was used.

Although NPC signalled compliance to the extent necessary to satisfy GOJ, an Exchange of Notes in March 1993 between the Coordination Council for the Philippine Assistance Program and NPC – following a shared regular bi-monthly meeting with line agencies and OECF – indicated that even after the ground-breaking ceremony OECF had again mentioned the suspension of disbursements if NPC failed to install remedial facilities to comply with the air ambient and emission standards (which NPC did in July 1993).

Yet, when OECF sent a mission in January 1993 to review the appraisal reports of the earlier mission for the second batch of the eighteenth yen loan package, the procedure for Calaca II had not yet been recommenced. While the discussions proceeded, GOP signalled to GOJ, in the same month, that it would take all necessary steps to protect the environment at the project site. This was responded to with a go-ahead by GOJ in the following month and with the re-establishment of the process. Therefore, upon receipt of the request for the second approval of the contract in March 1993 (including cost adjustments), OECF approved the contract up to the limits of the existing L/A. Before doing so, however, it requested the renegotiation of the contracts and the compensation agreements between NPC and the contractors (so far $1 million per month of delay) which resulted in a $3 million reduction in compensation costs for NPC. Immediately NPC issued the Notice to Proceed, with the ground-breaking ceremonies taking place only four days later on 29 March 1993.

Two days later, during the Tokyo visit of President Fidel Ramos, L/A No. PH-P130 for the environmental upgrading of the Calaca complex was signed, and GOJ pledged the remaining portion of the eighteenth yen loan. However, the package of ten projects again did not include the overrun costs for unit 2. Therefore, GOP requested it again with the first batch of the ninteenth yen loan package in December 1993, and again in January 1994 with the full ninteenth yen loan request. The request was considered by a fact-finding mission[55] in December 1993, the GOJ mission for the ninteenth yen loan package and the appraisal mission in February 1994. Although the possibility of a special yen loan for the overrun costs was considered in the wrap-up meeting, it was finally included in the pledge for the ninteenth yen loan package at the Paris consultative group meeting in July (the fourth MAI/PAP conference). E/N was signed in November 1994 and L/A in December 1994.

In terms of final implementation of the environmental measures for Calaca there is only space reserved in unit 2 for FGD equipment but the public acceptance programmes and environmental upgrading projects the GOJ and OECF missions had pressed for were mostly implemented or were on schedule by the end of 1994.

Conclusion

The Japanese case of Calaca highlights two crucial factors: that of the project and that of the donor. A power plant is a large-scale project that, in general, cannot be procured locally. It is likely to run into public controversies over ecological and – since it affects so many people – social issues. It invites political involvement – in this case from state visits and parliaments, to the media, down to the local level. As a landmark project it carries prestige from an international business perspective and offers profit opportunities that may make it worthwhile even for large multinational companies to do all that is possible to be awarded the project. In a country like the Philippines it sets the poorest directly against the most powerful, and in such a situation much happens during the process regardless of whether or not it is financed with an ODA loan.

The second factor highlighted is the general influence and the specific effects of the needs and the decision-making processes of the donor. Although OECF routinely deals with large projects and accompanying trouble-shooting activities, Calaca went beyond the normal and, therefore, offers rare insights into OECF's crisis behaviour.

Four stages can be roughly identified in OECF's decision-making. The first stage, during 1986–87 (request and appraisal), can be characterized as drawing and following a 'big picture': the support for President Aquino, the utilization of indigenous resources and the creation of a capital-intensive power project ready for implementation designed to translate political support into a boost for industrial reconstruction and development. Pledged only one month after the request, the loan agreement was signed ten months later. In the second stage (procurement) the project slowed down to 'business as usual', with OECF merely monitoring and approving NPC's decisions. Only after the award of the contracts (third stage) did the project run into a series of crises: the Guingona accusations, the environmental pollution of the commercial unit 1 affecting the ODA-financed unit 2, the missing ECC, and, finally, the Pinatubo eruption that split the eighteenth yen loan package. After addressing all these problems OECF's processing of the project did not return to normal until around the middle of 1993 (disbursement).

Of these stages, OECF's behavior in the first and third intervals appears most interesting and revealing. The initial phase shows that OECF reacted surprisingly quickly in concluding formal procedures in order to accommodate GOJ's wish to have an adequate gift ready for the state visit. The appraisal mission probably never had the chance to turn down the project, even if it had found faults in it, and most likely it participated in the mood of the times and never intended to find faults. By completely ignoring unit 1, OECF failed to realize the social setting in which it was to become involved. In addition, the F/S that JICA was simultaneously negotiating for unit 1 might have provided some comfort to OECF in the assurance that the problems of the other project would be taken care of.

During the crisis OECF's involvement differed sharply depending on the actual event. At all times the overall objective was to expedite an already much-delayed project with, where necessary, an overriding objective of self-protection clearly visible. Although OECF enquired about the accusations regarding the bid evaluation of Schedule 2, it did not interfere. OECF is a lending institution and not an investigative bureau. If there had been a court decision it could have acted. However, when OECF needed the ECC to demonstrate that formal rules and procedures were followed properly, it performed itself or encouraged others to undertake the necessary steps needed to obtain this ECC. This included applying direct pressure, an intelligent integration of the opposition into the implementation process at the cost of NPC and the unwanted adoption of unit 1 in an OECF-financed environmental upgrading study and project.

There is no doubt that these activities were a direct response to Senator Domoto's inquiries. OECF must follow its own and the Development Assistance Council's environmental standards. It emphasizes that environmental measures should be taken according to the regulations of the recipient country and be 'based primarily on the assessment of the potential damages to environment rather than political considerations'.[56] However, the above-mentioned episode shows the sensitivity of OECF and the Japanese administration to public opinion and political action. It was only when the issues had been raised by the opposition that its own environmental protection standards were applied. It also shows that OECF can pursue its own interests, if necessary – in this case to the benefit of the environment and the residents of Calaca, but at the expense of NPC. The FGD issue and consequently the additional emphasis on social acceptability that exceeded the OECF's direct concern, appears to have been pursued through GOJ missions and through more politicized channels (cf. the schematic overview of Appendix 6.1 which illustrates the difference in activities in 1991 and 1992 that followed Domoto's two interventions). In 1992, what NPC considered 'impositions' were no longer conveyed by OECF, and GOP's resentment assumed a more political stance. The issues brought up by the GOJ missions merely conveyed what had been raised in the Diet. Yet Senator Domoto maintains that she is not satisfied with the outcome, since her main objective, the installation of a FGD, was not realized.[57] In contrast to this episode, the rescheduling of the loans caused by the Pinatubo eruption was treated merely as a technical issue, which OECF addressed itself.

To conclude, the OECF's decision-making processes can be characterized as initially narrow in organizational self-consciousness and merely responsive to other developments, and proactive only where two dominant objectives are concerned: the protection of itself (and its funds) and the promotion of rapid implementation. OECF is a government organization that has to follow legal rules. Its role is not to set new environmental standards but to make sure that existing legal standards are met. Therefore, the ECC was only a document to prove the legality of action taken. Closely related to the first objective is the second objective, that of speed. The faster a project is implemented the better, as long as the standards are met and all issues are considered. Speed means progress, success, and protection for OECF – and development for the recipient country. In this respect the ECC served as a means to reduce complexity in a multi-dimensional social conflict. The early attraction of the FGD lay in the hope for an easy solution.

However, the rational application of these objectives requires power. And as the case clearly shows, OECF and GOJ wield surprisingly little of it. Only in the selection of a Japanese consultant and in pressing for necessary measures to require an ECC did the Japanese side prevail. Which consultant and which consulting services, which design, which required procedures, which environmental upgrading measures, which social acceptability, which participants in the monitoring group, which standards, and so on, were all beyond the Japanese realm. Rather, it appears that the Japanese administrators accepted the Philippine decisions or positions, and reinforced their application. The FGD intervention was not successful and little connection can be found between JICA-financed studies and OECF projects. GOP's change of preference to BOT[58] in power generation appears to be a change against all conditional loans that are burdened with little predictable social and environmental concerns.[59]

Yet there is the presence of well-prepared and well-informed Japanese trading houses, which possess experience in dealing with the Japanese administration once things do not go smoothly. The teaming up of big manufacturers, which usually do well alone, with Japanese general contractors, indicates a more general Japanese influence. But unlike direct and visible intervention, this kind of influence is by its very nature hard to pinpoint. It might be observable in a merely deferential and defensive attitude towards the Japanese that can be found among other bidders or in the recipient administration. Having a Japanese partner in a consortium or as a consultant obviously meant for many, playing safe. Japanese consultants have been said to be key influence peddlars, but in our case little supports such suspicions. Although the background of the initially tense relationship between NPC and the consultant is not entirely clear, the ability of the consultant to serve Japanese business interests appears to be more restricted than commonly thought.[60] Torn between conflicting loyalties with the customer being NPC, the consultant runs a high risk by taking its own initiative or by interfering for any third purpose (e.g. planting specifications in the bidding documents, that nobody but affiliated companies can meet). Even mediating in a conflict or trying to speed up the process might run counter to the consultant's own interests and in the Calaca case it appears that the consultant, eager to keep a low profile, did not go beyond facilitating smooth relations/communication. Therefore, in terms of visible interaction it was Japanese NGOs, the Japanese media and one woman in the Japanese Senate who certainly had more impact than the Japanese bidders with whom NPC is accustomed to dealing.

Certainly, Japanese assistance that leaves the responsibility entirely with the recipient administration supports the existing power, administrative and interest structure, including its shortcomings. However, it must be recognized that a more politically conditional and donor-administrated ODA, like typical US assistance, limits sovereignty to a much larger degree than has been reported in this case. The Japanese approach of self-help not only raises controversies between donors but ultimately plays the ball into the court of the Philippine administration, the public and democratic participation in its decisions.

CALACA, A PHILIPPINE CASE

Prior to commencing an examination of the Philippine story of the project Calaca, the two dominant perspectives involved should be introduced.

Energy planning and policy

Brown outs of two hours first occurred in 1989, but with the commission of two smaller gas turbines (combined output of 210 MW), the electrical power demand was met in 1990. In late 1991, however, sporadic brown outs recurred, and became endemic in the Luzon grid in 1992 (averaging four hours) and 1993 (8–12 hours), especially during the summer with its combination of a limited water supply for hydro power plants and a high demand for air-conditioning. A JICA-financed M/P on the rehabilitation of the Luzon grid blames 'faults due to deterioration of facilities and degraded performances of power generation, transmission, and substation due to insufficient repair and maintenance, aggravated by natural disasters' and states that installed capacity appeared sufficient for present demand only if it operated at full capacity.[61] However, NPC and GOP, assuming a sharply increasing energy demand in the near future concentrated on the extension of present capacity.

The 1993–98 Medium Term Philippine Development Plan placed heavy emphasis on power generation with a 4,596 MW capacity extension and the interconnection of the island grids of Luzon, Visayas and Mindanao. In addition, a rural electrification of 12,945 *barangays* (village communities) is intended to bring the rate of household electrification up from the present 48 per cent to 73.5 per cent in 1998. Although the Medium Term Philippine Development Plan does not mention financial resources like ODA for government projects, a preliminary Public Investment List 1994–98 schedules 66 of 91 power generating projects (P28 billion out of P32 billion, approximately $1.2 billion) for foreign assistance.

For the Luzon–Visayas grid the Power Development Programme 1995 has scheduled 6,559 MW additional capacity by the year 2000. About half of the scheduled plants up to 1999 are BOT or BOO (allowed with Executive Order No. 215, of 10 July 1987), revealing a new and heavy emphasis that Japanese ODA is reluctant to support but in which Japanese companies participate.[62] The latest available estimates, assuming NEDA's GDP growth rates, predict annual energy sales growth rates in Luzon of 9.4 per cent 1993–98, and 10 per cent 1993–2005. Sales in 1992 of 18,880 GWH are expected to grow to 32,420 GWH by 1998 and 65,360 GWH by 2005. For Luzon this translates into an average yearly increase of necessary installed capacity of 487 MW for 1993–98.[63]

Using earlier but similar estimates and attempting to fill the void of the mothballed nuclear power plant, NPC established the following priorities for implementation: short construction period; use of the country's indigenous resources; low cost per installed capacity; and sufficient plant capacity. The choice of Calaca II as the most feasible option was based on the following criteria: it was economical since basic facilities for a second unit were already installed; the site investigation and development were completed; the resettlement of a bordering village (Barangay San Rafael) was almost completed; and the close proximity to the coal mine.

Public participation through the EIA

Today, every project that requires a loan/investment of more than P300 million or $5 million is subject to the Investment Coordination Committee process (ICC, of which NEDA is the secretariat). This means that the implementing agency identifies a project and a possible financial source (in this case, OECF) and suggests the project to the NEDA secretariat where it is evaluated, co-ordinated with other projects (inclusion in development plans), and prepared for an ICC board meeting. ICC has both a technical level with under-secretaries and staff from the agencies concerned for issues, such as feasibility and co-ordination, and a cabinet level where political and budget implications are discussed. Endorsement of a project is subject to approval from:

1 DENR/EMB (which issues the Environmental Compliance Certificate – ECC);

2 NEDA-Regional Development Council (RDC);
3 Department of Finance.

To speed up the process projects are usually endorsed conditional upon later receipt of these approvals. After ICC approval the project is channelled through the Department of Foreign Affairs, via the Japanese embassy, to GOJ with a copy sent directly to OECF and to the NEDA Board, which is chaired by the President of the Philippines. Thereafter, the regular OECF process is adopted, with NEDA sometimes co-ordinating or mediating between the line agencies, hosting meetings with Japanese missions, as well as additional responsibilities. Japanese project pre-selection and appraisal missions deal directly with the line agencies and the staff involved. GOJ missions usually meet at the under-secretary level with the concerned agencies, discussing general issues with, in particular, NEDA and the Ministry of Finance. The Coordination Council for the Philippine Assistance Program, originally created to co-ordinate and accommodate all donors (especially USAID), has today assumed a monitoring function at the implementation stage.

Public participation in this process is assured through the ICC mechanism, that is, through the endorsement of EMB and RDC – and as a precondition for the latter, that of the Local Government Unit (LGU). The Calaca case shows that this does not always occur. Public participation was totally absent during martial law and then it was assumed to be guaranteed through the NEDA/RDC system. Together with the Mount Apo geothermal project in Mindanao, the Calaca experience is considered crucial in recent developments which extended the meaning of environment into social environment, and in so doing making social participation subject to an EIS. Presidential Decree 1151 of 1977 made a statement on environmental impact a requirement of almost every private and public activity. Decree 1586, which became operational in 1982, specified this earlier requirement, made an EIA a part of a project application, and required an ECC before an operation could start. Executive Order 192 of June 1987 identified EMB as the enforcing agency to which an EIA was to be submitted by the implementing agency and which would subsequently issue an ECC. In June 1992 the whole environmental impact statement system (EIS) was revised and amended in DENR Administrative Order 21, which also addressed socio-economic issues in an holistic approach.[64] The expansion from a more technical environmental assessment to an enlarged social and livelihood acceptability assessment as an inherent part of EIS has been a painful process[65] that was more or less enforced through a strong representation of a political culture dominated by the mushrooming of NGOs in the Philippines of the late 1980s. It is no secret that these NGOs were strongly represented in DENR, and that the then under-secretary Delfin J. Ganapin was regarded as an NGO activist himself.[66] Still, it is unlikely that EMB could reach this influence today if it did not also find strong indirect administrative support from OECF, for quite different reasons, as mentioned previously.

With a processing time of 56 months for an ECC, Calaca tops the complaints list of NPC. However, since then the time required has fallen often to less than one month. Certainly the power crisis and the need for speedy processing had some impact, but EMB considers that implementing agencies like NPC now anticipate public participation and the wishes of LGU. The engineers at NPC, pressed with power shortages, and in their daily work with technical requirements, rigid economic calculations and negotiations, were challenged by a new grass-roots culture inside the administration:

> Our health, our well-being, and our future are at stake. Many of us depend for our livelihood on clean unpolluted rivers, lakes and seas. If the air and soil are polluted, our health will suffer. We all want to survive, but more than that, we want a better life for ourselves, our families and our friends . . . . All of us have a stake in the future and in preserving a healthy environment. The issues facing us and our fragile planet are many and complex. No one has all the answers. Each one has something to share, to contribute, to answer the questions [regarding the project] that are posed . . . . Participation means dialogue. In a dialogue, we listen to one another and listen attentively so that we hear what each one has to say. We listen so that we may understand each other's concerns.[67]

While an OECF mission once asked EMB what kind of attitude NPC had in regard to the local people, there was no question that today this attitude has changed.

A Philippine history of Calaca

Pre-history and project identification

The history of a coal-fired thermal power station in Batangas dates back to the oil crises in the 1970s and GOP's resolve to develop nuclear and indigenous energy resources. The mothballing of the nuclear power plant in Bataan with its installed capacity of 620 MW blocked the first alternative. It concentrated the combined pressure of foreign debts, the lack of feasible alternative energy resources, and the mounting power crisis, on the second alternative: the half-developed utilization of coal from Semirara Island.

Calaca was the first project, and the coastal location between the coal mines and Manila reflected the overall concept developed in the 1979 F/S that NPC commissioned from the consultants WESTJEC and EDCOP.[68] As recommended in the F/S, NPC implemented the first unit and the common facilities for a second plant, awarding the contract to Mitsui & Co. as main contractor, with Foster Wheeler Energy Corporation (boiler) and Toshiba Corp. (turbine-generator and balance of plant) in accordance with the results of international bidding and procured on a full turnkey basis. Despite severe right-of-way issues and the need to forcefully resettle Barangay San Rafael residents, the first plant was commissioned in November 1984. From the point of view of NPC the problems during construction of unit 1 were resolved, but that meant havoc and disarray for the local residents. The displacement of an entire community enforced under martial law left bitter feelings, which only deepened when the operation of the plant resulted in serious pollution.

The poor performance of the plant led NPC not only into conflict with the residents but also with the contractors, who blamed the lower than specified quality of the Semirara coal and later insufficient maintenance. NPC, in turn, accused them of a non-performing technology and pressed for an upgrading of the first plant before the construction of a second unit could be considered. Since the consortium was lobbying for the immediate completion of the second unit, NPC used this continuing interest to strengthen its negotiating position for the upgrading measures to be adopted along with the blending of higher quality Australian coal in order to approximate the design coal specifications. The resulting $8 million arrangement allowed a satisfactory operation for NPC, that is, an operation at the rated capacity with an increased portion of the lower quality local coal. However, a side-effect of the coal blending was the overstocking of local coal. Forced to acquire a certain amount annually through a lift or pay provision in the coal supply contract with the mine, NPC annually bought up to 360,000 tons of local coal more than it needed. Overstocking and other coal handling problems resulted, especially in 1989 and 1990, in spontaneous combustion in the coal stacks. Unchecked burning of this kind resulted in serious ash, particle and smoke pollution combined with a foul smell. Moreover, the irregular operation caused enormous noise problems from the steam circle during shut down and start up, as well as heat and chemical water pollution, according to the complaints of the local fishermen.

These problems directly affected the local residents, whose living environment, crop and fishing grounds were seriously damaged. The complaints included fly ash over the houses from the freely combusting coal stacks, the foul odour coming from the plant and respiratory diseases affecting countless people. This heavy burden only added to their sad experience with the authoritarian way in which the site was chosen and the plant implemented. The residents of Calaca and the surrounding fishing villages did not want to bear the burden of an energy demand in the distant capital region, and they certainly did not look forward to more of the same. From the perspective of NPC this resulted in strong complaints from local residents and, with the support of regional NGOs, led to an all-out campaign against operation of the first and against the construction of a second plant. Certainly, the expansion plan crystallized an opposition movement that would directly associate the recent dictatorial experiences of the Marcos regime with a NPC subservient to the same elite, with the Japanese and Philippine business interests involved, and with a second Japanese 'invasion' that would not treat people very differently to the first.

Meanwhile, GOP, in need of energy replacements, had negotiated the loan from GOJ/OECF to fund the foreign exchange cost of the second plant. The L/A of September 1987 stipulated that the major part of the loan was untied and that NPC would be the implementing agency. However, for major decisions like the selection of contractors and the award of contracts the agreement of OECF was obligatory. NPC proceeded on the basis of this loan agreement up until the signing of the contracts in June 1991, which OECF would not approve.

Along the path to this dramatic turning point three distinct episodes should be mentioned: the selection of the consultants, the preparation and evaluation of the bid, and the slowly mounting conflict between EMB and NPC.

Procurement

The pressing desire not to repeat the experience of unit 1 can be recognized as NPC's dominant objective from the selection of the consultant onwards.

The new NPC team for unit 2 had no experience with coal of such comparatively low quality, which has only been used elsewhere, in

Germany and Canada. They therefore originally planned to hire a consultant from one of these countries to assure sufficient experience with the necessary technology for the preparation of specifications. However, although OECF agreed to untie the major portion of the loan, the leading consultant had to be Japanese.[69]

Obviously somewhat frustrated by this requirement, NPC began conducting its own research around 1987, including visits to Canada and Germany. It drafted a detailed design (which is usually not required for a compact project like a power plant) that would become the basis for its negotiations with the consultant and afterwards for the tender documents themselves.

The long period that NPC needed to reach a contract with NEW-JEC can be explained by difficult negotiations with the consultants. Due apparently to economic efficiency concerns, the consultant opted for a coal-blending approach employing standard technology while NPC insisted on the national policy of using 100 per cent indigenous resources. Although the quality and price of local coal is unfavourable, import substitution is in line with the macro-economic requirements enforced by foreign debt service. NPC's concept prevailed.[70] Despite OECF's significant influence in the selection of the consultant, NPC project management imposed its requirements regarding the design and made sure that there was no misunderstanding about who wielded the decision-making power. While the initial period could be characterized as one of difficult co-operation, in the end representatives of NPC found the arrangement the best deal they could get, relying greatly upon the work and support of the consultant. (When the crisis with GOJ arose after 1991 NPC was certainly pleased to have a Japanese consultant mediating and sending out for opinions in the various ministries in Tokyo on behalf of NPC's project management.)

NPC then proceeded with the preparation of the tender, requiring the consultant to use the NPC design as blueprint for the tender documents. Sixteen companies applied for the pre-qualification of bidders for the main plant during summer 1989. Eight were accepted for the first schedule (out of eight applicants), eight for the second (out of eleven), and all six applicants for the third.[71] The criteria applied were the experience of the manufacturer, the availability of equipment, and the civil work sub-contractors, which had to be local companies. For the preparation of tender documents NPC management set up an organizational structure that placed drafting teams of NPC and the consultant in a parallel structure of a 'chapter by chapter task force', that is, vertically along the schedules and horizontally along civil works, the electrical system, steam circle, etc. In this way the work of the teams could be cross-checked from both sides, the consultant could be effectively controlled and technology transfer be assured. The consultant spent almost 50 man-months just drafting the tender documents. The resulting documents extended to seven volumes (with 600 pages in Volume 4 for the boiler alone).

Following the invitation for bids[72] NPC held at least one pre-bid conference from 15–18 January informing the bidders of all important details. After the submission of bids and the public opening of the offers at 11 a.m. on 22 March 1990, the evaluation period began. The evaluation flow chart of NPC runs through seven separate stages, with the first exclusion criteria applied during the opening. A formality and responsiveness check followed resulting in the first evaluated price and time considerations. The three most favourable bids were then evaluated in detail, resulting in the final evaluated bid price. Here deviations from the specifications and time schedules are fined. After considering potentially cheaper alternatives once the evaluated price is calculated, the bid with the lowest and most advantageous evaluated price is translated into an estimated contract price, and included in the recommendations of the evaluation report to be submitted to various committees in NPC. For this evaluation procedure the project management sets up another organizational structure including staff from the Thermal Power Engineering Department, from unit 2 and experienced staff from unit 1, which parallelled the organization of the consultant who spent, altogether, 87 man-months until the conclusion of the evaluation and another 36 man-months for the consequent negotiations with the contractors. The organizational charts show that for the evaluation no one was placed at the same task as they had been for the drafting stage. This was to assure the tight control of the consultant, the training of different NPC staff at different tasks working side by side with the specialists of the consultant, and also can be seen as a cautious self-protection of the project management against any accusations of irregularities.

However, the outcome of the evaluation was challenged immediately. After several NPC committees the National Power Board finally recommended a winning bid and the chairman of the Parliamentary Energy Committee convened all responsible officials for a hearing in November 1990. In January 1991 the then Senate Pro-Tempore President Guingona who had called for banning the 'Japanese bribers' like Mitsui from GOP projects only two years before, accused NPC of irregularities in the evaluation of Schedule

2 in which the US–Japanese consortium of Combustion Engineering and Mitsubishi Corporation (CE/MC) was favoured. Calling it illegal and immoral, he indirectly but clearly assumed a continuation of the earlier illegal payments, such as those Mitsui paid to Marcos. A few days later he substantiated his accusations with exhibits.[73] However, what was intended as the launch of a Senate investigation failed when Senator Guingona suddenly lost interest and did not follow up his accusations. This brief appearance by him was interpreted by some in the Philippine administration as first the losing and then the winning bidder having approached him, and thus 'enlightened' he fell silent.

Indeed, there had been complaints from the losing bidder in Schedule 2, expressed to various involved committees and individuals inside and outside NPC during a time when information on the evaluation was still restricted.[74] Two weeks after Senetor Guingona's intervention the Presidential Complaints and Action Office received complaints of a similar nature. The evaluation was judged anomalous and highly irregular, in violation of Philippine and international bidding regulations, OECF guidelines and in disregard of NPC bid requirements and technical specifications. The detailed accusations included the preliminary acceptance of a prototype pulverizer, of longer completion time, of a less effective electrostatic precipitator incapable of operating with all specified coals and of a lean phase in ash and dust handling. The winning bidder was also allowed to improve its bid regarding the pulverizer and the ash handling to meet the specifications, while the electrostatic precipitator was accepted as offered.[75] Certainly, the other bidders would have also appreciated such a second chance.[76]

Some background information may help in understanding the general situation. The consortium with Mitsui as general contractor, that had built unit 1 and whose lobbying for unit 2 was used by NPC initially to assure its co-operation for the upgrading of unit 1, disbanded following the option of a repeat order being rejected. Instead, the former consortium partners participated in the tender for the second plant in different groupings for each of the three schedules – and lost.[77] (See Table 6.2.) This time the consortium with Marubeni as the general contractor won, but only in Schedules 1 and 3. In Schedule 2 CE/MC won on a narrow margin against the consortium of Marubeni/Babock & Wilcox (B&W, Canada) on the basis of the final evaluated price despite cost advantages if Marubeni had won all three schedules. It was B&W, ostensibly the Canadian Embassy, that launched the complaints, naturally only questioning the evaluation procedure in Schedule 2.[78]

Table 6.2 Overview of as-read, evaluated and first contract prices

Rank	Company	Bid opening price (as read, $ million)	Bid evaluated price ($)	Contract price (as of June 1991, forex plus local)
Schedule 1: Electric Generator				
1+2	GEC-Alsthom/Marubeni Corporation (France/Japan)	A (300MW): 109 B (350MW): 111	114,788,400.00 –	$109,934,165.00 plus P208,961,790.00 (approx. $7.6 million)
3	Chiyoda/ABB-Mannheim (Japan/Germany)	115	126,824,870.00	
4	Toshiba (Japan)	118	123,922,400.00	
5	Ansaldo GIE (Italy)	152		
6	Kanematsu/Fuji (Japan)	157		
Schedule 2: Boiler				
1	Mitsubishi Corporation/ Combustion Engineering (Japan/USA)	195	209,448,400.00	$183,832,110.00 plus P555,507,850.00 (approx. $20.2 million)
2	Babock & Wilcox/Marubeni (Canada/Japan)	204	216,391,980.00	
3	Foster Wheeler/Ishikawa Heavy Industries (USA/Japan)	211	222,284,560.00	
4	Mitsui/Stein (Japan/France)	216		
5	Sumitomo/EVT (Japan/Germany)	230		
Schedule 3: Transmissions and Substations				
1	Marubeni (Japan)	9	9,137,790.00	$8,505,182.00 plus P24,025,530.00 (approx. $0.9 million)
2	Mitsui (Japan)	11	11,819,030.00	
3	Kanematsu (Japan)	16	16,430,470.00	
4	Chiyoda (Japan)	17		

However, even the then Auditor-in-Charge of NPC adopted the criticism in a report of early January 1991: 'it is indubitably clear that the bid of CE/MC was non-complying and should have been rejected outright. Such being the case, it is, therefore, strongly recommended that should the Agency insist in finally entering into such contract and allow its implementation, all payments in connection therewith should be disallowed in audit.'

While judgement on this matter is neither an objective of this study nor should it be expected from the author, considerable time has been spent to get a grasp of the subject and its circumstances, on discussing the issue with 'insiders', and on the study of related documents. At first sight and when focusing solely on the bid of CE/MC most of the accusations appear sound. But a few doubts should be raised to question this impression. One should be reminded that a tender is not an absolute measurement but rather a relative estimate and that all arguments have to be considered in comparison to other offers, based on information prior to the evaluation, and on relative estimates of the possible performance of offered technology in the future. Therefore, complaints from an ex-post perspective that disregard other offers should be treated cautiously. For various reasons relating to the specially researched design necessary for the extraordinary low quality of the coal, all bidders had to make adjustments in their standard technology so that it could be judged either as an improvement or a prototype. Therefore, if all bids had been evaluated under the most strict interpretations of the tender documents, all bids would have had to be rejected as non-complying. Compared to the 199 deviations of B&W, the 150 of CE/MC appear favourable. Certainly NPC, by forcing the lowest bidder into specified requirements upon award at no extra cost, attained an even more favourable deal by pushing a normal procedure for minor adjustments to the limits. Further, as stated above (see note 41), OECF also made sure in its approval for the award of the contract that the electrostatic precipitator would meet the specifications.

The Presidential Action Team, created on 1 April 1991 in response to the above-mentioned complaints, began its investigation into the case three days later. After receiving the NPC reply to the allegations, in which OECF approval is mentioned to support its case, the team concluded its investigation. There was no further investigation or official objection which appears to be a proper decision.

Late Philippine appraisal

In the meantime environmental issues and the dispute between the Environmental Monitoring Bureau (EMB) of DENR and NPC had taken centre stage. NPC had applied for an ECC in October 1987 with an EIA (or EIS),[79] one year after the official request to GOJ and even after the L/A with OECF. The fact that the ICC meetings in April 1987 came six months after the official request might be explained by the haste in which the project was requested prior to the state visit and also by the fact that the new administrative procedure was not yet established.[80] The late submission of an EIS also suggests that at that time it was neither a major concern nor did an ECC seem difficult to obtain. An EIS/ECC was not even discussed at the ICC meetings. Instead, economic issues played a principal role, such as cost differences between Semirara and imported coal, the production cost of electricity and the expected return in comparison with the cost of the loan. The only relevant statement found among the actions taken asserts that 'environmental measures will have to be instituted to safeguard the welfare of inhabitants in the affected areas'. There is no mention of an ECC requirement and, therefore, the approval can be seen as not conditional upon it. Each of these events indicates a fairly significant deviation from Philippine and OECF formal procedures.

Up to 1989 there was a continuous exchange of letters between EMB and NPC, as EMB requested additional information on design specifications of unit 2. Only after EMB became aware of strong local complaints did it involve itself actively, treating the ECC application for unit 2 as an integral part of an overall change of policy regarding the site and therefore making it subject to prior improvements in unit 1. In May 1989 it conducted the first visual inspection[81] and SO_2 sampling at the plant, followed by an EMB–NPC meeting in January 1990. After another stack and ambient flue gas sampling in September 1990 revealed that not much had changed, EMB issued a Cease and Desist Order effective for January 1991. However, considering the power shortages and the rising oil price due to the Gulf Crisis, and encouraged by an NPC presentation, the President's Office intervened and the EMB order to stop the operation of unit 1 was lifted subject to a resampling. There had been no violation of the ambient air quality standard[82] due to the dispersion provided by the 120 m stack.

This episode, however, only led to an expanded involvement by EMB. A Review Committee meeting was followed by a second extensive investigation of the site in February–March 1991, with highly unsatisfactory results.[83] Consequently, in April 1991 EMB scheduled a public hearing in Calaca for the EIS. Of the many documents submitted, a letter from the attorneys representing the town of Calaca (dated two days before the meeting) best indicated the depth of the local resentment. It complained about the unbearably foul odour of the sulphuric wastes, the pollution of drinking water, the fly-ashes covering the houses, the spread of respiratory diseases and the reduced productivity of farm lands. It concluded: 'Likewise, please register the names of all members of the Municipal Council of Calaca as oppositors [sic] of the said project and they have all expressed their willingness to participate at the hearing on April 18, 1991 at 10.00 am.' The demands expressed at the meeting were that: the pollution should be addressed, NPC should pay taxes and extend assistance to the municipality, and the extension plans for a second unit should be scrapped. The results of this hearing were: EMB/DENR would issue an ECC contingent on a multipartite monitoring programme and the local acceptance of Calaca II [sic],[84] and NPC would initiate environmental control measures.[85]

One day after NPC submitted the application for approval of the contracts to OECF in July 1991, it met LGUs of Calaca and NGOs. The two meetings, arranged by the Presidential Management Staff, marked the beginning of NPC's all-out campaign to endear itself to the people of Calaca. Another meeting between the EMB Review Committee and the opposition, presided over by DENR Assistant Secretary Ganapin, followed one week later. It should be noted that these decisive meetings occurred one month before OECF's formal refusal to approve the contracts, and more than one year before the GOJ mission in October 1992 that ensured NPC's compliance with the outcome of these meetings even after the ECC had been issued.

The demands presented at these meetings were: property taxes, anti-pollution devices, the electrification of fourteen *barangays*, the placement of lighted posts along a seashore for the fishermen, a social hall, a small clinic, donations of scrap poles/drums, and domestic water for upland *barangays*. While the LGUs appeared to be seeking a gesture of respect and co-operation, the NGOs pressed for reparations to people and for a restoration of the environment (both of which NPC rejected). As a result of these meetings at least four memoranda of agreement (MOA) were issued during the following year:

1 An MOA between DENR, LGU, NEDA and NPC defined their respective commitments 'towards the promotion of national and

local development with concomitant concern on the protection of the environment and upliftment of social and economic conditions of the people'. It defined the composition and task of a multi-partite monitoring group[86] 'for the effective implementation of Calaca II and the efficient operation of the Calaca I, and subsequently Calaca II' up to 1995. It included in an appendix a list of ten agreed compensatory development projects worth more than P40 million (approximately $1.5 million, at $1:P27), and the above-mentioned environmental improvement programme that was to be partly financed by an OECF loan (altogether approximately $62 million). The former mayor of Calaca Casanova never signed the MOA, but when a supplemental agreement was added on 14 September 1992 to meet the new mayor Katigbak's request for additional assistance, it was ratified by him.

2 A MOA between NPC and *barangay* leaders for assistance from NPC worth P3 million (approximately $111,000) in small infrastructure projects in return for their endorsement of a second unit; the last leader signed in January 1993.
3 A MOA between NPC and National Electrification Agency for electrification of twelve Calaca *barangays*; signed on 14 July 1992.
4 A MOA between LGU, the Department of Public Works and Highways and NPC on the installation of potable water in an upland *barangay* (signed 28 May 1992).

On the suggestion of OECF, and with the assistance of NEWJEC, NPC began working on a long-term environmental improvement programme around the end of July 1991. It encompassed and expanded the in-house efforts of NPC that had been implemented to meet the DENR standards. A draft copy of the enlarged programme was sent to OECF via the consultant for comment, evaluation and further recommendation. This was then discussed with the OECF mission of October 1991. The resulting more comprehensive and capital intensive programme consisted of about 26 items or smaller projects that were all directly negotiated or purchased, with the foreign portion financed by OECF.

EMB remained involved. In August 1991 it conducted a consultative meeting with the DENR Review Committee presided over by Assistant Secretary Ganapin and participated in the first multipartite monitoring, together with LGU, NGOs, NPC and DENR-Region 4, between August 1991 and October 1991. The results and the requirements for an ECC, derived from this monitoring, were then discussed in an consultative meeting with NPC and the OECF mission at the end of October. In November 1991 NPC submitted the final draft of the environmental upgrading report to DENR, which opened the way for an ECC. However, in an interview in February 1992, Mr Ganapin still rejected the granting of an ECC so long as the municipal council would not endorse the project. He also lamented that the draft agreement still did not include compensation for Barangay San Rafael residents who had been forced to leave due to the pollution as well as the taxes that NPC should pay to the whole city of Calaca. Accordingly, local NGOs were asked to continuously monitor the existing plant.[87]

On 24 April 1992 DENR/EMB issued an ECC for the construction of unit 2. However, the conditions in it drew concerns from OECF and GOJ since the contracts for Calaca II could be approved only if NPC and DENR agreed upon their fulfilment. Regardless of this development DENR proceeded to issue the 'Authority to Construct' on 15 July 1992. Six days later DENR's EIA Review Committee met with NPC which submitted a ground water monitoring plan and a risk assessment study in partial fulfilment of the ECC conditions. A revised ECC was then issued three days later with reasonable and attainable conditions for NPC.[88]

Despite this development, OECF continued to resist the approval of contracts because of what NPC perceived as the opposition of Japanese to Calaca II and due to GOJ's effort to persuade GOP to request the installation of a flue gas desulphurization plant from NPC. Since an FGD is not required under Philippine standards, NPC was able to mobilize various GOP agencies including DENR, against what it considered to be unjustified foreign imposition. Some exchanges, in fact, show that the tone of DENR changed towards support of NPC after receiving the assurance that the desulphurization facility could not be financed by a Japanese grant. Reports appeared in the press indicating various investigations on whether a BOT scheme for Calaca II would be feasible – all indicating deliberate attempts to escape Japanese pressure.

NPC argued that Calaca II was designed to meet the ambient air quality standards for SOx that is required under Philippine law equivalent to the standard that applies in Japan to a smaller city like Kamakura; that a FGD was neither required for an ECC or by any OECF agreement; and that no other more-prosperous neighbours in Asia had ever been requested to install an FGD. In August DENR clearly stated that a FGD was not necessary for Calaca II. And finally on 18 August 1992 NPC approached the President himself protesting at GOJ's demand for an FGD[89] and also sent a letter to the Embassy of Japan requesting OECF's approval of the contracts.

Subsequently DENR turned to support NPC. In December 1992 it approved the coal blending. On 18 March 1993 it revised the Air Quality Standards of 1992 and the Air Quality Standards of 1978.[90] In December 1993 it re-defined the term 'existing source'[91] and in May 1994 it specified that power plants would be completely exempt from source-specific standards so that only ambient standards applied.[92] The power plants in Calaca never did have problems in meeting ambient standards.

Developments like this are difficult to interpret but it appears that the impositions of a foreign government led to unification of quite strong adversaries, once the social issues had been addressed. During the interviews, the tone of the Philippine agencies towards each other was remarkably different from what it must have been only two years before. It should also be noted that the institutional setting of loan assistance led to a break-up of what could have been a political alliance against global pollution, such as that between DENR and Senator Domoto.

The formalities were now settled while the social issues were not. NPC had commenced local programmes, but in early 1992 the city of Calaca still doubted the seriousness of NPC's intentions. Two developments reinforced the need for urgent NPC action. One was that now, once the contracts were signed, every day of delay became enormously costly.[93] The second was that GOJ, since it could not set a basis for directly requiring the installation of FGD, had turned to other environmental measures and to the issue of social acceptability, as presented by the crucial GOJ mission in October 1992. Regarding these local activities only a few highlights follow.

Following the local elections in September 1992 NPC again assured additional support for the development programme. This was endorsed by the new and even more critical mayor of Calaca and formalized in a supplementary agreement to the above-mentioned MOA (No.: 1 of 91/7) signed by the mayor, the provencial governor of Batangas and the congressman of the district which covers the town of Calaca. In the same month the city council of Calaca issued a resolution of approval for Calaca II and the project passed the review of Regional Development Council Region IV (RDC IV). Formal RDC IV endorsement was then subsequently given.[94] With these developments NPC assumed final and complete fulfilment of all conditions set out by OECF in August 1991, but still OECF's approval of the contracts remained pending.

Finally, in January 1993 all forty *barangay* leaders of Calaca City signed the MOA of approval for the construction of Calaca II. In February 1993 NPC and the mayor of Calaca City reached an agreement on the scheme of assistance to the municipality. Yet not all problems were settled. In March the mayor of Calaca requested the release of funds from NPC, agreed in February, and in an NPC-Coordination Council of Philippine Assistance Program exchange in July 1993 it is reported that the pledged resettlement of 19 families ('7 bonafide, 12 squatters') was still pending, threatening OECF action. The funds for the resettlement had been turned over to the LGU Calaca but problems with the acquisition of the intended land caused the delay.

Neglect of early local complaints proved costly. Besides the social acceptance measures, NPC estimates put the overall delay in project implementation for unit 2 at 41 months,[95] inflicting costs/losses of P4.6 billion (approximately $170 million) in quantifiable terms alone (Table 6.3 illustrates the difference in contract prices between 1991–93). On the other hand, the environmental upgrading measures brought the plant up to international comparative standards[96] and together with a more participatory concept, the power plant appears to be accepted locally. The multi-partite monitoring group, scheduled for a first official meeting in January 1993, presented its most recently available report (prepared in December 1993) to NEDA Secretary Habito on 24 March 1994. The findings showed significant improvements and general compliance with the (ambient) standards. The source of Cadmium pollution in one of the two rivers adjoining the plant could not at that time be determined, as oil/grease levels in the bay were traced to other industrial enterprises.

Commissioning tests for Calaca II were scheduled to start in July 1995.

Conclusion

Examining the project from the Philippine side reveals that – in contradiction to a common view about Japanese ODA – Calaca II was very much a Philippine project. The conflict, background and actual events that took place, suggest the importance of the country factor. On the NPC's side, preconditions for the conflict can be traced to the rule of martial law. The subsequent and collective rejection of the project by the local people was in response to NPC's criteria used for: the selection of the site and the feasibility estimate, its technocratic approach to development and an initial implementation schedule that

Table 6.3 Calaca II contract price difference, 1991 and 1993

Schedule	Contractor	June 1991 contract price		March 1993 revised contract price	
		Forex $	Local P	Forex $	Local P
1	GEC-Alsthom/Marubeni Corp.	109,934,165	208,961,790	134,156,329	216,223,405
2	Mitsubishi Corp./Combustion Eng.	183,832,110	555,507,850	219,189,553	571,991,772
3	Marubeni Corp.	8,505,182	24,025,530	9,544,677	24,657,750
	Total	302,271,457	788,495,170	362,890,559	812,872,927
	Grand total (exchange rate at contract date)	327,554,629.33		394,803,950.00	

ignored the people who were expected to bear the burden but whose empowerment and effective opposition were not anticipated. On the other side, following the revolution against martial law, a political self-affirmation emerged that encouraged local residents to express their fears and frustrations. It characterized a whole generation of Philippine NGOs for which Calaca became the fomentation issue.

There is a desperate need to provide electricity as a precondition for industrial development, but there is also the fight against an elite concept of modern capitalist development that excludes the poorest among the population. When these orientations clashed in this one energy project they revealed that there was little preparedness for the basic idea of participatory co-operation. Still, the way in which NPC adopted this concept of participatory co-operation once it was challenged from outside and inside the administration is remarkable, as is the willingness of the community to endorse the disliked power station for a reasonable return by way of compensation. Both sides recalled the crisis as a time 'where we had to learn the hard way' and where 'we finally had to get our acts together'.

However, several qualifications regarding the country factor should be addressed:

- The above-mentioned deviations from formal procedures (EIS even after the L/A, or the ICC meetings only after the official request to GOJ and without consideration of an ECC), and altogether the Philippine appraisal occurring, in effect, after the procurement, can be blamed for the later delays and crises. However, it is clear that circumstances often do not allow formal rules to be applied, limiting their validity as a rational rule and as a measurement of operational efficiency.

- It is doubtful to what extent the opposition and the strong stand of DENR/EMB would have prevailed, if there had not been strong outside support intensified by the sensitivity of OECF to its public image and institutional environment. This conclusion does not diminish the importance of the preconditions for such public participation, that is, the Philippine democracy and democratic spirit.

- EMB, to a large extent, represented and facilitated the articulation of the local residents and the regional people's organizations. However, the energy crisis placed DENR on the defensive, and it was accused of inflicting project implementation delays that caused more damage than it prevented. Although the EIS system is presented as a tool for promoting sound long-term investments, the exemption of power plants from the source standards in fact abolishes control of absolute pollution levels. With the recent change in preference to BOT/BOO, ODA financing might be the only counterweight to this development, since international (OECF or DAC) environmental standards can then be applied.

- The implementation of Calaca II began at a time when the survival of the government itself was not always assured and when administrative procedures experienced considerable changes. In this respect the project became a historical part of this process from no governance to an institutionalized appreciation of established rules and administrative procedures. It is evident that the outside pressure facilitated through OECF supported this institution building since it honoured and required formal rules in a strict and very costly sense. As mentioned above, it may be contemplated to what extent EMB would have succeeded without OECF, given the economic cost of the inflicted delays and the IMF-inspired import restrictions reinforcing the use of low quality local coal.

Some elements would be better related to a general state of development than to the history of the individual recipient country. Most of them add up to an agonizing delay and a frustrating waste of human effort. The whole energy situation was originally caused by: a mixture of external shocks and internal prestige projects; the insufficient and late analysis of the real quality of the coal; a loose administrative culture with many loopholes; and the extremely bad living conditions of the local people who were threatened by such a mega-project should also be remembered. When considering reports that the members of the extended family of one *barangay* leader caused long delays over small bargains, it should also be borne in mind that a complicated and difficult local setting existed under which a participatory process had to be established. It seems a tautological conclusion, yet if there were no such problems there might be no need to extend ODA loans.

Regarding benefits that accrue to Japanese companies operating in the Philippines, it is acknowledged that Japanese and especially small Japanese investors do indeed benefit from the supply of sufficient and affordable electrical power – but so does everybody else. NPC's treatment of the consultant, as well as contractors, cannot be described as a 'gravy train' or any other similar label. Even the trading houses were unable to expedite the process.[97] GOP received financing for an environmental upgrading study and programme for unit 1, as well as the overrun costs for unit 2, both exceptional gains. In addition, GOP successfully resisted FGD, which is regrettable from an ecological point of view, but is justified given the fiscal situation of the government. GOP played the ball back into the Japanese field by requesting grant aid that the current system was not able to deliver. The tragedy of the loan concept in this case can be measured by the delay it caused and the resulting costs inflicted on the recipient. Not only the loss in overall Philippine development but also the diminished attraction of such financial tools underlines this point: where BOT is available, even a conditional loan will not be requested if such stringent conditions are attached and if it must be drawn in a rapidly appreciating currency.

GENERAL CONCLUSION

An examination of the machinations of Japan Inc. in the aid business began with the search for a unifying master plan, enforcement power, and a rational story – all considered key assumptions of the donor factor in this case. What were the findings? Different institutional and individual actors; different objectives, rationalities and concerns guiding their action; and different levels of power and influence make some of those involved more successful than others in the pursuit of their interests. A study of the decision-making manuals of OECF, NPC, NEDA and DENR readily indicates how project implementation can become complicated. An examination of the chronology of events in the appendices, reveals many unusual yet relatively unexplored details, such as the fact that there was a NEDA endorsement for the environmental upgrading project one year after the official request to GOJ or the fact that GOP had to request the overrun costs three times – all contrary to the logic of procedures. These findings suggest the relativity of the aforementioned assumptions.

Possibly the best guide to the donor and country factors might be a listing of the participants. The main actors were the Japanese and Philippine Governments and their administrations (especially OECF, the Embassy of Japan/MOFA, the Japanese Exim Bank, JICA, NEDA, EMB/DENR, NPC), Japanese and Philippine senators, the media, NGOs and people's organizations, the local residents and LGU of Calaca, the general contractors and sub-contractors, bidders and consultants. Not mentioned are lesser actors, such as IMF, whose import restrictions made the use of local resources mandatory (that is, the worst coal for the highest economic and ecological price), or the Philippine New People's Army that once requested revolutionary taxes for the Calaca complex and threatened its construction, or the participants of the Rio Conference who presented an agenda where a Japanese ODA project in Calaca created a poor image of Japan, or the demonstrators in front of the OECF office in Makati. Neither was the focus on the essential role some individuals played, such as, Senator Domoto and Under-Secretary Ganapin; on occasions the Japanese Prime Minister or Philippine President him/herself, a representative in OECF, two or three project managers in NPC, the two mayors of Calaca, and two or three Japanese activists.[98]

Although an overall and strong Japanese influence cannot be denied, it would be naive to assume that one organization such as OECF can control the whole process, with or without guidelines, or with or without administrative manuals. That this case study could be conducted with support from all sides indicates that the system is much more open than its image suggests. However, it must be admitted that Calaca was an extraordinary case, not only for the institutions but also for the individuals involved. This might have encouraged such co-operation. While OECF sided with the opposition in this case, it might not in another.

Several discoveries were made in this extraordinary endeavour of Japanese loan assistance which demonstrate how the factors affecting the actual procedure are interwoven:

• Much was determined by the fact that the project was financed with a concessional loan: the whole procedure and standards of international competitive bidding, the attractiveness for contractors because of limited risks, and the pain the delays inflicted on the recipients. On the other hand, being concessional, the process invited public awareness, political interference (at little cost for the donor) and was subject to the standards of the international donor community.

• It was not a Philippine agency, but rather OECF, acting in its own defence, that reacted to the public outcry on the situation in Calaca and stopped the process because of a missing licence.

• In so doing, OECF enforced formal administrative behaviour, which probably has had a lasting impact on the Philippine administration by forcing it to appreciate its own rules and guidelines. In this respect the Calaca project reinforced the main objective of the Aquino administration, which was the establishment of a formal democracy.

● Formal democracy does not necessarily mean direct participation of the public concerned in administrative decision-making. That OECF involvement was supportive of direct public participation appears to be the result of GOJ's sensitive reaction to political pressure applied by the media, NGOs, and one senator. It turned its powerlessness regarding the FGD into an effort to strengthen public participation through EMB and LGU.

● In respect to the latter two points it can be concluded that this infrastructure project turned into an institution building process, an institutionalized appreciation by the implementing agencies of the need to follow Philippine government regulations in order to anticipate social and environmental concerns.

● The costs of this lesson were inflicted upon NPC, and in the end have to be borne by the Philippine public.

This occurred not as a part of Japanese post-colonial rule, but as part of a Philippine endeavour, in which the issues, the points of contention, the means of resolution and finally the solutions themselves were 'provided'. OECF was only one of several major players, albeit a significant one, whose actions could make an impact. However, in the end OECF merely enforced the conditions set up by EMB and supported the integration of the opposition in a remarkable manner. The apparent encircling of NPC by Japanese administrations, organizations, media, NGOs, consultants, and companies, etc. is only one way to view circumstances. One major unifying issue amalgamated almost all the actors in the end, and also helped OECF Manila to stay in the middle of the events by mediating between adversaries: all wanted electricity and, therefore, a power plant; all – from the contractors to the local opposition – wanted it to be a good project that would not repeat the experience of unit 1; and almost all wanted it as soon as possible. It just took a little time.

NOTES

1 This chapter is based on almost 40 interviews with all relevant Philippine and Japanese agencies and many individuals involved in the project. Most of the information was received on a confidential basis and the sources cannot be disclosed. Accordingly, only academic and genuine political references are presented. The author would like to thank Professor Yoshiyuki Hagiwara of Dokkyo University as well as the researchers and staff of the Institute for Developing Economics in Tokyo and in

Manila for their essential support. The critical comments of Mr Yoshio Wada guided the progress of the study.

2   The decision was a key element of Mrs Aquino's electoral platform in 1985/86. The project was haunted by many irregularities and safety questions that seemed to outweigh the imminent need for electrical energy supply. Consequently the country suffered a $2 billion debt burden that hindered possible costly energy replacements. See Roberto Verzola, *et al.*, 'The Philippine nuclear power plant: plunder on a large scale', in Amado Mendoza, Jr. (ed.), *Debts of Dishonor, Volume 1: Philippine Rural Reconstruction Movement*, Quezon City, 1991. For a generally accessible update see *Far Eastern Economic Review*, 3 June 1993 and 24 June 1993.

3   The public uprising in 1986 that brought President Aquino to power is usually named after the road where it all happened, the Epifanio de los Santos Avenue (EDSA).

4   According to the author's search at IBON (Data Bank and Research Center) data bank, Manila, 27/28 October 1994.

5   *Far Eastern Economic Review*, 28 July 1994.

6   Preliminary Board of Investment/Department of Industry (GOP) figures for 1994 were reported by the *Nikkan Kōgyō Shimbun* 14 February 1995. Accordingly, foreign investment rose 4.3 times to $1.47 billion, with the US in first place ($710 million for electrical products, energy), in front of Hong Kong ($304 million for a Hopewell Holdings power plant), Taiwan ($283 million, cement) and Malaysia ($169 million, tourism). Japan, with $190 million investments mostly in special export zones, reached only fourth position. The energy situation is still cited as the main reason for the minor 10 per cent increase in Japanese investment against an already low 1993 figure.

7   JETRO, interview 30 September 1994, Tokyo.

8   Renato Constantino *et al.*, *A Philippine Vision of Development: Proposals for Survival, Renewal and Transformation*, Foundation for Nationalist Studies, Quezon City, 1992, p. 45–7.

9   Kore de ii no ka Karabaaruzon-Kyanpeen Iinkai/Firipin Santama Shirō Sentā, *Kokonatsu wa kare, sakana wa kie, soshite . . . Firipin Karaka Sekitan Karyoku Hatsudensho – Kōgai Chōsahōkokusho*, Santama/Tokyo, 1992, p. 1.

10 Cf. Margee Ensign, *Doing Good or Doing Well? Japan's Foreign Aid Program*, Columbia University Press, New York, 1992, or, more cautious, Robert Orr, *The Emergence of Japan's Foreign Aid Power*, Columbia University Press, New York, 1990.

11 Renato Constantino, *The Second Invasion: Japan in the Philippines*, Karrel, Quezon City, 1989.

12 Edberto Villegas, *Japanese Economic Presence in Southeast Asia*, IBON Philippines, Manila,1993, p. 57–60.

13 BOI/DTI figures, Central Bank figures show the same trend but on a lower base.

14 JETRO Manila, *Firipin kyōwakoku shuyōkeizaitōkei*, Manila, 1994, p. 22.

15 Including author's calculations, cf. JETRO Manila op. cit., pp. 8–13; National Statistical Coordination Board, *Philippine Statistical Yearbook*,

Manila, 1993; JETRO, White Paper on International Trade, Tokyo, various years.

16 Takushi Ohno, *War Reparations and Peace Settlement. Philippines–Japan Relations 1945–1956*, Solidaridad Publishing House, Manila, 1986; Akira Takahashi, 'From reparations to Katagarawi: Japan's ODA to the Philippines', in Bruce M. Koppel, and Robert M. Orr (eds), *Japan's Foreign Aid, Power and Policy in a New Era*, Westview Press, Boulder, CO, 1993.

17 Annual commitments from 1987 to 1993 averaged close to $1.1 billion in grants and loans; if not for the absorptive capacity and for the delay of the IMF agreement in 1993 the figure would have been markedly higher.

18 Author's calculations based on National Statistical Coordination Bureau, *Philippine Statistical Yearbook*, Manila, 1993, tables 3–6/7, 7–3, and OECD *Geographical Distribution of Financial Flows to Developing Countries, Disbursements*, OECD, Paris, 1986–94; the figure is only a rough approximation because both currencies had to be converted into current US dollars.

19 Material and information provided by Akira Takahashi (Executive Director of the Institute of Developing Economics and chairman of both country study committees, see below), the Institute of International Co-operation, JICA, MOFA, the Japanese and the US embassies in Manila, NEDA (Deputy Director-General Dante B. Canlas, Public Investment Staff, Public Monitoring Staff), the Coordination Council for the Philippine Assistance Plan (Deputy Executive Director Orlando M. Cablayan), Asian Development Bank (Philippine Desk), and the World Bank Manila.

20 The MAI/PAP (Multilateral Assistance Initiative/Philippine Assistance Program) was suggested in 1987 by four US Senators and Representatives as a 'mini Marshall plan' for the Philippines, it was endorsed in 1989 by 16 donor nations and international institutions under the chairmanship of the World Bank. At a time when the US Government was negotiating the extension of the lease of its military facilities, the plan suggested a significant increase in foreign assistance and private investment of other donors, who were expected to share the burden in exchange for the global security umbrella the USA provided.

21 Carolina Guina, *Perspectives of Donor Behaviour Under the Multilateral Aid Initiative: A Philippine View*, German Development Institute, Berlin, 1991.

22 Perceivably the main bottleneck of the absorptive capacity, which in turn triggered the donors' unified pressure for increased government revenue, especially an improvement in tax collections. It is estimated that some 80 per cent of the budget of the Department of Public Works and Highways is allocated to counterpart funding, leaving maintenance and non-ODA projects pending.

23 There had been no MAI/PAP pledging session in 1993 because of the missing agreement. With this precondition all ODA is directly linked to debt management regardless of the social implications of IMF's 'structural adjustment cure'.

24 The ¥40.4 billion for Calaca II came with a package of ¥100 billion

(\$625 million), which included money that had already been pledged to Marcos but had not been disbursed.

25 *International Herald Tribune (IHT)*, 13 November 1986, *Asahi Shimbun (Asahi)*, 14 November 1986, *Washington Post*, 14 November 1986.

26 *Financial Times*, 14 November 1986.

27 The request included a \$500 million World Bank co-financing loan from the Japanese Exim Bank and about \$812 million for the fourteenth ODA yen loan package (including \$300 million for commodity loans).

28 *Nihon Keizai Shimbun (Nikkei)*, 19 and 23 October 1986, *IHT*, 7 November 1986.

29 Unlike the regular yearly loan packages where the appraisal follows the GOJ mission and the appraised projects are listed and pledged within the available budget (with some shifted to the next year), the appraisal for a special request usually results directly in a pledge.

30 *Business Day* 28 October and 4 November 1986.

31 'The Balthazar, A. Aquino papers', in M. Tsuda and M. Yokoyama (eds), *Japan, Inc. in Asia: A Documentation on its Operations through the Philippine Polity*, Akashi Shoten, Tokyo, 1992, pp. 325–571.

32 These are guesses that were discussed during the interviews but could not be verified in the strictest sense. Nobody could be found who could recall the administrative procedures at that time, but everybody assumed that there had been no change.

33 Although an ECC is not directly mentioned, one could draw this conclusion because of a later involvement of the Investment Coordination Council (ICC, see below) at that time. EIA regulations have not changed in principle but EMB was identified as the implementing agency only in June 1987, with executive order 192; for discussion of the old decision-making process see Romeo Reyes, *Official Development Assistance to the Philippines: A Study of Administrative Capacity and Performance*, National Economic and Development Authority, Manila, 1985, Appendix II–10 A (Flowchart for the Implementation of the OECF Project Loan).

34 JICA, *Firipin Kyōwakoku – Karaka Sekitan Karyoku Hatsudensho 1 gōki Kaizen Keikaku – Jizenchōsa Hōkokusho*, Tokyo, 1986, p. 8.

35 JICA, *Firipin Kyōwakoku – Karaka Sekitan Karyoku Hatsudensho 1 gōki Kaizen Keikakuchōsa – Saishuu Hōkokusho*, Tokyo, 1988.

36 OECF loan No. PH-P76: 4 per cent interest, 10 years' grace period, 30 years maturity, ceiling ¥40.4 billion (only about \$280 million at that time), for main plant, transmission and substations, and consultancy services.

37 For consulting services the 'two envelope system' of OECF guidelines applies whereby bidders are evaluated solely on the basis of qualifications and content of services and not price. They send in two sealed envelopes. First, all envelopes containing the service offer are opened. Only when a consultant is chosen is the envelope with the price offer opened and the price negotiated. Unsuccessful bidders have their second envelopes returned unopened.

38 NEWJEC (of Osaka), Hokuden Kogyo (Hokkaido), Monenco (today Monenco-Agra, Canada), and Internafil (Philippines).

39 *Nikkei* records the informal announcement of the award on 12 October 1990 (the NPC Board of Directors formal approval only came on 19

October) and mentions expectations that the contracts would be signed in January 1991.

40 This procedure appears to be enough to bring about what representatives of the business community perceived as generally 'cleaner' projects than others commercially financed. Otherwise the level of 'commissions' is said to be more country-specific and less project-specific.

41 The only condition stated in the letter of approval is that the NPC should ensure during the contract negotiations that a particle removal efficiency of the electric precipitator is not less than 99.5 per cent when firing any of the specified coals.

42 *AMPO Japan Asia Quarterly Review*, 1991/1.

43 *Nikkei*, 3 March 1991; *Mainichi Shimbun (Mainichi)*, 3 April 1991; *Asahi*, 3 April 1991.

44 Budget committe protocol from 28 March 1991, *(Dai 120kai Kokkai/ Sangiin Yosan linkai Kaigiroku Dai 20 gō)*, pp. 19–20; before entering politics in 1989 Senator Akiko Domoto had been a news director of TBS Television with a long history of reporting and writing on children's welfare, education, women's issues, welfare of disabled persons, development and environment. She is chairperson of GLOBE Japan (Global Legislators Organized for a Balanced Environment).

45 *Asahi*, 3 April 1991; *Mainichi*, 3 April 1991; Kore de ii no ka Karabaaruzon-Kyanpeen linkai/Firipin Santama Shiryō Sentaa, op. cit.

46 *Philippine News and Features*, 24 August 1991, p. 5; *Business World (BW)*, 24 August 1991, p. 6.

47 Republic of the Philippines/Department of Trade and Industry and Japan International Co-operation Agency, *The Master Plan Study of the Project CALABARZON*, Final Report, 1991.

48 Regardless of the actual contents of the M/P study emphasising a balanced agrarian development for the region. The original BOI/DTI concept of CALABARZON was indeed primarily promoting foreign investments while checking uncontrolled industrialization on the outskirts of Manila in mere terms of basic infrastructure, while the Japanese consultant favoured an agrarian and local development scheme. The actual M/P presents a compromise between both strategies.

49 1991 estimate according to the approval of the National Power Board.

50 Because of prolonged delays the amount changed; according to material provided by MOFA the pledge in July 1994 amounted to ¥5.5 billion, roughly $55 million at that time.

51 Change of the scope of the project (land for the originally intended route of the power line to Manila could not be acquired); a reduction of the construction period from 35 months to 31 months (considering the power crisis); the delay in implementation, already running at some two years at the time of the tender.

52 *Yomiuri*, 21 February 1992; *Mainichi*, 20 January 1992; *Asahi*, 9 February 1992.

53 Foreign Affairs Committee of the Upper House, 21 February 1992. The protocol of these enquiries reached OECF Manila the next day by fax. It appears that the questions raised by Senetor Domoto were then directly translated into conditions/requests to GOP which would explain their much more specific content from now on.

54 It is not entirely clear what the original task of this mission was since it is not documented in the OECF files on Calaca but only by the Philippine side.
55 The fact-finding mission gathers information in order to pre-select the 10–15 best prepared projects out of a GOP list of 30–40 projects, since a GOJ mission cannot deal with such large number of projects.
56 OECF comment to this case study, April 1995.
57 Comment to the author, 4 January 1995.
58 Build–Operate–Transfer, along with a mix of Build–Operate–Own, Build–Transfer–Operate, Rehabilitate–Operate–Lease, Rehabilitate–Operate–Maintain, Operate–Lease, see Republic of the Philippines, *Medium Term Philippine Development Plan, 1993–1998*, Manila, 1994, pp. 4-16–4-20.
59 The response from OECF: 'In regard to environment issues in the Philippines, the government might need to give due attention to the projects under private initiatives such as BOT/BOO as well.' (OECF comment to this case study, April 1995)
60 The practice of planting specifications in the tender documents is well known.
61 The Republic of the Philippines (and JICA), *Master Plan Study on Rehabilitation/Renovation and Operation/Maintenance Improvement of Power Facilities in Luzon Grid*, Final Report (Summary), 1992, p. 1–1.
62 Interviews with the Japanese administration and a Japanese trading house involved, a NPC brochure, *Historical Development of the Private Sector's Participation in Power Generation, and the Medium Term Philippine Development Plan, 1993–1998*, 1993.
63 National Power Corporation/Planning Services, Office of the President, *Power Development Program (1993–2005)*, (Revision 3.0) April 1993, cf. for the exploration of alternative energy sources: Republic of the Philippines, Department of Trade and Industry and JICA, *The Master Plan Study of the Project CALABARZON*, (Final Report), 1991, Appendix G: Energy.
64 Cf. Environmental Management Bureau/Department of Environment and Natural Resources, *Amending the Revised Rules and Regulations Implementing P.D. 1586 (Environmental Impact Statement System)*, DENR Administrative Order No. 21, Series of 1992; ibid., *A Primer on Environmental Impact Assessment in the Philippines*.
65 The definition of and responsibility for 'social acceptability' was the starting point of the complicated inter-agency struggle. The original confrontation between EMB ('majority of people must accept') and NPC ('RDC endorsement is enough') forced NEDA (acting also, as the formal window for the OECF) and the LGU to take positions. It appears that only presidential intervention ended the confrontation, with EMB prevailing. However, GOJ's final requirement of a 100 per cent approval of *barangay* (village) leaders in the municipality should exceed even EMB's demands.
66 Backed by the ambitious DENR secretary Fulgencio S. Factoran who is said to have welcomed the conflict and the upgrading of the EMB merely for his own personal advancement.
67 Sylvia Guerrero *et al.*, *Public Participation in EIA: A Manual on Com-

munication, Manila, 1993, pp. 11–12, (Published as part of an Asian Development Bank-financed technical assistance project, *Improving the Implementation of Environmental Impact Assessment*, in co-operation with EMB/DENR).

68 Japanese and Philippine. The other criteria used were topography, elevation, foundation conditions, economic costs; there were no social or cultural factors considered.

69 The minutes of discussion of the cabinet level ICC meeting in April 1987 reveal that GOP explored alternatives to OECF financing because of this question. NPC was also asked to present a list of Philippine and other consultants from Less Developed Countries to the OECF. The untying of consultancy services for OECF loans became standard only after 1991.

One estimate during the interviews among the consultants was that NPC could do the job well on its own but that having a Japanese consultant meant a comfort factor to OECF, being assured of the adequate quality of the work and smooth relations between the involved parties. In turn NPC's project management was described as using the consultants intensively, to learn from them, presumably its major objective and a smouldering bone of contention between NPC and the consultant.

70 During the negotiations even an alternative to international bidding was considered and brought up in the House of Representatives. This would have sought to speed up the process by some 18 months by a repeat order of unit 2 with the consortium that had built unit 1. The attempt failed since it violated Philippine law and the L/A with OECF. See *Manila Bulletin*, 9 February 1989, *BW*, 1 May 1989.

71 Approved by OECF in October 1989.

72 Documents are sent out to pre-qualified companies.

73 Cf. 'Teofisto T. Guingona, Jr Papers (Set A, D, E)', in *Tsuda and Yokoyama* (1992), op. cit., pp. 574–682; Mr Guingona afterwards became Executive Secretary in the Ramos administration, one of the highest positions in the Philippine government.

74 After the bid evaluation report of the NPC's Project Contracts Committee, dated 27 September 1990, similar letters reached the Board of Directors of NPC, the NPC President, the former Executive Secretary, the Executive Director of Energy Affairs, the Commission on Audit, and the Senate Blue Ribbon Committee. The leak of information before the award of the contract contradicts Section 5.04 of the OECF Guidelines for Procurement.

75 NPC board meetings 19 October 1990 and 6 November 1990.

76 An opinion still held by a representative of the contractors.

77 Place 4 for Toshiba in Schedule 1, place 3 for Foster Wheeler/IHI and place 4 for Mitsui/Stein (France) in Schedule 2, and place 2 for Mitsui in Schedule 3; cf. Table 6.2.

78 A quite common attempt, as managers of multinational corporations involved in the project confirmed in a discussion of the case.

79 A detailed description of project, estimated impact, and countermeasures; for the current procedure see DENR Administrative Order No. 21, Series of 1992 (of 18 July 1992), op. cit.

80 Only in June 1987 did Executive Order 192 identify EMB as the implementing agency of the EIS system.
81 There was an overflow of the ash pond, for which NPC blames a right of way problem hindering the completion of a dam.
82 While the source-specific standard measures the absolute pollution released, the ambient standard is only a relative measure of pollution concentration in the surrounding environment.
83 The validity of the sampling method was challenged by NPC.
84 Such an ECC requirement of social acceptability had never been raised by DENR in earlier negotiations NPC confirms. Since DENR would not issue an ECC without public acceptance and OECF would not act upon the approval of the contracts without an ECC, social acceptance programmes would subsequently became a decisive aspect for NPC.
85 'In-house' measures, 19 in all, included the full compartmentalization of the ash pond, water spraying at the coal unloaders, and the re-negotiation of the contract with the coal mine.
86 Consisting of representatives of DENR/EMB, LGU, NPC, NEDA/RDC. The MOA makes DENR responsible for encouraging the participation of those NGOs which are designated by the municipality.
87 *Philippine News and Features*, 1 February 1992, 'Still no go for Calaca II, town council agreement sought'.
88 The changes appear to be related to equipment rendred unnecessary by end of the overstocking of coal and improved technology in both units. It appears no less stringent.
89 NPC argues in this letter: 'Please know that the additional deSOx facility, with the Japanese as sole manufacturer and supplier, is estimated to cost $65 Million, enough to fund another 50 MW power plant. Moreover, the deSOx facility was not made a specific requirement by the OECF Japan, the main financier of the project. Its inclusion was proposed instead by Japanese trade officials and NGOs.'
90 DENR Administrative Order No. 14, Series of 1993.
91 DENR Administrative Order No. 14-A (Subject: Amendment to Administrative Order No. 14, Series of 1993 and Clarifying its Coverage and Scope).
92 DENR Memorandum Circular No. 29, Series of 1994 (Subject: Applicable Air Quality Standards to All Existing Geothermal and Thermal Electric Power Generating Projects).
93 Because contracts for unit 2 signed in June 1991 had gone beyond their validity period, NPC had to re-negotiate them in June 1992 resulting in additional costs of $1 million per month of delay.
94 RDC Resolution IV 2–92 of 15 October 1992 became possible because of the endorsement of Calaca II by the Calaca Sanguniang Bayan (city council) Resolution No 92–93 the month earlier.
95 As of December 1992; a detailed listing of delays shows however, that of this amount 9.25 months can be traced to the selection of the consultant and 12.25 months to the bidding process up to the signing of the contracts (the original target date was August 1989). Therefore, the total delay inflicted by DENR, the local residents and GOJ amounts to some 21 months until approval of the contracts in March 1993.

96 Author's personal judgement based on the interviews in the DENR and among the consultants at the construction site. That is except NOx (nitrogen oxide) and SO_2 (sulphur dioxide), against which measures are estimated to cost 20–50 per cent of the whole plant. Accordingly, without FGD equipment such a plant would not be operated in Central Europe or in Tokyo anymore, but its pollution level would be much better than its image.

97 The Combustion Engineering management once inquired of Mitsubishi about the cause of the delay and if they could help. Since Mitsubishi did not know much about it, they both came to OECF's Manila office and together with the OECF representative aproached NEDA. But they simply could not help.

98 The author's impression from interviews with NPC was that the Japanese government missions had told NPC – or had given the impression – that there were countless NGOs in Japan which rally round this environmental problem, suggesting that there was no other solution than giving in to public pressure. In reality there were only a few people active in Japan.

208 *Ben Warkentin*

APPENDIX 6.1

Map of events

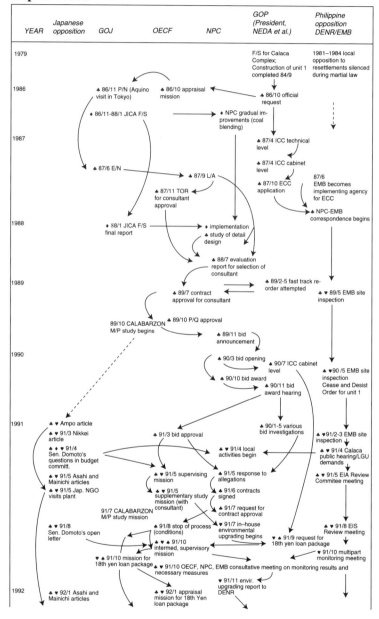

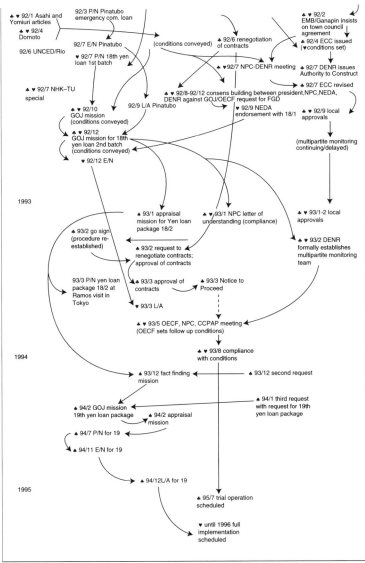

♣ ♥ 92/1 Asahi and Yomiuri articles

92/3 P/N Pinatubo emergency com. loan

♣ ♥ 92/4 Domoto

92/6 UNCED/Rio

92/7 E/N Pinatubo

(conditions conveyed)

♥ 92/7 P/N 18th yen loan 1st batch

♣ ♥ 92/6 renegotiation of contracts

♣ ♥ 92/2 EMB/Ganapin insists on town council agreement

♣ 92/4 ECC issued (♥conditions set)

♣ ♥ 92/7 NHK–TU special

♣ ♥ 92/7 NPC-DENR meeting

♣ 92/7 DENR issues Authority to Construct

♣ 92/7 ECC revised

♣ ♥ 92/10 GOJ mission (conditions conveyed)

92/9 L/A Pinatubo

♣ ♥ 92/8-92/12 consens building between president, NPC, NEDA, DENR against GOJ/OECF request for FGD

♥ 92/9 NEDA endorsement with 18/1

♣ ♥ 92/9 local approvals

♣ ♥ 92/12 GOJ mission for 18th yen loan 2nd batch (conditions conveyed)

(multipartite monitoring continuing/delayed)

♥ 92/12 E/N

1993

♣ 93/1 appraisal mission for Yen loan package 18/2

♣ ♥ 93/1 NPC letter of understanding (compliance)

♣ ♥ 93/1-2 local approvals

♣ 93/2 go sign (procedure re-established)

♣ 93/2 request to renegotiate contracts; approval of contracts

♣ ♥ 93/2 DENR formally establishes multipartite monitoring team

93/3 P/N yen loan package 18/2 at Ramos visit in Tokyo

♣ 93/3 approval of contracts

♣ 93/3 Notice to Proceed

♥ 93/3 L/A

♣ ♥ 93/5 OECF, NPC, CCPAP meeting (OECF sets follow up conditions)

1994

♣ ♥ 93/8 compliance with conditions

♣ 93/12 fact finding mission

♣ 93/12 second request

♣ 94/2 GOJ mission 19th yen loan package

♣ 94/2 appraisal mission

♣ 94/1 third request with request for 19th yen loan package

♣ 94/7 P/N for 19

♣ 94/11 E/N for 19

1995

♣ 94/12 L/A for 19

♣ 95/7 trial operation scheduled

♥ until 1996 full implementation scheduled

Symbols for individual projects/loans:
♣ Calaca II Main Plant (OECF L/A Nr. PH-P76)
♦ Calaca I Coal Utilization Performance Upgrading Project (NPC)
♥ Calaca Complex Environmental Upgrading Project (NPC/OECF L/A Nr. PH-P 130)
♠ Calaca II Cost Overun Loan (OECF L/A Nr. PH-P141)

APPENDIX 6.2

Time framework of projects/loans up to contract approval

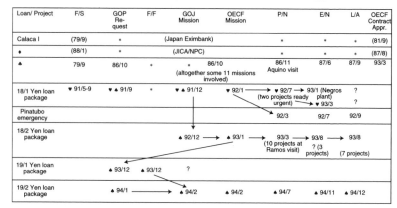

Loan/ Project	F/S	GOP Request	F/F	GOJ Mission	OECF Mission	P/N	E/N	L/A	OECF Contract Appr.
Calaca I	(79/9)	*		(Japan Eximbank)		*	*	*	(81/9)
♦	(88/1)	*		(JICA/NPC)		*	*	*	(87/8)
♣	79/9	86/10	*	* 86/10 (altogether some 11 missions involved)		86/11 Aquino visit	87/6	87/9	93/3
18/1 Yen loan package	♥ 91/5-9	♥ ♣ 91/9	*	♥ ♣ 91/12	♥ 92/1 ⟶	♥ 92/7 ⟶ 93/1 (Negros plant) (two projects ready urgent) ⟶ ♥ 93/3	93/1	?	?
Pinatubo emergency						92/3	92/7	92/9	
18/2 Yen loan package				▲ 92/12 ⟶	▲ 93/1 ⟶	93/3 (10 projects at Ramos visit) ⟶ 93/8	? (3 projects)	93/8 (7 projects)	93/8
19/1 Yen loan package		▲ 93/12	▲ 93/12	?					
19/2 Yen loan package		▲ 94/1 ⟶		▲ 94/2	▲ 94/2	▲ 94/7	▲ 94/11	▲ 94/12	

Symbols for individual projects/loans:
♣ Calaca II Main Plant (OECF L/A Nr. PH-P76)
♦ Calaca I Coal Utilization Performance Upgrading Project (NPC)
♥ Calaca Complex Environmental Upgrading Project (NPC/OECF L/A Nr. PH-P 130)
▲ Calaca II Cost Overrun Loan (OECF L/A Nr. P 141)

7 Shipping aid to China

Marie Söderberg

Where would you take your children if you wanted to show them something really luxurious? In Europe there is not much to be found in this category any more. Some hotels such as the Oriental in Bangkok or the Okura in Tokyo are a little better, but they are only bleak shadows of what you could find in 1994 in the People's Republic of China. As you step into the entrance hall of the Wang Fu Hotel in Beijing you realize that much has happened in China during the last ten years. Looking at the crystal, the lamps of the elevators travelling up the wall of the entrance hall, and the massive marble bridge, reputed to have cost more than $1 million, it is hard to believe that you are in a developing country with a per capita income of no more than $370.[1]

Construction work seems to be occurring everywhere. The Chinese eighth five-year development plan (1991–95) places a strong priority on infrastructure development, especially in the transportation sector. This case study examines one of these projects, namely, the Shenzhen Dapeng Bay Yantian Port project. This comprises the construction of three berths for containers, bulk and multipurpose use in Dapeng Bay in Shenzhen City, north of Hong Kong. An associated access road and a railway have also been built in order to meet the increasing demand for cargo transportation.

The study begins with a short review of the modern history and the aid relationship between Japan and China. A description of the process of receiving aid in China follows in which a number of country-specific factors are analysed and then the process of giving aid to China where a number of ODA- and OECF-specific factors will be considered. The case study itself will follow the entire process in detail from the original plans of the project, its progress, the conclusion of contracts and finally what subsequently happened.

FROM A POLICY OF 'SELF-RELIANCE' TO EXTERNAL AID

The development to be found in Beijing and some other cities that have experienced strong economic growth is not the whole picture of this huge country with its population of 1.2 billion people. As is generally the case in developing countries, economic growth is an uneven process and does not occur with the same speed in the countryside. Outside the cities conditions are as poor as ever and sometimes even worse.

Being the 'Middle Kingdom', with a long cultural tradition and the largest population in the world has led to a number of country-specific factors as to how the Chinese viewed the world and their own role. The People's Republic of China followed a policy of 'self-reliance' from its foundation in 1949 until the end of 1978. Under this policy all foreign borrowings and acceptance of outside assistance were denounced as humiliation of the country and in most cases rejected.[2] It was only after China declared its economic reform and open-door policy in 1978 that multilateral organizations and various OECD countries began to give aid in 1979. The amount of aid steadily increased until the military crackdown on pro-democratic demonstrations in Tiananmen Square in June 1989. This led to economic sanctions against China, including the suspension of ODA.

Japan was the first country to restore friendly relations with China and at the Group of Seven meeting held in Houston in July 1990, Prime Minister Toshiki Kaifu announced that Japan would gradually resume aid.[3] Since then other countries have followed and ODA to China has gradually increased again. In fact, in 1993 China was the world's largest recipient of ODA, being the only country to receive more than $3 billion.[4]

The most significant bilateral donor, in a class of its own, is Japan. In 1993 it disbursed in excess of $1.3 billion to China.[5] The second-largest donor in 1990 was Germany, France in 1991 and Italy in 1992, each extending aid of around $200 million.[6] Bilateral aid accounted for 58 per cent of all ODA to China in 1992[7] and multilateral aid, 42 per cent. The largest multilateral donor was the World Bank[8] which alone accounted for 30 per cent of all ODA to China in 1992. Second among the multinationals was the Asian Development Bank with 7 per cent and third were UN organizations with 5 per cent of total ODA.

HISTORICAL RELATIONSHIP

The mutual importance of the relationship today between China and Japan is not in doubt. This seems only natural, since they are geographically close to each other and complementary in many ways. Japan, a small island country with only one-tenth the population of China, is advanced both economically and technologically and can supply China with machinery, steel, and chemicals. China with its vast territory can supply Japan with raw materials, textiles and light industry products.[9] Japan possesses huge amounts of capital and China has an abundance of cheap labour.

Historically, the Chinese cultural influence on Japan has been significant and has led, among other things, to the adaptation of Buddhism as well as the Chinese writing system. During the last 100 years relations have soured and erupted into war twice, in the 1890s and later in the 1930s. On both occasions this has occurred on Chinese territory. The invasion of Manchuria, where over 500,000 Japanese colonists subsequently settled, as well as the great numbers of Chinese who died at the hands of the Japanese during World War II, still creates a great deal of negative sentiment among the Chinese. Notwithstanding that, there is a shared concern today in fostering peace and prosperity in Asia. China has opened its market to stimulate economic growth and the enormous potential of the market has led many Japanese companies to invest in the country. The early commitment of Japanese trading companies after 1979 has been demonstrated by the substantial number of offices opened not only in Beijing but also in other major cities. However, very few Japanese companies appear to be satisfied with the financial returns resulting from their business with China.[10]

Apart from the opening of trading house offices, statistics reveal that Japanese investment was not particularly impressive in the early years. The Japanese are not the largest foreign investors on a cumulative basis, but lie fifth after Hong Kong, Macau, Taiwan and the United States. (see Table 7.1).

Japanese direct investment to China has increased considerably and in 1993 this investment was $1.7 billion.[11] Trade between the two countries is also considerable. In 1993 China was Japan's seventh-largest export market[12] and China was second only to the United States in imports. Similarly, in 1993 Japan was China's third-largest export market after Hong Kong and the United States and Japan was China's main source of imports.[13]

214   *Marie Söderberg*

Table 7.1 Direct foreign investment to China (contract basis) 1979–92

Country	Amount ($ billion)	Percentage of total
1 Hong Kong, Macau	73.9	66.7
2 Taiwan	8.5	7.6
3 USA	8.1	7.3
4 Japan	5.8	5.7
5 Others	14.5	12.7
Total	110.8	100

Source: Compiled from *Yearbook of Chinese Foreign Trade*

JAPANESE–CHINESE ODA RELATIONS: PAST TO THE PRESENT

Following World War II both Chinas renounced reparations. The Japanese Peace Treaty was not signed by the People's Republic of China in 1951. A year later Japan signed a treaty with Taiwan. As an ally of the United States, Japan extended assistance to Taiwan from the inception of its aid programme until the initiation of diplomatic relations with the People's Republic of China in 1972.

An ODA programme to the People's Republic commenced after Prime Minister Ohira's visit to China in 1979, after he declared that Japan would co-operate with the efforts to modernize China. Since that time ODA has grown enormously. Between 1982 and 1986 China was the single largest recipient of ODA from Japan. The incident in Tiananmen Square in 1989 led to a temporary cessation of new ODA projects but aid has now resumed and continues to grow. In 1993 China was the number one ODA recipient and is expected to remain so until the turn of the century. OECF yen loans make up 78 per cent of Japanese ODA to China (see Table 7.2). The providing of ODA can be divided into three time periods, following the three OECF loan packages. The first yen loan package, from 1980 to 1984, included five projects (two ports, two railway projects and a commodity loan) and had a value of ¥331 billion ($1.3 billion). The second package, from 1984 to 1989, promised financing for sixteen projects at a total value of ¥470 billion ($2 billion). However, as the value of the yen rose, much more could be financed with that sum, and so another nine projects were added to the original sixteen. Further funding was also provided in 1988 by an additional loan of ¥70 billion ($550 million) through the so-called 'yen recycling programme'.[14] The third yen loan package, covers

Table 7.2 Japanese ODA to China ($ million, (%))

Year	Grant aid		Technical assistance	Loan aid	Total
1989	58.01	(7)	106.10 (13)	668.07 (80)	832.18 (100)
1990	37.82	(5)	163.49 (23)	521.71 (72)	723.02 (100)
1991	56.61	(10)	137.48 (23)	391.21 (67)	585.29 (100)
1992	72.05	(7)	187.48 (18)	791.23 (75)	1,050.76 (100)
1993	54.43	(4)	245.06 (18)	1,051.19 (78)	1,350.67 (100)
Total	494.96	(6)	1,187.34 (15)	6,114.12 (78)	7,796.41 (100)

Source: Waga Kuni no Seifu Kaihatsu Enjo

the period from 1990 to 1995. When it was announced in a meeting between the Chinese and Japanese heads of state in August 1988, it listed 42 projects with a value of ¥810 billion ($5.5 billion). It is obvious now that this is insufficient to cover all the projects, so it is probable that some will not be realized within this period.[15]

As is the usual case, infrastructure is the main thrust of OECF loans (see Figure 7.1). What is country-specific for China is the extremely

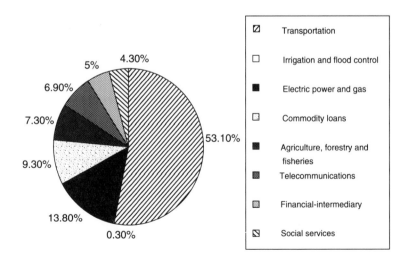

Figure 7.1 OECF loan commitments to China by sector
Source: OECF

heavy emphasis on the transportation sector which is also the first priority in the eighth Chinese state plan. As a principle, all OECF loan aid is on general untied conditions.

THE FUTURE

The Chinese have already specified 69 projects[16] at a value of ¥1,400 billion ($13.7 billion) which they wish OECF to finance during the next five-year period. The Chinese want the five-year system since this follows their own state planning which is also for consecutive five-year periods. The Japanese, however, would prefer to change the OECF loans to a system of yearly negotiations. They claim that the five-year system is too rigid and that with the current rapid economic growth it is difficult to predict Chinese needs for the year 2000.

When Prime Minister Hosokawa visited Beijing in the spring of 1994 the two parties agreed to a compromise according to which the next yen loan package would be divided into three plus two years. In January 1995 it was determined that the amount of money for the first three year period (1996–98) would be ¥580 billion ($5.7 billion).[17] This amount is considerably less than the original Chinese request. For the next package, Japan has agreed to support more inland projects and those aimed at western regions to help narrow the gap between the rapid development in the eastern coast areas and the relatively slow growth occurring inland and in the western parts of China. The total amount of money spent on infrastructure will probably remain the same although the proportion of funding for infrastructure within the total aid package may decrease while other areas, such as the environment, will receive greater emphasis.[18]

PROCESS OF RECEIVING AID

The process of receiving aid in China has its own country-specific factors which reflect the Chinese view of themselves as well as the way they perceive the role of donors. The process is extremely complex and lacks any form of formal co-ordination for bilateral and multilateral donors. The Chinese government has made it clear that they do not want any external agent to co-ordinate or control aid to China. As a result they have decided not to join the World Bank's consultative group or the UNDP (United Nations Development Programme) donor round table discussions.[19]

All types of co-ordination are also complicated by the fact that there are different Chinese ministries, departments or divisions within the departments that handle contacts with and aid from the different donors (see Table 7.3). All these bodies tend to have their own interpretation of national development policy. China also has one system for receiving grant aid and technical assistance and another for loan aid. All grant aid and technical assistance is dealt with by the Science and Technology Commission. Loan aid is handled by the State Planning Commission. It determines the total amount of money that China is allowed to borrow from abroad. To be able to receive external financing for any project, the ministry responsible or the Provincial Planning Committees must first apply for permission from the State Planning Commission.

The State Planning Commission has a rough idea of the level of funding that can be expected from different sources and compiles a list of projects that it considers should be financed by foreign loans. It also decides which source of finance would be suitable for each project. This depends on the nature of project and whether it is likely to suit the loan conditions of the various donors. Other important factors are what financial resources are available at a particular time and how favourable conditions need to be to make a certain project feasible. The State Planning Commission also determines the amount of money that can be borrowed from abroad for each project, that is, the proportion of local and foreign financing appropriate for each project. This list of projects prepared by the State Planning Commission must then be formally approved by the State Council.

Table 7.3 Different ministries handling different donors in China

World Bank	Ministry of Finance (World Bank Department)
Asian Development Bank	Bank of China (International Department)
IMF	Bank of China (International Department)
JICA (Japanese grant aid and technical assistance)	MOFTEC (Ministry of Foreign Trade and Economic Co-operation)(Foreign Relations Department)
OECF (Japanese loan aid)	MOFTEC (Foreign Financing Administration, Fifth Division)
UNDP	MOFTEC (China International Centre for Economic and Technical Exchanges)
UNICEF	MOFTEC (Department of International Trade and Economic Relations)
WHO	Ministry of Public Health (Foreign Affairs Department)

Source: UNDP

How OECF yen loans are handled by the recipient

Following completion of the above process, the State Planning Commission and the Ministry of Foreign Trade and Economic Co-operation (MOFTEC) begin consultations with the Japanese government representatives, that is, representatives from the Ministry of Foreign Affairs (MOFA), Ministry of International Trade and Industry (MITI), Ministry of Finance (MOF) and the Economic Planning Agency (EPA) as well as OECF.

In the past OECF loans have been announced in five-year packages, roughly following the Chinese five-year long-term planning. Since Japanese loan aid is request-based, the procedure has been that the Chinese present a number of projects for which financing is needed. In the last five-year package 60 different projects were presented to the Japanese but following discussions the number of projects was reduced to 42.

The number of selected projects as well as the amount of funding is subsequently announced for each package. The Chinese rely on this money and incorporate it into their five-year planning. At the time of announcement of the packages, estimates are only rough and indicate the sum of money that Japan is willing to lend to China during a certain period rather than which projects will actually be implemented. After the five-year 'frame' has been decided, negotiations are held on an annual basis between the Japanese government representatives (the same grouping as above) and representatives of the same Chinese together with representatives from the relevant ministries of both governments on a case-by-case basis. These make up what the Japanese term 'government missions'. On those occasions new projects can be included if there is sufficient funding available, as occurred during the second yen loan package. Some projects can also be removed, if there is insufficient funding, which is likely to happen during the third loan package. It is at these annual meetings that decisions are made concerning which projects should be implemented first, that is to say, which projects the appraisal missions should evaluate. At least a few months in advance or usually in January, the Chinese submit a formal request for the projects they wish to proceed with during the forthcoming year. The final decision on which projects are accepted and the level of funding that should be allocated to each is made after the appraisal mission.

Throughout the process, in addition to the formal missions, there is close contact between Chinese and Japanese officials. On such occasions preparations are made well in advance so that the government mission becomes a mere formality. Usually the delegates do not take more than 20 minutes to decide whether to proceed with the appraisal mission for building a new harbour, a railroad or other such project. Prior to this meeting, many hours have been spent by OECF and MOFTEC officials discussing each project. Relevant ministries have also been involved and consulted in these discussions.

MOFTEC has a special department, the Fifth Division of the Foreign Financing Administration, that deals only with Japanese OECF yen loans and foreign aid from the Netherlands. Four people work in the department and they are supposed to meet weekly with OECF. Sometimes they meet more often and sometimes less, but they are in close contact at all times.

MOFTEC is the implementing agency that signs on behalf of all other ministries concerned. Before any loan agreements are signed with OECF, however, there is a yearly Exchange of Notes between the governments . These are usually signed in Beijing by the Japanese Ambassador and the Chinese Vice Foreign Minister. The notes specify the projects and the amount of loans provided for each, as well as the total sum. Conditions for the loans are also specified. Following this, a loan agreement is signed for each project between MOFTEC and OECF, usually by a Chinese delegation which travels to Tokyo. The relevant ministry for each project then becomes the so-called executing agency. In this case study this is the Ministry of Communication. It also has a special department that deals only with OECF loan projects and is staffed with Japanese-speaking officials.

Procurement itself is not carried out by the implementing agency, but rather by one of the three procurement agencies under MOFTEC, that is, the China National Technical Import and Export Corporation, the China National Machinery Import and Export Corporation or the China National Instrument Import and Export Corporation. These procurement agencies also have departments dealing especially with OECF loans. Other procurement agencies exist in China but these are the only ones that are allowed to handle OECF loans.

China has a number of country-specific factors. It is in a strong position, relative to many other recipients and has a long history of state directed planning. It also allocates a number of officials with expert knowledge to deal with Japanese aid officials. At every level there are special departments that concentrate only on this form of aid and their staff easily fill the gap caused by the shortage of staff at OECF. Japanese experts are, however, not lacking in number. In fiscal year 1994 there were around 1,160 people employed by JICA in China dealing with grant aid and technical assistance.[20] The studies that JICA conduct are provided free of charge to the Chinese. Co-operation between OECF and JICA is not always easy because widely different views are held on what is considered to be a suitable project. The Japanese engineering consultant firms to be found all over the rest of Asia are not allowed to open offices in China. This limits the firms' access to the Chinese market. However, they are allowed to participate in various JICA financed projects.

Aid-giving process

The five-year loan packages are special treatment that so far has only been extended to the Chinese. They do not match with OECF budgetary procedures which are done on a yearly basis. In fact, the five-year packages are merely oral commitments that have been made by Japanese Prime Ministers to Chinese leaders on different occasions. This can be seen as a proof of the political importance of ODA loans to China. Such matters are not delegated to OECF officials to handle completely on their own, according to standard regulations, but are presented by Japanese prime ministers to Chinese leaders in connection with meetings where other matters are also discussed.

These five-year loan packages are preceded by a great deal of work, and involve negotiations between MOFTEC and OECF as well as OECF and the different ministries concerned. The Japanese Embassy in Beijing, representing the Government of Japan, is regularly involved and all the Four Ministries are included in the process before any commitments on loan aid are given. There has never been any written Exchange of Notes or anything formally signed in connection with the oral commitments. Yet the promises have been kept, even when there was a temporary interruption in the implementation of new projects in connection with the Tiananmen Square incident in June 1989.

The concession by the Japanese to accommodate the Chinese five-year plans has a number of practical implications as well. One is that the amount of aid for specific projects is based on rough estimates and is, therefore, imprecise. At the time of request for the five-year packages, feasibility studies do not exist for many of the projects. This displays a strong political commitment rather than one based on facts and figures. Another implication of the five-year system is that the amount of aid for China is decided in advance, irrespective of the total amount of Japanese ODA. Even though the five-year goals are set in dollar terms, the Japanese budget is decided on a yearly basis. The five-year commitment also means that it has been difficult to make major changes during this period, even if the priorities of Japanese ODA policy changes. The ODA charter introduced in 1992 (see Chapter 1) emphasized that environmental issues, military spending, development and production of weapons of mass destruction as well as human rights issues, should be considered when extending foreign aid. However, this has not altered the implementation of the five-year loan package to China since all its projects were agreed upon prior to the new charter.

In both the Chinese Eighth Development Plan and the third Japanese yen loan package priority was given to the transportation sector, especially on the eastern coast. In that way the Shenzhen Dapeng Bay Yantian Port construction was a project typical of its time.

SHENZHEN – ECONOMIC DEVELOPMENT SPEARHEAD

Economic development in Shenzhen began at about the same time as Japanese ODA to China. As early as 1979 the Shenzhen Economic Zone was created as a special industrial zone where foreign as well as local companies, through tax deductions and various economic incentives, were encouraged to build facilities especially for export production.

Shenzhen's location, directly adjacent to the border to Hong Kong, proved most advantageous. The Hong Kong economy was at that time overheating because of rising wages and land costs. This prompted many companies to relocate production to Shenzhen where costs were lower. It was also seen by many companies as a first step into the Chinese market with its enormous potential.

In 1979 there were around 40,000 people living in Shenzhen. Today the city of Shenzhen, and Shenzhen Economic Zone, which comes under the same local government, boast a population of around 3 million people.[21] The small houses have disappeared to be replaced by modern high-rise buildings, factories and terrible traffic jams. Construction seems to be in progress everywhere.

According to information from the Shenzhen government, there were 5,757 industrial enterprises in the area in 1992 including light industry, textiles, electronics, petrochemicals, machinery, building materials, foodstuffs and beverages. The industrial output was valued at $7 billion, 446 times the 1979 levels.

In 1992 Shenzhen was the number one exporter in the Guangdong Province and the second among all cities in China, next only to Shanghai. The area boasts a mixed population with immigrants from other parts of China. Salaries are generally higher than in other places and many of the people living there have specifically chosen to work in Shenzhen as this, according to them, is 'where the action is taking place'. Shenzhen is considered to be the spearhead of China's economic development and many of the inhabitants are convinced that their own future as well as China's future is very bright.[22]

Old plans for a new harbour

Plans for building a harbour in the north-west of Dapeng Bay date back further than the Shenzhen Economic Zone. A survey conducted by the Chinese government in 1953[23] chose the location as suitable for a harbour for the southern part of China (see Map 7.1). The water in the bay is extremely deep and to the south, on the opposite side of the bay, is the Kowloon peninsula of Hong Kong. To the north stretch the Wuting Hills which prevent typhoons from sweeping into Dapeng Bay. The water in the bay is sufficiently calm to serve as a natural shelter for ships.

At that time, however, there was no funding available and the plans were not realized.[24] Once the Shenzhen Economic Zone was inaugurated and industrial production began in the area, discussions for the harbour were renewed. This time the initiative came from the local people who wanted a deep sea port. Representatives from the Shenzhen Shipping Company, Shenzhen SEZ Co. Ltd, and Shatoujiiao Co. Ltd wrote to the Shenzhen and Guangdong governments as well as to the Ministry of Communications requesting a harbour. In 1985 these three companies created the Shenzhen Dongpeng Industry Co. Ltd for the purpose of building a harbour.[25]

In China there are country-specific factors that govern the way companies of the People's Republic are formed and what kind of authority they have. Shenzhen Dongpeng Industry is an industrial company with the legal rights to conduct trade and sign business contracts. Creation of the Shenzhen Yantian Port Construction Command was linked to it. This consists of roughly the same people but it is the agency that officially signs on behalf of the Shenzhen government. The general director of Shenzhen Yantian Port Construction Command is the mayor of Shenzhen. The vice-general director of the Shenzhen Yantian Port Construction Command is Mr Liu Dingtong, who is also the general manager of Shenzhen Dongpeng Industries. (For the sake of simplicity these two organizations will be treated as one company from now on.)

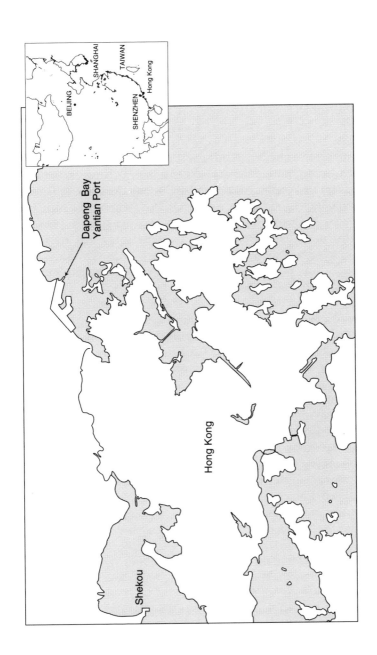

Map 7.1 Shenzhen Dapeng Bay Yantian Harbour

Need for a feasibility study

In order to construct a harbour, calculate the cost of it and seek assistance with financing, a feasibility study was first required. Shenzhen Dongpeng Industries asked the organization officially responsible for technical assistance, the State Scientific and Technology Commission, for a feasibility study which, in turn, requested it from JICA.

JICA prepares a number of different studies every year in China.[26] These are decided during the annual consultations between the Japanese Ministry of Foreign Affairs and JICA, and the Chinese Science and Technology Commission and MOFTEC. The study of a port construction in Shenzhen was agreed to in a meeting in 1985 and was started in January 1986. It was the only study that JICA performed in this geographical area[27] at the time.

The study was prepared by the Japan Port Consultants Ltd[28] in conjunction with Toko Consultants and in co-operation with representatives from the Chinese Ministry of Communication, and in this case, the Water Transportation Planning and Design Institute,[29] the Shenzhen city government and Shenzhen Dongpeng Industries. The Japanese study team was based in Tokyo and was dispatched to China four times for data collection and consultations.

The work was divided between the Japanese and Chinese participants so that there was co-operation on land development, a railway and a highway that was to be connected to the port. The Japanese assumed the main responsibility for the development of the harbour itself and the Chinese for the city that was to be connected with it. The final report, which was based on both Chinese and Japanese findings, was completed in March 1987. It pointed out the importance for continued Chinese economic development of removing bottlenecks in the transportation sector, especially in the four Economic Zones and the fourteen economic and technical development areas. The harbours planned in the Chinese seventh economic Five-Year Plan were important in this respect and the port in Shenzhen was seen as playing an important role in the long-term development of the entire southern region of China.

The study began with this long-term view and in fact formed a kind of master plan for the development of the harbour and related facilities to the year 2000. It outlined a grand scenario with large-scale devlopment in Shenzhen[30] which would, on completion, include a harbour with more than 50 berths. This is followed by a description of the first part of the harbour development in Yantian Bay (scheduled for 1990) and specified six berths of certain sizes which were evaluated and found to be of importance as well as financially feasible.[31]

When the Ministry of Communication submitted a list of projects to be approved for yen financing to the State Planning Commission in 1987, the harbour in Shenzhen was not included. The request for listing of the harbour did not occur until the end of 1987 and it was added to the original list in the beginning of 1988, the same year that the Chinese State Council also approved it. The list was then presented to the Japanese Government and in August 1988 the harbour in Shenzhen was one of the 42 projects agreed upon between Japanese and Chinese leaders in connection with the third yen loan package.

Case process

In 1989 the plans for a harbour in Shenzhen were returned to the Ministry of Communication, which then turned to the Shenzhen local authorities as well as Dongpeng Industries for confirmation and further studies on the site. These were carried out by the Ministry together with the local Water Transportation and Design Planning Institute.

At this time it was obvious to many that the financial issues were likely to be resolved and that the construction of Yantian Port stood a fair chance of being realized. Several companies started, therefore, promoting their products by approaching local people involved in the project on the basis of supposedly assisting in planning activities by supplying product specifications and listing product merits. The companies were all endeavouring to establish a favourable position prior to the bidding process even though the project was still only in the design stage.

In July 1989 the new study by the Ministry of Communication was completed but the massacre in Tiananmen square which had occurred the previous month led the Japanese Government to impose a temporary halt to all new ODA projects in China. This would delay the process for some time.

OECF APPRAISAL MISSION

A formal request for OECF yen loans to finance the Yantian Port as well as other projects was submitted by the Chinese Government in January 1990 but it was not until October of that year that the Japanese Government sent a mission to discuss the requests. The list of projects requested was substantial. For Shenzhen the Chinese side[32] requested money for the construction of a total of three berths for containers, bulk and multipurpose use in Dapeng Bay as well as an access road of 72 km and a railway of 24 km, to meet the increasing demand for cargo transportation. The same month an appraisal mission arrived to study the port project. This consisted of two people, a technical expert and an economist, who stayed for about one month. An appraisal of the whole project was needed even though all the funding would not be supplied in the first year but would be included in three different loan agreements, each with slightly different conditions.

One of the items that an appraisal mission considers are the proportions of local and foreign currency. OECF loans do not usually cover the whole cost of infrastructure projects in China, but generally only part of the foreign currency proportion. The Chinese contribution is, in most cases, around 60 per cent. This is country-specific in the sense that it is a much higher percentage than that found with OECF loans in other countries. The Chinese provide a shopping list of what is needed for the project and discussions commence with what is to be financed locally and with OECF money.

According to the appraisal mission the construction of the Yantian Port project needed total financing of ¥35,679 million ($246 million). The foreign, that is OECF, part of this was to be ¥14,681 million ($101 million) and the balance, around ¥21 billion ($144 million), was to be financed locally.

In addition to the economic appraisal and calculations of internal rate of return, a technical appraisal was also performed. The report from the appraisal mission is an internal OECF document and its contents are not open to the public. On the basis of the decision of the Japanese government to proceed with the project, the findings of the appraisal mission was that the project must have been viable. This was in accordance with the feasibility study.

SIGNING OF THE LOAN AGREEMENT

On 21 December 1990 an Exchange of Notes for the twelfth yen loan[33] was completed between the two governments. Included in this, among a number of other projects, was ¥7,613 million ($53 million) for the Yantian Port project. On 22 January a first loan agreement was signed between MOFTEC and OECF for this sum. The interest rate was 2.5 per cent, with a repayment period of 30 years, including a grace period of ten years. The rest of the money was to follow when it was needed, that is, when there was a need for further procurement for the project. The second loan agreement of ¥3,691 million ($27 million) was signed as part of the thirteenth yen loan on 4 October 1991. The third and last agreement of ¥3,377 million ($27 million[34]) was signed on 15 October 1992. For these two loans the interest rate was 2.6 per cent and the repayment period of thirty years include a grace period of ten years.

All OECF loans within the third yen package are untied. All contracts should, in principle, be decided through international competitive bidding although in some cases international shopping may apply.[35]

FORMAL STRUCTURE ON THE CHINESE SIDE

MOFTEC always signs OECF loans. After this the Chinese have a country-specific process for handling procurement: MOFTEC appoints a procurement agency and, in the case, of OECF loans, it is one of the three National Corporations under MOFTEC with authority in procurement. The agency most often used is the China National Technical Import and Export Corporation (CNTIC) which handles around 70 per cent of all procurement for OECF loans.

CNTIC was indeed also chosen to handle procurement for the Yantian Port. Of its six different business divisions, the third was set up to deal with Japanese OECF loans and, to a lesser extent, government loans from the Netherlands. This third division is further divided into four sections which deal with different kinds of procurement. The third section is responsible for communications and procurement in connection with port and highway construction and was, therefore, responsible for procurement for the Yantian Port project.

The official executing agency for the project was the Ministry of Communication but the actual end-user, the one that CNTIC would sign contracts with at the same time as they signed with the suppliers, was Shenzhen Dongpeng Industries. This company was the actual borrower and the one expected to repay the loans. Consequently, Shenzhen Dongpeng Industries was, of course, interested in receiving as much as possible for its money and so it was heavily involved in the procurement phase with preparation of all the technical documents as well as with the evaluation of the tenders at a later stage.

The Shenzhen Dapeng Yantian Port project was divided into three parts to make construction and procurement easier. These parts were: (1) the harbour itself and associated equipment; (2) the railway and (3) the highway. To manage each of these, Shenzhen Dongpeng Industries established three subsidiary companies with responsibility for the respective areas, namely the Harbour Service Company, the Railway Company and the Highway Company. Dongpeng Industries also created a special Japanese loan division to deal with the OECF funding.[36]

PROCUREMENT PHASE

The procurement for Yantian Port project resembles that of many other infrastructure projects in China. For example, no Japanese or other engineering consulting company supervised the progress of the project. Instead, this was done by Shenzhen Dongpeng Industries, performed in co-operation with CNTIC during procurement, and with overview by the Ministry of Communication.

Another aspect of note was that the project was not contracted in large parts with, for example, one company receiving the order for the railway and another one for the highway. Instead, it was broken down into numerous smaller contracts. For the loan signed in 1991 there were approximately fifty different contracts, many with sub-contractors specified within them. Altogether there were around 90 different contracts signed for the OECF loans. The reason given for the Chinese end-users operating in this way was that it gives them more complete control of the process and ensures that they receive exactly what they want.[37] On the other hand, this also makes the bidding process of less interest for large foreign companies.

All technical specifications needed for the preparation of tender documents were supplied by the subsidiary companies of Dongpeng Industries in Shenzhen. They were ultimately responsible but occasionally used consultants such as the Water Planning Design Institute. A consultant was also used for the finalization of the tender documents. Dongpeng Industries calculated how much equipment and material were needed and at what time, i.e., the scheduling. It was reported to the Ministry of Communication which then allowed CNTIC to proceed with purchasing.

The actual issue of tender documents was performed by CNTIC. As bidding occurred for different parts of the project at the same time, they were often grouped together into the same tender documents. In other words, there could be as many as ten different items to bid on in one document, but sometimes there were fewer items, or even only one. Tender documents, according to OECF legislation, should be checked by them. This was stipulated in the loan agreement and, according to OECF, reviews occurred in accordance with the agreement. The Chinese view it a little differently and claimed that this no longer happens, except in unusual cases. CNTIC now has had 15 years of experience of working with OECF and is usually trusted to handle tender documents alone.[38] In fact it is difficult to imagine that OECF had enough staff to accomplish any thorough checking as it had only four Japanese and eight locally employed people in its office in Beijing and there were about 70 different projects with numerous contracts in progress at the time. Besides checking all the tender documents it was to check tender evaluation, agree to each contract and give notice to proceed as well as check the projects upon completion. Indeed, this was only part of its responsibilities which, among other things, included guiding different appraisal missions and government missions, and keeping in regular contact with MOFTEC as well as a number of other ministries.

There were six different tender documents for equipment and three for material for the Yantian Port. International competitive bidding was used for all tenders except for two of the equipment packages where international shopping was used. These included the communication system for the harbour (September 1992) and the communication system for the highway tunnel (February 1993).[39] The announcements for the international competitive bidding was done according to the timetable shown in Table 7.4.

No pre-qualification was needed for the international competitive bidding process. Cases where it is needed are rare but in technically complex large projects this can sometimes occur.[40] It also means that with no pre-qualification all bids received must be evaluated. In the final tender document for the Yantian Port, 14 pieces of equipment were to be purchased and 58 suppliers submitted their bids.

The time period from an announcement of a bid to the opening of tenders varies. For simple tendering it can be 40 to 45 days while in more complicated cases the time varies from 60 to 120 days.

Table 7.4 Bidding announcement for Yantian Port project

1	March 1991	Material 1
2	June 1991	Equipment 1
3	November 1991	Equipment 2
4	November 1993	Equipment 3
5	October 1993	Equipment 4
6	March 1992	Material 2
7	November 1993	Material 3

Source: Japanese Loan Office at Dongpeng Industries

Tender opening ceremonies were held at CNTIC's office in Beijing. All the companies that had submitted bids were invited to attend. At the opening of each tender the bidding companies were ranked according to the tender price submitted. These rankings were, however, in no way the final ones. After opening tenders were evaluated. This can, in simple cases, be accomplished in less than a month. In more complicated cases it can take six months or even up to a year. Evaluation meetings are usually held at the end-user's offices, or in this case at Dongpeng Industries' office in Shenzhen. Participating at those meetings were representatives from:

1 CNTIC, which among other things was to check the foreign suppliers. CNTIC representatives were economists and not technicians so their main responsibility was economic evaluation of the tenders.
2 Dongpeng Industries, which was responsible for, among other things, the technical evaluation.
3 The Ministry of Communication, in case of the Yantian Port its representatives did not attend all meetings and sometimes arrived only at the end. The Ministry's opinion was considered important, however, since it had experience from similar projects elsewhere in China.[41]
4 Technical experts, who were also included whenever needed for different kinds of technical evaluations.

The usual procedure in the evaluation process[42] was that the group convened for a first meeting to inspect the bids. After this the companies which supplied bids were visited or contacted as a part of a checking procedure. The number of bids was then shortlisted to around five. These companies were then the subject of more detailed checks and were able to make clarifications of unclear points in their bids. If sub-contractors were to be used, a list of those was also to be submitted and approved by CNTIC as well as Dongpeng Industries, as part of the evaluation process. Price was never discussed during the process but companies could 'clarify' what is included in a bid. Once it was determined who had won the tender, Dongpeng Industries was allowed to add or subtract 5 per cent to the value of the bid.[43]

Fifty-nine different contracts were executed through international competitive bidding for equipment for the port project in Shenzhen. (For a complete list of the contracts see Appendix 7.1.)

Japanese companies won 22 per cent of the orders for equipment and 33 per cent were won by other OECD countries (see Table 7.5).

Table 7.5 Nationality of contractors for equipment

	Contracting amount (¥ million)	Percentage
Japan	1,953	22
LDC	4,026	45
OECD (except Japan)	2,929	33
Total	8,908	100

Source: Compiled from CNTIC information

The main part of the orders to OECD countries went to the Finnish Corporation Kone which, besides the main order for the container cranes, won another order for additional cranes. In total the Kone contracts were valued at ¥2,127 million ($16.7 million).

It should be noted that the LDCs' share was not all awarded to Chinese companies but to other Asian countries as well. Chinese companies won orders with a value of ¥2,107 million and other LDCs won orders worth ¥1,919 million. Other LDC orders were made up of 19 to companies in Hong Kong and one to a Korean company. The fact that only the main contractors were listed makes the figures misleading (see Chapter 2) and the Chinese share was much larger than indicated since many of the other contractors used Chinese sub-contractors.

An overwhelming majority of the contracted material went to Chinese companies, although some steel pipes were purchased from Belgium, steel construction from the United States, asphalt from Singapore, log wood from the United States and steel construction from Germany.

PROCESS OF THE MAIN CONTRACT

The single biggest contract in terms of value was the contract for the three container cranes in the harbour. This was announced for bidding in the second tender documents for equipment in November 1991. The contract worth ¥1,694 million ($13 million) was, after a lengthy evaluation process, won by a private Finnish company, Kone. There were 12 companies bidding for that contract of which three were Japanese (see Table 7.6). The lowest bid was submitted by a Chinese state company. It was based on old heavy technology and was in the end rejected on these grounds. The second-lowest bid was submitted by Kone corporation.[44]

Table 7.6 Bidders for the container cranes

---

1 Kone (Finland)
2 Mitsubishi (Japan)
3 Hyundai (Korea)
4 Mitsui (Japan)
5 Ansaldo (Italy)
6 Vulkan GmbH (Germany)
7 Impsa (Argentina)
8 IHI (Japan)
9 Ederer (Germany)
10 PHB (France)
11 MGM (Italy)
12 Shanghai Port and Machinery (China)

Source: Dongpeng Industries

Kone had already began selling cranes to China in 1989 when it received orders for several small-scale cranes and, thereafter, became a leading crane supplier to China. Kone, which at the time was a privately owned Finnish company[45] specializing in elevators and cranes, did not establish an office of its own in China but worked through an agent in Hong Kong. This agent became aware of the Yantian Port project approximately two years in advance of the tendering[46] and, like many other suppliers, provided specifications for Kone cranes when the project was still on the drawing board. This agent apparently not only worked for Kone on the Yantian Port project but was itself found on the contracting list for other equipment. Supplying specifications that were later used as the basis for the tender documents was an advantage to Kone since it was then able to use its standard cranes for the project which made costs much lower than if special cranes had had to be offered for the Yantian Port.

In 1991, the year before it received the Yantian order, Kone had sold two container cranes to Shekou, the other major port in the middle of the industrial zone in Shenzhen. This was financed through Finnish export credits. Through this project Kone become well established and known, at least in this region of China. It also had developed all the channels and contacts for sub-contracting within the country, a necessity since the cranes would have been far too heavy to ship to China. Although steel from Finland was used, Kone sub-contracted the steel construction, transportation and erection on-site. This was carried out using Modern Engineering Trade Company acting on behalf of Xingang Shipyard, which produced parts, and

Sinhe Shipyard which performed the main construction as well as erection on-site.

It took more than six months from tender opening before contracts were signed for the three container cranes on 31 August 1992. Negotiations took place with the three leading bidders during the whole of this period. At the evaluation meeting when the final decision was made representatives from the Ministry of Communication were also present.

The fact that there were three Japanese companies participating in the tender did not make any difference according to the officials of the Japanese Loan Office. All that was done here was to check the Japanese tenders carefully and inform the companies why they did not win the tender.

SMALL OR LARGE CONTRACTS?

The Yantian Port project was divided into many smaller contracts for tendering. This seems to be the way that contracting is most often done for OECF-financed projects in China, but not in every case. In Qinghuangdao, OECF financed a coal transportation project. The value of the tender was ¥9,870 million ($97 million) and this was allocated in one contract.[47] A similar coal transportation project in Shanghai was not kept to one tender but divided into several contracts.

According to the Ministry of Communication it actually prefers larger contracts. In the Qinghuangdao port it was important that the different machines were compatible and it was only one type of function that was to be performed. In the Shanghai case the machines were to perform different functions. What is more, Ministry of Communication was not the end-user.

At CNTIC the explanation as to why the whole project in Qinghuangdao was offered in one package was that the end-user lacked the technical capability necessary to divide the project into smaller parts for tendering. Therefore, it preferred to leave the responsibility to another party to whom it could complain if it was not satisfied.

Whether a project put to tender is divided into several small contracts or contracted in one part actually seems to depend on the wishes of the end-user – what it considers is the cheapest and best way to handle a project, as well as what qualifications the end-user has to administer the process.

THE BIDDING PROCESS AND THE BUSINESS COMMUNITY[48]

OECF regulations state that no bargaining of price should occur after tender opening in OECF international competitive bidding. The company with the lowest price conforming with the specifications in the tender documents should, in principle, be awarded the order. According to the business community, this is not always the way it works in reality. Sometimes the end-user has determined what it wants in advance. It holds a powerful position in the evaluation process and can influence the outcome to coincide with its wishes. In other cases it can be a ministry that has definite opinions about which of the bids should be chosen. Therefore, the large companies must also maintain good relations with the various ministries. One businessman claimed that even the State Planning Commission and senior Chinese leaders can influence the process if Chinese political relations are at stake. When a leader from a foreign country visits China and a contract signing ceremony is needed as a token of the countries' friendship and good relations this might favour a company from a particular country.[49]

At which level – State Planning Commission, the relevant ministry, the procurement agency or the local end-user – most power is concentrated is difficult to determine and probably varies from case to case. Companies must satisfy all of these players to assure themselves of a favourable treatment. A reasonably priced conforming tender is, of course, essential as no one ever wants to make a bad deal. Generally agencies and officials are well prepared and have information about companies' previous bids for similar projects on other occasions and in other parts of the country. This data is all computerized and easy for Chinese state officials to access. They can simply ask their colleagues in other agencies. At times considerable bargaining is reported to occur at different levels, even for OECF projects.

WHO DECIDES THE LOAN AMOUNT?

The loan agreement for Yantian Port projects was signed for a sum of ¥14.7 billion. This was the foreign currency cost that the appraisal mission considered necessary for the project. However, only ¥13.3 billion was received for them. Who made this decision and why?

OECF in Beijing claims that the loan agreement was for ¥14.7 billion and no other amount. It claims that there must be some miscalculation at Dongpeng Industries in Shenzhen.

In Shenzhen, Dongpeng Industries is of another opinion. It insists that only ¥13.3 billion was received and since Dongpeng Industries have all the contracts, it has the papers to prove it. No more money is expected as the project was officially finished on 14 August 1994, according to the Ministry of Communication. According to Dongpeng Industries,[50] the third allotment of the loan was reduced because the State Planning Commission needed the money for other projects.[51] Funds to cover this shortfall had to be found from other sources. MOFTEC confirms that Dongpeng Industries did not receive all the money and claims that it, MOFTEC, determined that the new sum should be ¥13.3 billion.

A second check by OECF[52] showed that the full sum of the loan was not actually paid out. In the end some of the equipment that OECF had agreed to finance was not needed and therefore not purchased. Who decides what is needed? This raises the question of who has decision-making power over the loans, OECF or MOFTEC and the State Planning Commission?

Costs, in general, have risen in China to the level where all 42 projects chosen for funding in the third yen loan package will not be implemented. Is it possible then that the State Planning Commission has decided not to let projects financed by OECF use 100 per cent of their allocated loans with the purpose of trying to save some money for other projects? In that case what can OECF do about it? Who is governing the process?

PRIVATIZATION – KNOWN PRIOR TO FINAL CONTRACT SIGNING

In the feasibility study financed by JICA, a first phase with six berths was suggested for Yantian Port. Shenzhen Yantian Port Construction Command and Shenzhen Dongpeng Industry Co. also wanted six berths and started to build three for bulk and cargo on their own initiatives. The OECF loans were to cover the costs for the next three berths as well as the railway and the highway. By November 1992 the first three berths were ready and the State Council officially approved the opening of Yantian Port to foreign-flag vessels.

There was only one problem. There were virtually no ships interested in using the harbour. Although it was located near to busy Hong Kong harbour, no one had heard of Yantian Port. The Chinese company, Dongpeng Industries, had no contacts in the shipping business. Even though it was newly built and modern, there was a maximum of one ship per week docking there.[53] Meanwhile, construction of the other three berths, a railway and a highway had already started. Something had to be done to prevent an economic catastrophe and ensure some activity in the harbour.

To Shenzhen Dongpeng Industries the solution was to sell the harbour. It established a joint venture with the prominent business-man and shipping magnate from Hong Kong, Mr Li Ka-Shin. By October 1993 Yantian International Container Terminals Ltd was established. The privatization was sanctioned by top leaders in China and President Jiang Zemin attended the signing ceremony. This was even before the announcement of the final tender for the OECF project, which occurred in November 1993.

One of the conditions of ODA is that it can only be government-to-government aid. Chinese regulations also would not permit the selling of the harbour. Therefore, the government still formally remains the owner of the harbour. What were sold and became privatized were the rights to operate and maintain the harbour.

Since the project was unfinished at the time of sale, the berths were not ready and the equipment not in place, Mr Li Ka-Shin's company had to wait some time before it could commence operations. This period of time was spent, among other things, on erecting a new administration building on the premises.

CONCLUSIONS FROM THE PORT PROJECT

The idea of building a harbour in Yantian was an old Chinese one that was revived in connection with the economic zone and the economic development of the area. It was an idea promulgated locally by the people of the area. It was also a project which was well in line with the type of project that OECF wants to finance.

No evidence could be found in this case that Japanese companies were given any special favours just because the project was financed by OECF loans. On the contrary, the main contract was won by a Finnish company in competition with such giant Japanese companies as Mitsubishi, Mitsui and IHI. These are all major Japanese companies with supposedly good connections among influential circles at home, but which were unable to influence the Chinese decision-making process.

It could be argued that the sum of the main contract of the project, ¥1,694 million ($12 million), is insufficient to make it worth any major efforts by these companies and that this is why they did not bother to try and use their good connections among influential circles at home to win the order. Yet the division of the project into smaller contracts is not unique. This seems to be the rule rather than the exception when it comes to projects financed by Japanese loan aid in China, and Japanese companies still exert great effort to bid for them. It has often been argued, especially by the Japanese trading houses (see Chapter 3), that foreign companies should use trading house services to receive a share of the orders for Japanese ODA. This might be reasonable for grant aid that is all tied, but cannot be proved from this case study. On the contrary, a Hong Kong agent who was well connected in the area seemed to be as competent or, in this case, perhaps even more skilful. Political pressure does not seem to have played any major part in this case, since the winner was a Finnish company. Its political strength with respect to China does not seem overwhelming. It should be pointed out, however, that Finnish export credits for two similar cranes in the area the year before may have had some importance.

The feasibility study by JICA concluded that there was a market for a harbour at this site and encouraged the Chinese to go ahead with the construction. This was apparently an overly optimistic view of the Chinese capability of handling international shipping. It is doubtful whether the consultants had any knowledge in this field either. The Chinese also overestimated their own capabilities in the shipping trade. Many developing countries do likewise. What was different here was that once the mistake was realized the Chinese were skilful and adept in adjusting to changed circumstances. The OECF appraisal mission apparently also placed too much faith in the feasibility study since they did not reject the project.

On the whole, this project appears to have followed typical business practice where economic and technical concerns are placed first. OECF financed less than 40 per cent of the project, the rest was funded by the Chinese themselves. That meant that the larger portion was not ODA and this might explain why some of the ODA-specific factors are missing. That considerable bargaining occurs after tender opening of OECF financed contracts is clear. The perception that the project adhered to typical business practice is further strengthened by the fact that the right to operate the harbour was sold as soon as the Chinese had difficulties attracting customers there themselves. This was a solution not normally expected in connection with ODA. The Chinese did not hesitate on any moral grounds such as it being an aid project given to the Chinese government by the Japanese government. Legal grounds, however, prevented an outright sale of the harbour, and to circumvent this problem they sold the right to operate and maintain the harbour instead. To the Chinese end-user, Dongpeng

Industries, the sale of the harbour must have been the most logical solution at that time.

MOFTEC officially signed the loan agreement and the Ministry of Communication was the formal executing agency but when the harbour was sold the money was retained by Dongpeng Industries in Shenzhen. That the money was not returned and used for other infrastructure projects indicates the strong position of the real end-user, that is in this case Dongpeng Industries. China is in great need of capital and after all MOFTEC was the official borrower. This also raises questions as to what interest Dongpeng Industries in their turn is paying on the loans. Would MOFTEC allow Dongpeng Industries to profit alone? This is something this study failed to discover.

A country-specific factor is the lack of foreign engineering consultantcy firms. In other parts of Asia there are many foreign engineering consultants, especially Japanese, undertaking work in relation to OECF loans. In China this is lacking and foreign engineering consultants are not allowed to open offices. The Chinese perform these services themselves.

OECF has limited staff in China. The Chinese compensate for this shortage of Japanese aid officials with their own people. At every step there are departments that specialize in dealing with Japanese loan aid. MOFTEC and the Ministry of Communication have such departments and at CNTIC the department even has several sections. Dongpeng Industries has a special Japanese loan aid division employing seven people. Many of these people now have considerable knowledge and experience with dealing with the Japanese loans.

Another conclusion that can be drawn from this case study is that it is not easy for OECF to control the process. OECF agrees to a loan of ¥14.7 billion for the project but if the State Planning Commission and MOFTEC suddenly decide that certain equipment is not needed and that only ¥13.3 billion should be used and give such a directive to the end-user, OECF cannot do much about it. This raises questions of who is actually governing the process. The Chinese seem to be especially powerful in this respect and this must be regarded as a country-specific factor.

China has made it abundantly clear that it wants to control the ODA process and do not need any co-ordination activities by donors from different countries. In its dealings with OECF the Chinese have taken command of the procedure and forced OECF to deviate from its regular procedure of annual commitments to be replaced instead by commitments of five years at a time adjusted to the Chinese five-year plans. These five-year aid packages are announced by Japanese Prime

Ministers in their meetings with Chinese leaders which points to the political dimension of the packages.

In the case of Yantian Port project OECF staff followed the operational guidelines. The sale of the rights to operate the harbour could not have been prevented by the guidelines. Not all OECF projects directly generate income for loan repayments, for example, roads, schools and rural development. Yet the OECF staff, besides having a responsibility to disburse money as quickly and effectively as possible, have to consider operations from a financial point of view. Therefore, there is an incentive to find projects that are sufficiently profitable to begin loan repayments within ten years. This is something OECF has in common with end-users in the recipient country.

YANTIAN PORT – EPILOGUE

The OECF project was officially finished in August 1994. At an on-site inspection in November 1994, the railway was not working because there was still no cargo to carry and almost no ships docking. New construction was underway in the harbour area because the quay had to be brought up to international standards, according to Mr Li Ka-Shin. More cranes had also been purchased and he had started to bring in his own people from Hong Kong to administer the port.

Mr Li Ka-Shin now owned 70 per cent of the rights to operate the port. He purchased this right for 1.8 billion Hong Kong dollars. This is approximately equal to 70 per cent of the total construction cost.[54] Dongpeng Industries has retained 30 per cent ownership of the port[55] and seemed satisfied with the deal, convinced that the harbour will become a profit-making enterprise and that it will be able to commence loan repayments to Japan in ten years' time. Meanwhile, Dongpeng Industries were considering what to do with its personnel and their money. Many people were now out of work since the Hong Kong people had taken over. The Japanese Loan Aid office could not remain forever either since the project is now officially finished. Some of them claimed that the money received from selling the harbour would be used to develop a new satellite city linked to it. Everyone was positive that the future was bright and things could only become better and better.

NOTES

1 Figures from Japan's Ministry of Foreign Affairs, *Waga Kuni no Seifu Kaihatsu Enjo*, 1994.

2 Tong Xiangao, 'Japan's ODA and the People's Republic of China: Strategic Aid?', in Chulacheeb Chinwanno and Wilaiwan Wannitikul (eds), *Japan's Official Development Assistance and Asian Developing Economies*, Institute of East Asian Studies, Thammasat University, Bangkok, 1991.

3 Although not promising any new aid Japan had, in August 1989, already lifted its freeze on ongoing aid to China. In October that year the World Bank also resumed its lending to China for humanitarian aid. Japan was quick to follow in December by releasing $35 million of new grant aid.

4 Figures from DAC, *Annual Report 1994*.

5 Figures from Japan's Ministry of Foreign Affairs, op. cit.

6 UN Figures are different, see its *Annual Report of the Resident Coordinator for 1993*, Beijing, March 1994. Japanese bilateral aid amounted to $887 million (62 per cent of all bilateral aid) and Italian aid to $182 million (13 per cent). The trend is the same though and the difference is probably largely due to the different fiscal years where Japanese counting starts from 1 April 1992 and does not end until 31 March 1993.

7 UN *Annual Report*, op. cit.

8 According to Japan's Ministry of Foreign Affairs, op. cit., IDA (that is, the World Bank) aid amounted to $790 million.

9 Nigel Campbell, 'Japan's success in China', in Hellmut Schutte (ed.), *The Global Competitiveness of the Asian Firm*, St Martin's Press, New York, 1994.

10 Ibid.

11 Figures according to Keizai Koho Center, *Japan 1995: An International Comparison*, Keizai Koho Center, Tokyo, 1994.

12 The first six are USA, Germany, South Korea, Hong Kong, United Kingdom and Singapore according to the IMF *Direction of Trade Statistics Yearbook 1988–1994*, Washington, DC, 1995.

13 Ibid.

14 This was a programme Japan started to recycle part of the huge surplus in the trade balance.

15 Interview with official at Commercial and Development Co-operation Department, Embassy of Japan, Beijing.

16 The 69 projects comprise ten agriculture and water projects, six railway, eleven road, seven airport, three harbour, three information-telecommunication, nine energy, four subway, six city water supply, nine enviromental and one fertilizer.

17 *Far Eastern Economic Review*, 12 January 1995. Conversion to dollars is done on the 1994 rate of 102 yen to the dollar.

18 Ibid. Interview with official at Commercial and Development Cooperation Department, Embassy of Japan.

19 Interview with UNDP Representative in Beijing. Donors still meet about twice each month to exchange information and ideas about different sectors and topics.

20 Interview with representative of JICA in Beijing. In August 1995 Japan cut grant aid to China in protest at Chinese nuclear testing.
21 Interview with official at the Development Department, Shenzhen Dongpong Industry Co. Ltd.
22 This was what was stated by at least all the whitecollar people the author interviewed.
23 Interview with official at the Japanese Loan Office, Shenzhen Dongpong Industry Co. Ltd.
24 Ibid.
25 Interview with official at the Development Department, Shenzhen Dongpeng Industry Co. Ltd, op. cit.
26 JICA feasibility studies started to appear first in connection with the second yen loan package.
27 Interview with representative of JICA Beijing. According to officials at OECF in Tokyo the Chinese are very experienced in planning and no Japanese feasibility studies were done before 1985. A few have been performed since although the Chinese usually prefer to carry out their own.
28 In Japanese Kokusai Rinkai Kaihatsu Kenkyu Centa. Only Japanese engineering consultant firms were at the time eligible for work of this kind, financed by JICA.
29 A legal body under the Ministry of Communication. Approved and found qualified for this kind of job by the Ministry.
30 The grand scenario include the development of a Port District and a hinterland area of more than 30 square kilometres. This area should it was suggested, be open to warehouses, industry, commerce and residences. Around Yantian Port there should be a modern satellite town built for a population of around 100,000 people.
31 See the feasibility study for the Dapeng harbour by JICA, March 1987.
32 That is, representatives from the State Planning Commission, MOFTEC and most probably the Ministry of Communication.
33 This was the first in the third yen loan package.
34 As the value of the yen had increased. Although this sum in yen is considerably less, the amount in dollars is the same.
35 In the case of Yantian Port international shopping was also used on certain occasions.
36 The Japanese loan division was still staffed with eight people in November 1994 although the project was officially finished in August of that year (Interview with an official at the Japanese Loan Aid Division).
37 Op. cit.
38 Interview with an offfical at CNTIC.
39 Japanese Loan Aid Division, op. cit.
40 CNTIC, official, op. cit.
41 Japanese Loan Aid Division, official, op. cit.
42 CNTIC, official, op. cit.
43 Japanese Loan Aid division, official, Op. cit.
44 This is according to information from Kone Corporation.
45 Since then the company has been divided into two parts and the crane division has been sold to the Swedish company, Export Invest.
46 This part is built on information received from Kone Corporation.

47 The contract was won by the Japanese company Tomen Corporation.

48 This part is built on several interviews with Japanese and other foreign businessmen with experience in OECF-financed projects in China.

49 During the conclusion of the two case studies in November 1994, the Canadian Prime Minister Jean Cretien visited Peking together with a Canadian trade delegation of 400 people. He and Premier Li Peng attended the signing cermony of contracts worth $6.6 billion between the two countries. (see *China Daily News*, 11 November 1994).

50 Japanese Loan Aid Division, official, op. cit.

51 According to the Japanese Loan Aid Division official the last loan only amounted to ¥1.9 billion.

52 This was done after written correspondence with the authour.

53 Most ships travelling to the area still preferred Shekou, the other port in Shenzhen which is located in the industrial zone and from where there is a river on which cargo can be taken further inland.

54 That is both the local and the OECF financed parts, total estimated cost of the project was ¥35 billion.

55 Later another 5 per cent was also sold to the Danish company Maersk.

APPENDIX 7.1

Contracts for equipment at Yantian Port construction projects

Company	Country	Amount (Japanese yen)
1 China Mfrcinats (Hekou) Imp. & Exp. Corp.	China	8,869,868
2	Belgium	606,514,981
3 Eckoxa Co. Ltd	Hong Kong	77,042,360
4 China Harbour Engineering Company	China	341,600,000
5 CMEC Hunan Co. Ltd	China	5,963,340
6 Momac GmbH	Denmark	99,181,110
7 China Engineers Ltd	Hong Kong	49,180,482
8 Hoi Tung Marine Machinery Suppliers	Hong Kong	13,385,356
9 Marubeni Corp.	Japan	149,644,900
10 Heavy Equipment International Ltd	Hong Kong	17,838,043
11 Sumitomo Corp.	Japan	115,667,098
12 Sumitomo Corp.	Japan	36,283,822
13 Sumitomo Corp.	Japan	113,186,809
14 Sumitomo Corp.	Japan	183,262,203
15 China Communications Imp. & Exp. Corp.	China	50,938,620
16 China Communications Imp. & Exp. Corp.	China	272,672,334
17 China Communications Imp. & Exp. Corp.	China	292,653,934
18 China (SZ) Material & Industrial Trading Group Co. Ltd	China	9,369,000
19 Holding Luck Ltd	Hong Kong	325,159,100
20 Lucky Goldstar Int'l Corp.	Korea	53,100,000
21 Kone Corp.	Finland	432,880,000
22 Kone Corp.	Finland	1,694,110,000
23 Pacifra (Hong Kong) Co. Ltd	Hong Kong	66,081,630
24 Hefei Forklift Truck Works	China	21,319,000
25 CMEC Hunan Co. Ltd	China	18,927,392
26 CMEC Hunan Co. Ltd	China	9,242,622
27 Ekpac Engineering	Hong Kong	50,732,000
28 Hoi Tung Marine Machinery Suppliers	Hong Kong	36,822,240
29 Marubeni Corp.	Japan	130,000,000
30 Hongda Technical Imp. & Exp. Co.	China	11,415,300
31 China National Building Material & Equipment	China	22,863,600
32 Tomen Corp.	Japan	871,769,000
33 Patrick Ho Co. Ltd	Hong Kong	192,020,000

APPENDIX 7.1

Continued

Company	Country	Amount (Japanese yen)
34 Tomen Corp.	Japan	28,000,000
35 CMEC Hunan Co.	China	30,063,094
36 China Harbour Engineering Co.	China	33,581,095
37 Xian Electric Machinery Imp. & Exp. Corp.	China	305,324,000
38 Hoitung Communication & Navigation Co. Ltd	Hong Kong	126,000,000
39 Shangdong Technical Imp. & Exp. Corp.	China	116,118,000
40 Choka Trading Co.	Japan	32,830,290
41 Liaoning Machinery Imp. & Exp. Corp	China	182,829,000
42 Morf Joys (Hong Kong) Co. Ltd	Hong Kong	134,820,000
43 China National Machinery I/E Shenzhen Corp.	China	61,025,400
44 Sumitomo Corp.	Japan	192,408,000
45 Tamrock (Far East)	Hong Kong	83,791,000
46 Ekpac Engineering	Hong Kong	95,988,000
47 Ekpac Engineering	Hong Kong	92,860,000
48 Wisfchefr China Investment Ltd	Hong Kong	138,000,000
49 Patrick Ho Co. Ltd	Hong Kong	40,590,827
50 Ekpac Engineering	Hong Kong	181,888,000
51 China Communication Imp. & Exp. Corp.	China	45,500,000
52 China National Machinery I/E Shenzhen Corp.	China	70,112,722
53 China Engineers Ltd	Hong Kong	55,287,000
54 Hoi Tung Marine Machinery Supplier	Hong Kong	88,833,000
55 Humatt Engineering	UK	96,243,000
56 CMEC Hunan Co.	China	52,440,000
57 China Harbour Engineering Co.	China	139,424,000
58 Sumitomo Corp.	Japan	100,237,481
59 China National Construction & Energy Machinery	China	13,898,000

Source: CNTIC

8 Rail aid to China

*Gang Zhang**

The railway sector figures prominently in the portfolio of Japanese ODA to China given that it has attracted nearly one-third of the total OECF yen loans to China. This case study illustrates how OECF yen loan financed railway projects are administered in China by using as an example the Hengshui–Shangqiu railway project. In so doing due regard to the particularities of China's railway sector is given.

The study proceeds as follows. First, OECF yen loans to China's railway sector since 1980 are reviewed within the context of the overall railway sector including past investment spending and sources of investment. Formal procedures for railway construction and for seeking OECF loans are then described. The above-mentioned OECF railway project is studied in the subsequent two sections: the first section describes the project's history up to the finalization of loan agreements, and the second describes the procurement phase of the project including a discussion of rules and practices common for all OECF railway projects. Finally, concluding remarks are given to summarize the study.

INTRODUCTION

When China started its current modernization drive in the late 1970s, the transportation sector together with other sectors suffering from bottlenecks, such as agriculture, energy industry and communications were made strategic development priorities by the government. However, the phenomenal rate of economic growth experienced by China in the 1980s which continued into the 1990s has instead meant that the country's transport sector has been further outpaced by the economy as a whole.

Despite its efforts to modernize the transportation sector by devel-

oping more modern modes of transport such as air travel and highways during the last 15 years or so, China still relies heavily on its
railway system. The respective shares of China's major transportation
modes are given in Appendices 8.1. and 8.2. As of 1993, railway
transport was responsible for almost 40 per cent of the country's
freight transportation and 44 per cent of passengers' transport.[1]
These figures demonstrate the importance of railways in the transport
sector, although there has been a decline since 1980 when railway
transport was responsible for 48 per cent and 61 per cent, respectively.

China has a total of 53,600 km of railway lines, of which some
13,700 km are double-track lines and only 8,400 km are electrified
lines. Railway freight transport is mostly of staple goods and raw
materials, of which coal accounted for some 31 per cent, other mining
products 15 per cent and oil 4 per cent in 1992.

Each year, huge amounts of coal are transported by railway across
China, from the north to the south and from the west to the east. This
coal provides 75 per cent of China's energy consumption. From 1980
to 1993, the railway transport capacity more than doubled for both
freight and passengers. Yet it still falls behind ever-increasing
demand. For the most overloaded railway lines, for example, those
between Beijing and Guangzhou and between Beijing and Shanghai,
it is estimated that only 40 per cent of the demand for railway
transport can currently be met.

CHINA'S RAILWAY SPENDING AND SOURCES OF INVESTMENT

Because China's economy is developing rapidly, there is a huge need
for the expansion as well as the upgrading of the country's railway
system. Although the Chinese government has made transportation
construction a priority of its development strategy, investment in the
sector has still been far from sufficient. Between 1980 and 1990,
investment in the transport sector was only 1.3 per cent of China's
GDP, a level below that of other comparable countries, such as India.
Moreover, investment in transportation as a share of GNP declined in
the 1980s from 1.7 per cent to 1 per cent by 1990.[2] This trend has
reversed in the 1990s, and investment in the transportation sector has
increased to 2.6 per cent of China's GDP between 1990 and 1993.[3]

It is estimated that an investment of $47 billion in the railway
sector is required by China in the period 1994 to 2000.[4] However,
there is a lack of funds for financing this investment. China has

maintained a highly centralized railway system which is fully controlled by the central government in which the State Council, China's cabinet, sets the level of railway charges. In 1991, the central government raised the charges for freight transport from 0.0165 yuan to 0.0265 yuan per ton kilometre, while the rail fare for passengers increased 50 per cent to 0.04 yuan per kilometre in 1990. At the time these prices were set, they were only intended to cover costs, not to generate profits. By 1993, the railway system as a whole was operating at a deficit due to increased input costs coupled with a price freeze of railway charges caused by the central government's fear of pushing up the general price level. The railway system continued to operate in the red with a total loss of 7,000 million yuan in 1994.[5]

This situation means that the railway system cannot operate independently in terms of its requirements for investment funding. In the past, the railway system distributed all its profits to the central government and in return relied on the state budget for investment capital. For a period in the 1980s, the railway system was supposed to be self-financing. Construction funds were to be generated from retained profits and there would be no need for investment capital to be allocated from the state budget. However, being forced to operate at state controlled price levels resulted in insufficient investment capital.

In 1991, a special investment fund, namely the Railway Construction Fund, was established with the approval of the central government in order to generate sufficient re-investment funds within the railway system. Consequently, the railway system was allowed to add an extra charge of 0.012 yuan per ton kilometre for the Construction Fund to the standard charge for railway freights.[6] From that time onward, the railway system started to draw investment capital from the Fund. The surcharge increased to 0.027 yuan, giving a total of 0.0535 yuan per ton kilometre, in 1992, and has remained at that level to this day.

This source of funding is estimated to cover 65 per cent of the above-mentioned $47 billion equivalent worth investment required for railway development to the year 2000. Thus, there is a shortfall in available development funds. Foreign capital is assessed to provide some 5 per cent of the total estimated investment need. However, the lack of market pricing mechanisms in the railway system have been, and will continue to be, a deterrent to direct foreign investment in railway construction. Despite the emerging possibility that foreign investors may be allowed to own a stake in the local railway lines, the national railway system is, in principle, not ready to open to foreign direct investments in the near future.

Therefore, the foreign capital that China needs for the railway system can only be raised through foreign borrowing. Multilateral international organizations, especially the World Bank and Asian Development Bank (ADB), have provided a major part of the foreign capital for infrastructure construction while commercial loans accounted for a marginal share in total foreign capital inflow.[7] With regard to bilateral aid to China, Japan, which contributed 50.1 per cent of it in 1991, is of particular importance.

JAPANESE OECF YEN LOANS TO RAILWAY SECTOR

There is an apparent priority with Japanese ODA given to China's transportation sector. It has absorbed 53.6 per cent of the cumulative total OECF yen loans to China as of March 1993.[8] In terms of total project numbers, the transportation sector accounted for 11 of the total 23 projects of the first two OECF yen loan packages, and 24 out of 42 projects in the third one.[9]

Within the transportation sector, railway construction, which claims 58.7 per cent of total loans, is given a further priority for Japanese OECF yen loan aid to China. The Japanese government has provided loans and technical assistance for railway constructions in China since 1979.[10] Japanese OECF yen loans to China started in April 1980.[11] In cumulative terms, Japan alone claims financial responsibility for 4,407 km (part of it is still under construction) of either newly built railway lines or electrification of existing lines during the period from 1981 to 1995. There are 2,735 km electrified rail lines included in the total of these rail lines financed by the OECF yen loans, accounting for 25 per cent of the 10,875 kilometres electrified during that period. Of the total $9.69 billion (¥1,610.9 billion) OECF yen loans granted to China in the 15 years up to 1994, nearly $2.65 billion (¥440 billion) or, 27 per cent, have been for railway construction.[12]

There is a long list of railway construction projects that are financed by OECF yen loans. Major projects are listed in Appendix 8.3.

There is speculation about the rationale for the absolute priority that Japan gave to yen loans granted to China's transport/railway sector. According to previous studies, when Japan began giving ODA loans to China in 1979, it had been severely affected by two oil crises and had gained a renewed understanding of the importance of coal supply to its economy.[13] Based on its understanding of the significance of China for its own coal supply, Japan intentionally made the first yen loan package (1980–85) focus on coal transportation from the coal-rich Shanxi province to the Qinhuangdao port, which is not only one of the major harbours to Japan, but is also located in the old Manchuria area. Later OECF yen loan packages also focused on the expansion of railway coal transport capacity. Such a purposeful and persistent application of OECF yen loans has improved railway coal transport capacity directly between the coal-producing regions to the major outlets on the east coast of China.

The decision of the Japanese Government in giving the first (¥50 billion) OECF loan to China in 1979 was subsequently explained at a later occasion by the Japanese Foreign Minister in the following manner. The construction of the Datong to Qinhuangdao railway, the modernization of the Qinhuangdao port, and the construction of the railway between Yanzhou and the Shijiusou port in the Shandong peninsula are all aimed at transporting coal from the inner regions, and hence it (that is, Japan's policy of giving ODA loans to China) will, among other things, assist in the supplying of coal from China to Japan.[14] It is, of course, also closely related to Japan's energy policy, the Foreign Minister concluded.[15]

The focus of Japanese OECF loans on the development of China's coal transport capabilities is obvious, and that Japan has had a vested interest in this development, was well understood by the Chinese. However, it was never mentioned by Chinese officials in interviews for this case study. It may be too sensitive to comment on such a matter, but a more likely explanation is that Japan's self-interest with the application of OECF yen loans is passively accepted by the Chinese, at least for the time being. If this interpretation is correct, it suggests that China has not only accepted Japanese OECF yen loans as aid, but also as business, in accordance with the principle of reciprocal benefits.[16]

RAILWAY CONSTRUCTION PROCEDURES IN CHINA

As mentioned earlier in this study, the railway system is highly centralized in China, and so too is the procedure for railway construction. There are some standard railway construction procedures that apply to all cases including those financed by OECF yen loans. Given that the administration of a OECF yen loan is effectively an additional part to the standard process, it is useful to start with the general procedures before examining OECF yen loan financing in this case study. The formal railway construction procedures that have been in force since 1990 in China include the following phases.[17]

1 A preliminary feasibility study (P F/S) of the proposed project is carried out by one of the engineering and design institutes under the Ministry of Railways (MOR). The Department of Planning at MOR then performs an on-site investigation to evaluate the P F/S. The P F/S is then submitted by MOR to the Department of Transportation and Department of Borrowing at the State Planning Commission (SPC) for consideration on whether to initiate the project.

2 SPC entrusts China International Construction Consulting Company with the task of evaluating the P F/S of proposed railway projects. SPC bases its appraisal of the P F/S primarily on the consultation report prepared by the consulting company.

   If the project is a major construction in terms of investment size, degree of technical complexity, or practically any railway construction more than 200–300 kilometres in length, the P F/S (with the recommendation of SPC) is subsequently submitted by MOR to the State Council (SC) for approval. The approval document, among other things, specifies the gross total sum of the investment and divides the source of financing between domestic and foreign sources, if the project is to be financed with foreign capital. When foreign financing is involved, only the projects on the five-year state development plan are to be considered for funding.

3 Upon approval by the SC, the formal feasibility study is carried out and is submitted to MOR and SPC, and, if necessary, to SC for approval. The procedure for requesting OECF yen loan formally begins at this stage.

4 After the formal feasibility study is approved by SPC and SC, SPC issues a ratification document to MOR to enable it to begin preliminary design work, including estimates of total costs, time schedules for start and completion of construction, designs of preparatory work, such as access roads, construction premises on-site, etc. [The preliminary designs must be evaluated by an appraisal mission which involves various departments of MOR and is administered by the Technical Appraisal Center (TAC), an authorized body under MOR for performing technical appraisal of railway constructions.]

5 Detailed technical designs are prepared on-site, and must be submitted for appraisal by the TAC appraisal mission.

6 Construction working designs, including working drawings, time frames for the construction work, etc., are prepared and evaluated by the TAC appraisal mission.

7 Construction commences.

PROCEDURES FOR OBTAINING OECF YEN LOANS FOR RAILWAY PROJECTS

The request, approval and use of OECF yen loans for railway construction projects follow the general procedure outlined in Chapter 7. For railway projects, the Foreign Capital and Technical Import Office (FCTIO) at the Ministry of Railways is in charge of foreign capital financing, and some officials in this office specialize in the administration of Japanese OECF yen loans.

At the government level, the procedure is a well-organized planning process. The SPC plans the allocation of OECF yen loans between sectors in terms of the total five-year commitment by the Japanese government, and informs MOR and other ministries in advance about the availability of OECF yen loans for the railway and other sectors. Based on this information, MOR then prepares a yen loan credit plan for a selected number of railway projects and submits it to SPC. The yen loan credit plans from MOR and other ministries are amended and finalized at SPC. A list of projects to be proposed by the Chinese government for OECF yen loan funding is finalized after the above process. The SPC and Ministry of Foreign Trade and Economic Co-operation (MOFTEC), on behalf of the Chinese Government, officially approaches the Japanese Government through its Embassy in Beijing to request OECF loans for the proposed projects.

On the Japanese side, the proposed projects are preliminarily examined by OECF. Then a Japanese Government mission formed by representatives from the Four Ministries as well as an observer from OECF, holds meetings with a Chinese delegation from SPC and MOFTEC to discuss these projects.[18] In such formal meetings the Ministry of Railways is involved only to the extent of answering queries on specific issues concerning the railway project under discussion.

At the project level, the request for foreign funding to the potential lenders, as designated by the SPC, commences when the formal feasibility study of a proposed project is completed. In the case of Japanese OECF yen loans, the formal feasibility study together with other loan application documents are submitted to the OECF Beijing Representative Office by MOFTEC.

These documents are then forwarded to OECF headquarters in Tokyo for appraisal. An appraisal mission is formed, normally consisting of a technical expert in the field concerned and an economist, and sent to China to evaluate the formal feasibility study in terms of technical, economic, and social effects as well as the repayment ability of the proposed project. If the appraisal mission recommends the project for approval and an OECF loan is arranged, prior notification is sent by the Japanese Government to the official borrower, that is, MOFTEC, of the decision. Thereafter, an Exchange of Notes, which often covers a number projects rather than just one project in the case of China, is signed between the two governments.

A formal loan agreement between OECF and MOFTEC on behalf of the two governments is then signed for the given railway project. The size of the loan and other conditions are specified in the loan agreement. Subsequently, SPC issues a 'red-heading' decree to the MOR specifying finally the amount of foreign capital permitted for actual use in the given project.[19]

FCTIO at MOR then takes over the responsibility for executing the loan agreement. It co-operates with OECF local officials in the implementation phase and its main duties include the organization of international bidding for procurement, assistance of the OECF officials in monitoring the use of OECF yen loans and reporting of the project's progress, amendment of loan agreements on a yearly basis in connection with the preparations for releasing funds in coming years, etc.

In general, MOR considers the OECF yen loans more suitable for railway construction projects than other loans due to its low interest rate and the long repayment period. The OECF yen loans have a much lower interest rate at between 3.25 to 2.5 per annum than, for instance, the World Bank loans, which carry interest rates just slightly below the market rate.[20]

As important as the low interest rate for MOR is the OECF's repayment scheme, which is normally 30 years including a period of grace of 10 years. It is particularly helpful for railway projects since the construction of railways always takes a few years, and the new railway line normally requires some years before it can operate smoothly and produce profits. The total time required from the construction start to the beginning of profitability takes on average seven years in China, according to MOR.

THE HENGSHUI–SHANGQIU RAILWAY CONSTRUCTION PROJECT

The Hengshui–Shangqiu Railway, hereafter referred to as the H–S railway, is 400 km long from Hengshui in Hebei Province to Shangqiu in Henan Province (see Map 8.1). It is a small part of the major railway construction project between Beijing and Jiulong (that is, Kowloon, Hong Kong), named the Great Jing-Jiu railway. Since the H–S railway is part of this larger main railway project, it may be helpful to study the history of the Great Jing-Jiu railway project before examining the H–S railway project itself.

History of Great Jing-Jiu railway project

The history of the Great Jing-Jiu railway project dates back to the late 1970s.[21] In 1978, the MOR started planning for the construction of a railway between Beijing and Jiujiang (Jiangxi Province), which was later nicknamed, the Little Jing-Jiu railway. In August 1982, MOR submitted a proposal to the State Planning Commission requesting approval to start design work for the planned railway construction.[22] In the proposal, the importance and necessity for construction of the new railway were assessed on the basis of growth forecasts of increased demand for railway transportation between the south and north along the new line. Furthermore, the technical standard of the new rail line was suggested as well as the estimated amount of investment required.

The proposal was approved by the State Council in July 1983. The Little Jing-Jiu railway project was thus included in the seventh five-year state plan between 1985–90, and pre-phase preparatory work was carried out. However, since MOR at that time lacked the funding needed for main railway construction, the project had to be shelved.

As the Chinese economy continued to develop, the need for fundamentally enlarged railway transport capacity was strongly voiced by local governments, and the plan for the Little Jing-Jiu railway received strong support from the provinces that were to benefit from it. For several reasons that are discussed below, the planned railway project was extended to Jiulong (Kowloon, Hong Kong) instead of the original destination at Jiujiang. Thus, the nickname Little Jing-Jiu railway is used to refer to the original plan and the Great Jing-Jiu railway to refer to the present project (see Map 8.2).

In October 1990, MOR submitted to SPC the proposal for the Great Jing-Jiu railway, which is 2,370 km long excluding (until 1997) a 30 km

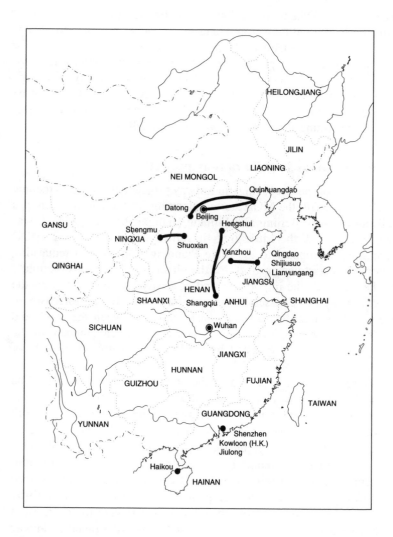

Map 8.1 Hengshui-Shangqiu railway and major OECF-financed coal transport projects in China

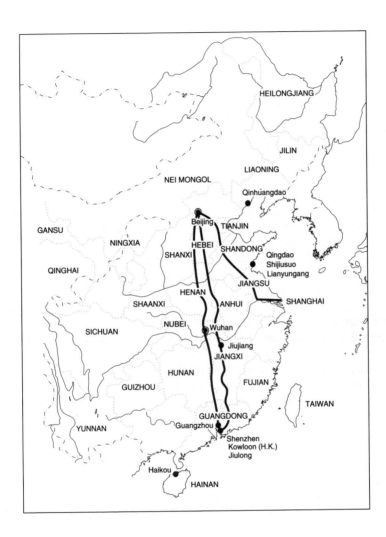

Map 8.2 Little Jing-Jiu and Great Jing-Jiu railways

section between Shengzhen and Jiulong and has a total budgeted cost of 21.2 billion yuan.[23] The proposal was further submitted by SPC to the State Council, which gave its approval to SPC in February 1992. SPC, in turn, approved the project advising MOR in March 1992 of its decision.

While the proposal took time to work its way through the various bureaucratic layers and approval steps, on the basis of the preparatory work done previously, the construction of the new railway started from the 10-km Sunhekuo bridge on the Yellow River in 1991. Gradually, the construction of all ten sections of the Great Jing-Jiu railway, excluding the part between Shengzhen and Jiulong, was started. The entire project is to be completed by the end of 1995, and trial operations are expected to begin in 1996.

There are a number of significant reasons for China's decision to construct the Great Jing-Jiu railway at this time. First, the booming economy of the coastal regions is facing constraints, especially regarding coal supply, caused by limited transportation capacity and the expansion in the exchange of goods and raw materials between the developed south and resource-rich north. Second, the existing hub national railway lines connecting the south and the north namely, Beijing–Shanghai line and Beijing–Guangzhuo line, are critically overloaded. The southern section of Beijing–Guangzhuo line, for example, has transport capacity of just 60 per cent of demand.[24] Even a temporary breakdown due to excessive burdens placed on the railway would be catastrophic, with severe economic and other consequences. Lastly, the return of Hong Kong to China after 1997 and the accompanying economic and political considerations underlie China's determination to construct a railway direct to Hong Kong.

History of the Hengshui–Shangqiu railway project

Since the H–S railway was part of the plan for the Little Jing-Jiu railway project in the 1980s, much of the pre-phase preparatory work was already completed at that time. In 1990, within the framework of the Great Jing-Jiu railway project, the H–S railway project was approved by the State Council. Meanwhile, design work started in February 1990. Technical designs were finished in June 1991 and all other design work was completed by August 1992. The design work was carried out by the No. 3 Design Institute of MOR located in Tianjin.

The construction teams broke ground at the Sunhekuo Yellow River Bridge in 1991, and gradually the work proceeded to the full extent of the railway line. Apart from the Sunhekuo Bridge, the H–S railway is completed and was scheduled to open for traffic in 1995. Construction has been divided between several companies, all of which belong to MOR's organization. Since local economies adjacent to the new railway line will benefit from the railway, its construction has been facilitated by direct local government participation in issues such as land acquisition and other local supplies.[25] Environmental issues, which more often than not cause problems with the implementation of large infrastructure projects in other countries, are not reported as creating problems to the Great Jing-Jiu railway. This is due in part to the fact that railway transport, especially with electrified lines, is relatively environment friendly, and partly to the fact that environmental issues are not yet a priority on the development planner's agenda in China.[26]

The OECF yen loan financing

In May 1989, a formal feasibility study of the H–S railway project was submitted to OECF as part of a request for yen loan financing.[27] It is evident that the feasibility study submitted to OECF at that time was a different version than the one that the Chinese themselves were using.[28] The fact that the one submitted to OECF was different suggests two possibilities: the OECF version was adapted to specific OECF requirements for format and contents; or it was a special 'tailor-made' version to make the project appear more in line with the criteria for OECF yen loan financing.[29] The latter possibility implies that there could be substantial deviations between the two feasibility studies.

It is noteworthy, however, that unlike most other ODA recipient countries, China has demonstrated strong technical capability when carrying out feasibility studies and technical designs for its OECF loan financed projects.[30] It is commonly recognized, as will be shown in this case study, that China is not only able to only carry out its own preparatory work, but it also has the experience and technical competence to implement projects. This is a country-specific factor that applies to most of the OECF yen loan projects in China.[31]

The significance of the H–S railway project becomes obvious when it is understood that it is considered to be a section of the most crucial railway project for China's economic development. To the Chinese officials, the Great Jing-Jiu railway is the most important railway project in the eighth Five-year Plan. This viewpoint is the underlying reason for the H–S railway being financed by OECF yen loans. When asked why the H–S railway project received OECF yen loans, the interviewed official of MOR instead discussgd the importance of the Great Jing-Jiu railway. It seems natural for government officials to assume a parallel between the priorities of Chinese government's five-year plan and that of Japanese OECF yen loans. To them, the H–S project exists only in relation to OECF yen loans, otherwise it is merely a part of the Great Jing-Jiu project.

It appears that the Japanese ODA to China has given priority to China's five-year development plans[32] or, at least, this has been the case regarding OECF yen loans for infrastructure constructions.[33] Officially, however, the OECF states the purpose of the H–S railway project as expansion of the coal transport capacity from the coal producing areas, a similar purpose to other OECF railway projects in China.[34]

Since discrepancies appear within the Japanese official publications as well as between the Chinese and Japanese interpretations, further enquiries were made in interviews with Chinese officials regarding the importance of H–S railway construction to coal transport. As it turns out, the opinions of MOR's officials on this matter are as divided as the Japanese. The FCTIO believes that the construction of the H–S railway is not at all for the sake of coal transport, particularly as coal transport capacity has been satisfactorily improved by the construction of the two special coal transport rail lines extending directly to the expanded harbour facilities at Qinhuangdao and Shijiusuo (Rizhaogang) port (see Map 8.1). The Planning Department of MOR, however, appears to have a different understanding and points to the two following explanations. First, although the capacity of the new special coal transport rail line between Datong and Qinhuangdao is as high as 100 million tons per year, it is still inadequate to meet demand. Second, whereas the new special coal transport rail lines have eased the crisis with coal transport from the north to the eastern coast of China, the Great Jing-Jiu railway, of which the H–S railway is a section, is particularly useful for enhancing the railway coal transport capacity between the north and the southern provinces, such as, Guangdong, Fujian, and Jiangxi, where economic development has been most rapid.

Beyond these differences in opinions, it seems clear that (1) coal transport is not the primary reason for the Chinese government building the H–S railway, especially when it is considered as being separate from the Great Jing-Jiu railway project; (2) an enhanced coal transport capacity is certainly to be a *de facto* underlying benefit derived from the new railway, including the H–S section. Thus, the fundamental difference in views of the various parties can be summarized as being the relative importance of coal transport attached to the construction of the H–S railway. Whether OECF's genuine opinion of the purpose of the H–S railway project is stated in its annual report, in which case it seems to be a partial opinion, or if coal transport is mentioned in the report to serve some other purposes, is difficult to tell from the information available.[35]

As specified in the OECF document, the subject of the OECF yen loan financing is the construction of 400 kilometres of non-electrified single-track railway between Hengshui to Shangqiu. The design of the railway was later changed by the Chinese authorities to a double-track railway. OECF did not object to this change. The expansion from single- to double-track construction was partially financed by a loan from the Asian Development Bank. This gives the project the appearance of a collaboration between the Chinese government, the OECF of Japan, and the ADB rather than a OECF yen loan project to China.

The loan agreements

The total sum of the OECF yen loan for the H–S railway project is ¥23,603 million ($187.4 million) bearing an annual interest rate of 2.5 to 2.6 per cent.[36] The total investment of the project is ¥80,785 million ($649.7 million), of which the OECF yen loan provides close to one-third and the domestic portion is two-thirds.[37]

The OECF yen loan financing is divided into four parts, for which there are four loan agreements (LA). The first loan was scheduled for 1990, but the loan agreement was not signed until 1991.[38] Consequently, there were two loans in 1991, and then one in 1992 and another in 1993. The loan agreement proceedings are summarized in chronological order in Appendix 8.4 of the study. The OECF yen loans provide for the provision of steel products, rails, sleepers, construction machinery, and survey and drawing instruments.

After the construction of the H–S railway began, MOR signed another loan agreement with the Asian Development Bank (ADB) to borrow $200 million in addition to the OECF yen loans. The borrowing was made for the double-track expansion of the original design. The loan from ADB was to finance the purchase of rail, signal system equipment and railway maintenance machinery.

THE PROCUREMENT PHASE

This section contains two parts.[39] First, the general rules and common practices of procurement for all OECF yen loan financed railway projects are addressed.[40] The second part illustrates the case of the H–S railway construction during the procurement phase.

General rules and practices

OECF yen loans to the railway sector, as was the case in China generally, were tied or partially tied during the first yen loan package (1980–84) and the second yen loan package (1985–89). During the periods of first and second yen loan packages, purchases of computers, consulting services and electric engine locomotives were tied to Japanese suppliers. These conditions were to some extent relaxed during the second loan package. Since 1992, all OECF yen loans to China have become generally untied and procurement using OECF yen loans must, by OECF regulations, be handled through international competitive bidding (ICB).[41]

In the implementation phase, two types of contracts, one for construction work and one for procurement utilizing OECF yen loans, are to be conducted through competitive bidding. Although competitive bidding is used for identifying contractors for construction work, this competition has been only between construction companies within the system of MOR. Thus, the competition is not international, but only internal. Reasons for this are twofold. First, China's railway system is still closed, possessing its own huge construction arm, and construction companies outside the MOR system have not yet been allowed to compete with it. Second, the companies within the MOR system have always specialized in railway construction, and this specialization implies technological and cost advantages over other potential competitors.

Unlike contracts for construction work, contracts for procurement using OECF yen loans must be concluded through international competitive bidding. The FCTI at MOR assumes the overall responsibility for ICB of railway projects. The actual conduct of the ICB is handled by a procurement agent. For an OECF yen loan project, the choice of procurement agent is restricted to one of three state-owned foreign trade corporations under MOFTEC; namely China National Technology Import and Export Corporation (CNTIC), China National Machinery Import and Export Corporation (CNMIEC), also known as CMC outside China, and the China National Industrial Machinery

Import and Export Corporation (CNIMIEC), a subsidiary of CNMIEC. These companies, which are state monopolies in designated areas of import and export businesses, are the ones that are accepted by OECF to work as procurement agents for its projects in China. There are divisions in each of these companies that specialize in the procurement of OECF yen loan financed projects.[42]

The monetary value of all OECF yen loan financed procurement is divided as a proportional share, 70, 20 and 10 per cent between CNTIC, CNMIEC and CNIMIEC, respectively.[43] In terms of the number of projects, seven of the eight OECF yen loan financed railway projects implemented by MOR was handled by CNTIC and only one by CNMIEC. OECF's restriction on the number of procurement agents and its acceptance of MOFTEC's administrative appointment of procurement agents for OECF projects are directly responsible for the above situation as well as for the consequences of this system that are illustrated below.

An unhappy arranged marriage

MOR cannot select a procurement agent by itself for an OECF yen loan railway project, but rather it is MOFTEC that decides. The Planning Division of FCTIO at MOR is responsible for preparing a shopping list for each OECF yen loan railway project. The shopping list is then sent to the Fifth Division, Department of Foreign Financing Administration at MOFTEC, which appoints either CNTIC or CNMIEC as the procurement agent for the project. This arrangement of principal–agent relationship is ironically called an 'Arranged Marriage' by MOR. Apparently, MOR is often unhappily 'married' and appears to be suffering from it in all aspects.

Ailing relations and ill effects

There are a number of ill effects of this arrangement, according to MOR. The present system impedes competition between agents and it creates disputes and problems between MOR, MOFTEC and the procurement agent. Disagreements and problematic relations tend to cause procurement delays, which may slow the progress of construction. MOR complains that the worst aspect of this arrangement is that since the agent is not appointed by them as the purchaser, it tends not to be loyal to and responsible for their interests. Instead, it often acts as if it were an agent for the sellers. The long-time monopoly of the two companies conducting procurement for OECF yen loan financed projects has led to the building of personal relationships with the companies bidding for the contracts. This directly affects the outcome of the ICB.

The way that procurement is handled in China is apparently rooted in China's state monopoly of foreign trade and in its legacy as a former planned economy. These are the country-specific factors that distinguish China from many other, more market-oriented, ODA recipient counties. It appears that the situation in China can be improved if OECF made changes in its policy so that more competition is introduced in this business, and procurement agents for OECF yen loan projects are no longer assigned administratively.[44]

Yearly reunion of unhappy couples

Although MOR, MOFTEC and the procurement agent can often find themselves in an unpleasant, troublesome and rather sensitive relationship, they nevertheless must often meet each other during each procurement phase since OECF railway projects are usually divided into several years. Based on the progress of construction, MOR routinely submits the following year's shopping lists for ongoing railway projects to OECF for approval. To secure the funding needed to proceed with procurement, however, MOR must rely on MOFTEC to request that OECF release the portion of loans necessary for the coming year. OECF sends the appraisal missions to inspect the progress of ongoing projects. Based on an evaluation of the progress of these projects and the submitted shopping lists, the yearly portion of loans is approved by OECF at the formal request of MOFTEC. The yearly portion approved can be utilized at any time during the following five years. This is, in principle, how OECF railway projects are divided within the procurement phase.

The process is time-consuming and occasionally the yen loans are not made available in time to keep up with the progress of construction. These loan delays further affect the progress of construction, requiring MOR to either draw on its own financial resources and material provisions or to find temporary remedies to reduce the impact caused by the delays. Complaints about OECF's delay in loan approval were purposefully voiced by an MOR official during an interview for this study.

Organization of ICB

Responsibility for organizing ICB formally lies with the procurement agent.[45] Each ICB includes a number of contracts, and both the procurement agent and OECF prefer them to be large contracts because too many small contracts would mean too much work. For instance, with the H–S railway project each steel contract is for at least 9,000 tons, or $3 million. There is no pre-qualification required for foreign companies, though the possession of export and import licences is a minimum requirement for Chinese companies to participate.

Preparation of bidding documents

There are two major sections in every bidding document: one technical and one commercial. The commercial section is always prepared by the procurement agent, and the technical part is, in principle, prepared by different end-users depending on the products in question. For procurement of building materials, the technical section can be prepared either by China Railway Materials Import and Export Corporation under MOR or by the material procurement department of the construction contractor. When it concerns the procurement of machinery, the technical bidding document is prepared by the actual end-users, that is, the ones that are to use the purchased machinery and equipment. Tenders must be submitted within 40 days for materials and 60 days for machinery and equipment.

Evaluating the tenders

The evaluation process may take up to six months, depending on the nature of procurement, but in most cases the process requires three months. First, the three foremost tenders, on a comprehensive basis, are selected. Then the procurement agent and, in the case of machinery procurement, end-users discuss the tenders with each of the three companies short-listed. The discussion is followed by on-site inspections of product quality of these potential suppliers. Finally, the procurement agent and end-users evaluate the tenders behind closed doors.

Tenders are always evaluated on both technical and commercial terms. The procurement agent is responsible in all cases for carrying out commercial evaluation. Technical evaluation for the procurement of materials is also done by the procurement agent with normally no participation by MOR or end-users. In the case of machinery procurement, end-users, that is, those having prepared the bidding documents, make technical evaluations of the tenders. In this case, MOR may also participate in the evaluation to control product quality and to ensure compatibility between machinery. End-users make the final decision, though other participants' opinions can also be essential to that decision.

Price is an important factor, but not the only factor in the evaluation. Other factors, including performance, technical standards and qualifications of the producers, are also taken into account. For example, among all manufacturers and sub-contractors specified in the tender documents, CNMIEC prefers larger to smaller companies.[46] Although previous tenders are not used as a reference in evaluation, the performance of previous contractors is actually assessed in connection with the evaluation of their present tenders. Thus, there is clearly a reputation effect derived from the name, size and past performance of different contractors. Although all these factors may give rise to bias in evaluation results, the use of a company's past performance as a reference in evaluation is justifiable, while the use of its name and size is not.

Appraisal of tender evaluation

For machinery procurement, the result of tender evaluation is subject to approval by the Machinery and Electric Appraisal Office (MEAO) under the State Council. A senior appraisal mission formed by representatives of MOFTEC, SPC and MEAO checks the tender evaluation results. This process normally takes no more than one day.

Approval of procurement contracts

In accordance with the results of the tender evaluation, procurement contracts are signed between the procurement agent with OECF authorization and the company winning the tender. All procurement contracts must be approved by OECF. For contracts below ¥500 million (approximately $5.1 million by the 1994 exchange rate), the OECF Beijing Representative Office has the authority to approve them. Above this amount, contracts have to be reported to OECF headquarters in Tokyo for approval. The process typically takes half a month in Beijing, or otherwise a month in Tokyo.[47]

The procurement for the H–S railway project

The procurement agent for the H–S railway project is CNMIEC, which has only been assigned one out of eight OECF yen loan financed railway projects. CNMIEC believes it was chosen this time because the H–S railway project is not a very big project. Insofar as CNMIEC's fortunes in receiving OECF projects is concerned, the company's frustration at receiving so few projects was observed during interviews and reflected in the lack of pride exhibited by its staff, especially when compared to the evident self-confidence of CNTIC employees.[48]

The H–S railway project has so far had seven ICB's and one more is scheduled for mid-1995 (see Appendix 8.5). At the conclusion of the first seven ICBs, 80 per cent of procurement value was expended on materials, such as, steel, cement, timber, etc., and only 20 per cent for machinery and equipment. The same proportions between materials, of which 70 per cent is steel, and machinery and equipment should apply for final procurement value.

Each time an ICB is held, tenders are called for more than ten contracts. From the procurement agent's point of view, it is better to have more contracts than less in each ICB, in order to reduce the agent's work as well as to decrease operating costs. Some 80 contracts have been handled through the first seven ICBs, and 10 more contracts are to be signed by the ICB in 1995. In the end, there will be a total of 90 contracts concluded by ICBs.[49]

International shopping (IS) is used by the procurement agent for purchasing materials of low value or in small quantities. In such cases, CNMIEC sends enquiries to known international suppliers and assigns the contract to the one willing to supply needed goods at a reasonable price. CNMIEC prefers IS as a procurement method to ICB because it saves about 10 per cent in operational costs by this method. However, OECF does not accept large-quantity procurement through IS.

The total contract value is distributed into 40 per cent Chinese suppliers and 60 per cent foreign suppliers. This pattern of contract value distribution closely follows the average pattern of 30 versus 70 per cent between Chinese and foreign companies for all OECF yen projects handled by CNMIEC. As much as 70 per cent of the foreign portion, equivalent to more than 40 per cent of the total contract value, has been awarded to Japanese companies. In fact, it can be stated that the Chinese and Japanese companies have split the total contract value with approximately 40 per cent for each, leaving the remaining 20 per cent or so to companies of other nationalities.

Chinese companies have had an advantage in competing for contracts of low-tech building materials as well as ordinary construction machinery and equipment, while Japanese companies, among other things, have been very competitive in rail contracts. A much-cited example of a Japanese company awarded a major contract is Sumitomo's rail contract won in early 1994, worth $32 million. Sumitomo's contract was no less than 14.3 per cent of the total OECF yen loans for the whole project, and in the OECF annual report for 1993, Sumitomo is listed as the principal contractor of the H–S railway project.[50]

All procurement contracts are subject to OECF approval, and OECF has not just rubber stamped contract recommendations. It checks and sometimes queries contracts. In the procurement phase of the H–S project, for example, OECF contacted the procurement agent to enquire about two contracts for similar products, one of which was awarded to a Japanese company and the other to a Korean company. It is understood that the OECF representative was concerned about why both contracts were not awarded to the same company, presumably the Japanese one. It was told by the procurement agent that although the products were all steel plates, one was thin and the other was thick, and that each of the two companies in question excelled in making only one kind of plate. The OECF Beijing office accepted the explanation and did not reject the contracts.[51] It remains an open question as to whether this incident shows that OECF carries out its duties seriously, or if it also shows that OECF tries to serve the interest of Japanese industries in its programme.

CONCLUDING REMARKS

The Chinese railway sector, which has absorbed close to one-third of the total OECF yen loan to China since 1980, is an important recipient of Japanese ODA to China. Furthermore, the Japanese OECF yen loan has particularly focused on the enlargement of railway coal transport capacity to the major harbours on the east coast of China. Admittedly, the expansion and technical upgrading of coal transport facilities are badly needed in China. It has nevertheless been noted, by Chinese scholars and by Japanese politicians, that the emphasis of OECF loans on the construction of railway coal transport lines is partially motivated by the Japanese interest in paving the way for coal exports from China. Japan's pursuit of its vested interest in the OECF yen loan funded railway construction projects is an interesting subject worthy of further research effort.[52]

The railway sector is still highly centralized and regulated in China, and there are standard planning procedures for establishing railway construction projects. Due to the level of centralization and to the nature of infrastructure investment, railway construction projects are normally listed in China's five-year development plans and are subject to approval by China's State Council. This implies that the OECF yen loans to the railway sector are generally confined to the projects on the Chinese government five-year plans. This characterizes the way in which OECF yen loan financed railway projects have been generated in China.

The H–S railway project is a 400-km-long section of the new Great Jing-Jiu railway line. The original plan for constructing a railway between Beijing and Jiujiang (Jiangxi Province), which was later referred as the Little Jing-Jiu railway, was first initiated in the late 1970s. However, it was shelved due to lack of funding until 1990. The present project, the Great Jing-Jiu railway, which is an expansion based on the little Jing-Jiu railway, is a 2,380-km-long railway line between Beijing to Jiulong (Kowloon, Hong Kong). The project is a top priority of China's eighth Five-year Plan between 1990 to 1995.

From the Chinese point of view, the H–S railway project is part of the vital railway construction project in China's current five-year plan and, therefore, it is financed partially by OECF yen loans. However, OECF stresses that the purpose of this railway project is to strengthen the coal transport capacity of China, hence its yen loan finance. The coal transport argument may be a true statement, or it may only be rhetorical signalling issues other than 'coal transport' in Japanese ODA politics with China. In either case, the H–S railway project seems to indicate that OECF is, in effect, confined to the Chinese five-year plan when it comes to the choice of which railway projects to finance in China.[53]

The fact that China has a strong sovereign government with technical capabilities and experience in development planning has enabled it to perform an active role in influencing Japanese ODA to China. It is commonly recognized, as is shown by the present case, that China demonstrates an unusual ability to perform the major parts, from feasibility study to technical design to project implementation, etc., of its OECF yen loan financed projects. This stands in sharp contrast to how OECF loan projects are generated and implemented in many other recipient countries and is clearly a country factor that depicts how the yen loan based Japanese ODA projects are being implemented in China.

Only three Chinese state trading companies are designated procurement agents for OECF loans projects. MOFTEC, which represents the Chinese Government in implementing the yen loan agreements, administratively assigns one procurement agent to the agencies executing each project. This practice has some shortcomings. By designating only a few state trading companies, it strengthens the monopoly position of the state companies and this long-term monopoly tends to give rise to corruption. By administratively assigning procurement agents, it hampers competition between procurement agents, which in turn leads to lower quality services. All of this affects the fair conduct of international competitive bidding which is the basic procurement policy of OECF. OECF declines responsibility for the situation by claiming that it has never restricted the number of procurement agents for its own sake, and by attributing the present system to the Master Agreement between OECF and MOF-TEC. It has, nevertheless, failed to recognize that the current system cannot be improved unless necessary changes are made to the Master Agreement. This is where OECF has an important role to perform. Thus, there is a need for OECF to reconsider its policies in this regard.

Another area identified for improvement is OECF's procedure of loan administration which is based on yearly loan requests and appraisals for all projects, including ongoing projects. The procedure is criticized for being too complicated and time-consuming, and that occasionally loans cannot be made available for disbursement in time. Although these are only the opinions expressed by recipients, it could be useful, or at least it would not be detrimental, for OECF to listen to and evaluate these comments, if it wishes to improve efficiency in loan administration.

Japanese companies have taken home approximately 40 per cent of the total procurement contract value for the H–S railway project. This case study finds no sign indicating that the Japanese companies in this case have benefited from the fact that the project is financed by OECF yen loan.

NOTES

*   The author wishes to thank the many people interviewed during this case study, in particular those at the Ministry of Railways and the China Naional Machinery Import and Export Corporation. Excellent research

support and assistance provided by the Swedish Embassy in Beijing is acknowledged. This study has benefited from comments by Marie Söderberg and other participants in the seminars organized by the European Institute of Japanese Studies, Stockholm.

1 Figures used in this section are, unless otherwise stated, based on the report 'Zhongguo Jichu Jianshe' [China Infrastructure Construction], Peregrine, Hong Kong, May 1994.

2 See *Financial Times*, 'China must raise transport spending', 6 December 1994.

3 See Peregrine, op. cit. p. 2.

4 Ibid., p. 11.

5 *Zhongyang Ribao* [Central Daily News] (Taiwan), 13 January 1995, p. 4.

6 The railway passenger fare is not subject to the collection of the construction fund (interview with Ministry of Railways), but it is to increase by 50 per cent in 1995, as reported by *Zhongyang Ribao*, ibid.

7 As of 1994, the World Bank financed seven railway construction projects in China, six national lines and one regional line in the Inner Mongolia Autonomous Region, with a total lending of $1,699 million, interview with World Bank official (Beijing), 9 November 1994.

8 OECF, *Annual Report 1993*, p. 32.

9 OECF, official correspondence with Marie Söderberg of European Institute of Japanese Studies, Stockholm, on 21 April 1995. This source is hereafter referred to as OECF correspondence (1995).

10 Figures used in this section from here onward, unless otherwise stated, are from the Japanese Embassy in Beijing, 'Riben dui Hua Jingji Yuanzhu' [Japanese Economic Assistance to China], August 1994. This source is referred to as Japanese Embassy hereafter.

11 OECF, *Annual Report 1993*, op. cit., p. 31.

12 The total is taken from *Guoji Shangbao* (International Commercial Newspaper), *Riban Zhengfu Daikuan de Xianzhuang yu Tedian* [The Present Situation and Characteristics of Japanese Government Loans] September 1994, and hereafter *Guoji Shangbao*; and the figure for railway sector was given during the interview with an official of Ministry of Railways on 2 November 1994. Considering the appreciation of yen over the period concerned, the exchange rate (166.2 yen/dollar) used here is a 12-year average of rates from 1983 through 1994, as published in the IMF's *International Financial Statistics*.

13 See Zhang Guang 'Riyen Daikuan Lun', (Study on Japanese yen-loans) in *Riben Xue Kan* (Journal of Japanology), No. 4, 1994, pp. 48–63. Hereafter it is referred to as Zhang (1994); also see Ono, Shuishi, *Sino-Japanese Economic Relationships, Trade, Direct Investment, and Future Strategy*, p. 2, World Bank Discussion Papers No. 146, China and Mongolia Department Series, The World Bank, Washington: 1992. According to Ono (1992), one of Japan's threefold strategies towards China in late 1970s and first half of 1980s was to expand oil and coal import from China as part of its energy diversification plan.

14 China's coal export to Japan is dealt with in the framework of the Japan-China Long-term Trade Protocol signed in 1978, which concerned Japan's exports of technology, etc. to China in exchange for China's oil and coal exports to Japan. Consequently, China's coal export to Japan

increased at an annual average of 32.1 per cent during the period of 1978 to 1985, but the increase slowed down after 1985. However, despite a rise in domestic demand, coal exports to Japan increased 3.4 per cent annually between 1985 – 89. As of 1990, China's coal exports to Japan amounted to $261.6 million per year, up from $19.9 million in 1977, and accounted for 2.2 per cent in China's total export to Japan, down from 4.2 per cent in 1983, see Ono, op. cit. pp. 2, 8 and 63, respectively.

15 See Zhang (1994), op. cit., p. 61. These two remarks were cited in Chinese in Zhang (1994) and translated into English by the author of this study.

16 While having expressed disagreement about the interpretation proposed here, OECF none the less admits that '[I]t is true that Japan's ODA has not only contributed to the economic and social development of developing countries, but in the medium- and long-term, has also served for the national interest of Japan in the sense as an instrument of the foreign policy and international contribution', OECF correspondence (1995).

17 This section builds on the information gained through interviews with officials of Ministry of Railway on 2, 16, 17 November 1994.

18 The four ministries are Ministry of Foreign Affairs, Ministry of Finance, Ministry of International Trade and Industry, and Economic Planning Agency.

19 The so-called 'red-heading' decrees (*Hongduo Wenjian* in Chinese) are government documents with headings in red ink, which signifies their importance and status. Presumably, the use of the red colour is influenced by the habit of Chinese leaders who used to make endorsement in red ink on government documents. They are normally issued only by the central government for final decisions on important issues, and they have the power to govern all government agencies at all levels concerned in implementing the decisions in question.

Taking a railway construction project as an example, the MOR has no power to issue orders to the provincial governments or other ministries concerning co-ordination efforts necessary for the construction of main railways. Therefore, a decree must be issued by SPC or by SC to oversee the needed co-ordination between these government agencies.

In the present context, the function of MOFTEC and its relation with the MOR may appear unclear, and hence needs to be spelled out. Since MOFTEC is the so-called 'uniform window' in dealing, on behalf of the Chinese government, with OECF, it signs the loan agreements with OECF for all other ministries concerned, which in this case study is MOR. But MOFTEC is at the same administrative level as MOR, and hence not in the position to finally decide the size of the loans for various railway projects. That is why the red-heading decree is issued by SPC to ratify MOR about the approved sum of the yen loan for a given railway project.

20 Loans issued by the International Bank for Reconstruction and Development, the commercial lending arm of the World Bank, carry a floating interest rate of 7.8 per cent as of 1994, while the International Development Association, the development assistance arm of the World Bank, charges 1.5 per cent for lending, according to an interview with the World Bank official in Beijing, 9 November 1994.

21 Since the history of this project extends beyond 1990, from which year the new construction procedures have been in force, at some point, the history of this project may deviate from the procedures outlined in the sections 'Railway construction procedures in China' and 'Procedures for obtaining OECF yen loans for railway projects'.

22 The proposal (*Sheji Renwushu* in Chinese) is equivalent to the subsequent preliminary feasibility study of the standard procedure outlined above, but in the 1980s the document was not called by that name. Another difference is that there was no financial evaluation in the proposal previously but it is a necessary part of the preliminary feasibility study today.

23 The cost figure is taken from Peregrine (1994), op. cit., p. 8.

24 See Sun Jingzhi (ed.), *The Economic Geography of China*, Oxford University Press, New York, 1988, p. 334.

25 In fact, as the most important railway construction project for China, the Great Jing-Jiu railway has received great publicity in the media. The *People's Daily* (overseas edition), the country's biggest newspaper edition aimed at overseas readership, has opened a column on its front page for special reports on the construction of the Great Jing-Jiu railway, see, for example, *People's Daily* (overseas edition) 9 April and 4 May 1994.

26 Since the author's access to the feasibility study was denied, no assessment about to what extent and how the environment issues have been treated in it can be made.

27 It is worth noting that the request for ODA loans was made before SPC approved the whole project in 1990.

28 This is not suspicion but is based on reliable information obtained during the case study.

29 After numerous repeated efforts, neither MOR nor OECF agreed to make the feasibility study of the H–S railway project available for this study. Therefore, a comparison of the two versions is not possible.

30 This may account for why the Japanese consultant companies, which are heavily employed by other major ODA recipient countries, are not yet allowed to open an office in China, see Chapter 7 of this volume.

31 This reflects also the Japanese opinion on China's ability and performance as an ODA recipient country, see Zhang (1994), op cit., p. 62.

32 In the publication by the Japanese Embassy in Beijing, the Chinese government's eighth Five-year Plan is treated in such a manner as if it also guided Japanese ODA to China, see Japanese Embassy 1994, op. cit., pp. 17–18. In an interview with an OECF official in Beijing, the five-year plan was also cited to help explain the OECF yen loan given to the H–S railway project.

33 OECF *Annual Report*, op. cit., p. 31, states '[T]he areas covered by projects under the Third Round [OECF yen] loans – which were mainly economic infrastructure projects . . . are designated as key areas in China's eighth Five-Year Development Plan'.

34 See OECF *Annual Report 1993*, op. cit., pp. 94–5. This standpoint of OECF is further stressed by OECF correspondence (1995), op. cit.

35 What can be considered is the possibility that coal transport helps OECF to demonstrate its adherence to Japan's policy on ODA to China, which has traditionally emphasized the building of coal transport capacity in

272   *Gang Zhang*

China. Or 'coal transport' is used as a tactical device aimed at gaining better publicity for ODA at home, since to certain interest groups the phrase may spell Japanese interest.

36 See Appendix 8.4 for the amount of the four loan agreements which are added to the sum here, and for the exchange rates used in calculations.

37 The size of total investment is given in Japanese yen by OECF Beijing Office without reference to the exchange rate used between yen and yuan. The exchange rate (124.3 yen/US$) used here is an average rate based on yearly rates of 1991 to 1993 published in the IMF's *International Financial Statistics*.

38 After the political incident on 4 June 1989, the implementation of the OECF loan agreement was suspended until July 1990 when the Japanese government announced its plan to resume aid relations with China. This presumably is the background for the delay in signing the loan agreement due in 1990.

39 This section builds on the interviews with officials of MOR on 2 and 16 November 1994 and with staff of CNIMIEC on 11 November 1994.

40 While focusing on the case of railway sector, this part complements, albeit with minor overlaps, the case study on China in Chapter 7 of this volume.

41 Interview with officials of MOR on 2 November 1994; also see *Guoji Shangbao*, op. cit.

42 These are the Third Business Division of CNTIC, Business Division No. 6 of CNMIEC and two sections with 12 employees in CNIMIEC, respectively.

43 Although CNIMIEC was recently spun off to become a subsidiary of CNMIEC, the difference between them is vague and unimportant to the present study. Therefore, they are treated as one company, referred to as CNMIEC, in this study.

44 While complaining about OECF's policy in this regard, MOR praises the World Bank for not having the same regulation for appointing procurement agents. However, according to a World Bank official, most of the shopping for their projects in China has been done by three Chinese state trading companies, that is, the two mentioned above plus China National Instrument Import and Export Corporation. It shows that although not many choices can be had within the confines of the present trade regime in China, aid donors can have an impact and improve the situation by their own policies.

45 However, according to the MOR, the Procurement Division of the FCTIO at MOR shares the responsibility of organizing ICB for machinery and electrical equipment.

46 According to the CNMIEC staff interviewed on 11 November 1994.

47 According to the official of FCTIO at MOR interviewed on 16 November 1994.

48 One can actually sense the competitive tension between CNMIEC and CNTIC by talking to their employees, even though the competition does not seem to follow market rules and is, as complained about by MOR, hampered by the practice of administratively appointing procurement agents for OECF projects.

49 According to OECF Beijing Representative Office, the total number of

contracts is 100 for the H–S project divided by the four loan agreements as follows: 30/1st LA, 20/2nd LA, 30/3rd LA, 10/4th LA. The difference between the total contract number and the sum of contracts divided by the four loan agreements is presumably the number of contracts concluded through international shopping.

50 OECF *Annual Report 1993*, op. cit., p. 137. (See also appendix to the Introduction of this book) Only contractors for over ¥100 million contracts for consulting services, and over ¥1,000 million for other contracts are listed as principal contractors in the OECF *Annual Report*. Ironically, Sumitomo Beijing Office was unaware of the company's eye-catching success in the H–S railway project, as it was found out from an interview with an assistant manager at Sumitomo Beijing Office.

51 According to MOR and the procurement agent, OECF has not rejected any procurement contracts of the H–S railway project.

52 It needs to be noted that the choice of ODA projects in such context is not a zero-sum game between the interests of China and Japan. Hence, the issue of interests is not whether it is Japan or China that has benefited most from such railway projects. Instead, it is whether and to what extent Japan's vested interests have played an important role in determining ODA projects in China. However, to analyse this question is beyond the scope of this case study.

53 This does not mean that Japan has lost its control over the choice of OECF project in China totally, in which case the issue of Japanese vested interests in the railway coal transport lines would become irrelevant. Note that even on the request basis and being confined to the choices of the Chinese five-year plans, Japan is still in the position to choose the ones such that its own interests may be best served.

APPENDIX 8.1

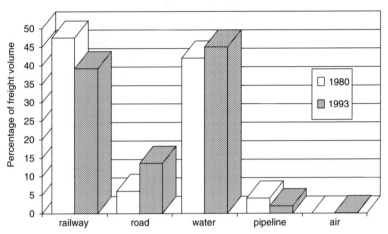

China's freight transport,1980 and 1993

APPENDIX 8.2

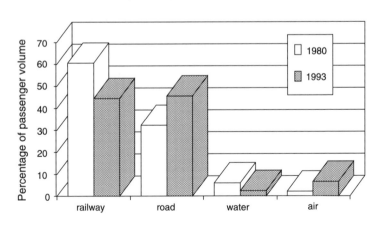

China's passenger transport,1980 and 1993

APPENDIX 8.3

Major OECF loan financed railway projects in China, 1980–94

Name and subject of projects	Implementation period(s)	Amount of approval (¥ million)	Amount of approval ($ million)
Beijing–Qinhuangdao double-track expansion and electrification (273 km)	1979–83	87,000	(367.1)
Principal coal transport line: Yanzhou–Shijiusuo (Rizhaogang port) railway (303 km) construction	1979–83	39,710	(167.6)
Hengyang–Guangzhuo railway expansion	1979–80 1984–87	81,914*	(564.9)
Zhengzhou–Baoji railway (684 km) electrification	1984–88	69,191	(540.6)
Principal coal transport rail line: Datong–Qinhuangdao (242 km) railway construction	1988–89	18,410	(133.4)
Beijing subway construction	1988–89 1991–93	17,335*	(156.2)
Shengmu–Shuo Xian coal transport railway (269 km) construction	1990–93	26,985	(243.2)
Baoji–Zhongwei railway (500 km) construction	1990–93	29,800	(268.5)
Hengshui–Shangqiu railway (400 km) construction	1990–93	23,603	(212.6)
Nanning–Kuongming railway (873 km) construction	1991–93	38,707	(348.7)
Zhangqian railway (Fujian Province) construction	1993–	6,720	(60.5)
Total		439,375	(3,063.3)

Source: Japanese Embassy in Beijing
Note: Figures in US dollars are converted by using yearly average exchange rate of the latest year shown in the table of the respective projects.
* Sum of the two implementation periods quoted

APPENDIX 8.4

Proceeding and amount of loan agreements (LA) (¥ million)

	LA I	*LA II*	*LA III*	*LA IV*
Formal request	Oct, 90	Jan, 91	Jan, 92	Nov, 92
Government mission	Oct, 90	May, 91	Mar, 92	Feb, 93
OECF appraisal mission	Oct, 90	Jun, 91	Apr, 92	Mar, 93
Exchange of Notes	Mar 15, 91	Sep 27, 91	Oct 06, 92	Aug 24, 93
Loan agreement	Mar 28, 91	Oct 04, 91	Oct 15, 92	Aug 25, 93
Amount	5,695	6,550	4,951	6,407
	(42.2)	(48.5)	(39.0)	(57.7)

Source: OECF Beijing Representative Office
Note: Figures in brackets are US dollar (million) equivalents converted by using yearly average exchange rate of the signing year of the respective loan agreement

APPENDIX 8.5

Time schedule of international competitive bidding held for H–S railway project

Serial No. of ICBs	Time
1	End 1991
2	Mid 1992
3	End 1992
4	Beginning 1993
5	Mid 1993
6	End 1993
7	Beginning 1994
8	Mid 1995 (to be held)

Source: CNMIEC, November 1994

Conclusion:

Working the two-way process

Marie Söderberg

The process of Japanese loan aid is nothing to study. Anyone interested in it can read *Operational guidelines on OECF loans*. This
document gives a detailed description of how the process works. It
is equally applied everywhere so there is no need to make case studies
in different countries. This was the initial reaction to this project
from OECF. What this research project found was something quite
different.

There is no 'one' image of how the aid process works. Instead it is
a picture with considerable variations. For instance, one loan aid
project encouraged formal democracy and forced the Philippine
government to negotiate with left-wing NGOs while another one, in
China, was sold even before the last OECF contract was signed.
Nothing of how this happened could be understood from reading
Operational guidelines on OECF loans.

It was not that OECF in Tokyo did not try to follow the guidelines.
The reason for such a varied picture is that Japanese loan aid is not a
uniform process directed from Tokyo. Aid policy is formulated in
Tokyo but at the implementation level matters become more complex. This is why, if what is actually happening in the recipient
countries is what matters, one has to leave the study of Japanese
white papers and guidelines and start looking at reality.

The recipient countries all have their own policies on how to
develop their countries as well as guidelines for how to receive aid.
Both the donor and the recipient must adjust to each others' policies
as well as to the specific circumstances surrounding each project to be
able to move it through the pipeline. Aid implementation is not
something static but a process which is formed through the interaction between the donor and the recipient.

These case studies clearly show that many of the recipient
countries exert considerable influence in the process and that aid is

not simply something given by a donor to a passive recipient, but indeed a two-way trade.

A first factor contributing to this lies in the choice of countries. These case studies were conducted in independent and relatively strong recipient countries in Asia. Besides being the main recipients of Japanese aid, they have a long history of extensive dealings with Japanese aid officials. Aid to Indonesia began with war reparations and China, with the least experience, has received aid for more than 15 years now. They all have considerable knowledge of OECF's processes and know what can be achieved within the system. They all have OECF offices located in their countries and, therefore, easy access to information as well as informal contact. These countries have gained experience over the years and in this way they have established their own processes of receiving aid.

The contact between the recipient and the donor is a close one in other fields as well. ODA is only one part of the concept of economic co-operation which also includes other official flows as well as private direct investment. Most of the recipients, with the Philippines being an exception, also have a considerable amount of Japanese private direct investment as well as trade. What is happening in these countries affects Japanese interests. This also gives the main recipients a certain amount of bargaining power. This power is demonstrated by the fact that the Japanese ODA charter is not strictly enforced on the main recipients in Asia. With the exception of Thailand, these countries have experienced war with Japan, and still have some lingering anti-Japanese sentiments that the Japanese government is careful not to provoke. That is why they do not stop all aid even if military spending increases, the development of mass destructive arms goes on and the security of basic human rights is violated. In Asia there is just too much at stake, whereas in countries like Haiti, Sierra Leone and Malawi aid can be stopped overnight.

China's strength is in a class of its own. Oral commitments are given for both specific projects and the amount of loan aid in 'five-year packages', when feasibility studies do not exist. This is completely contrary to OECF standard procedure and is unthinkable for any other recipient. China is not only strong in relation to Japan, but is also strong in relation to other donors. It has an extremely complex system of receiving aid that has resulted from the government's decision not to let any external agent control aid to China.

A second factor contributing to this two-way trade is surely the type of ODA studied, namely, loan aid. If grants had been examined, the results might have been different. It is relatively easy for a recipient to agree to a project and any accompanying conditions as long as it does not have to pay for it. Usually the recipient does not care if it is tied aid or who the contractor is as long as it receives the benefits. Similarly, the recipient country does not care whether the cost of a project is twice the normal price.

With loan aid things are more complicated. This is money the recipients know they will have to repay one day. Many of them have already experienced difficulties in connection with this. All of the countries studied have built up special processes through which loan aid projects must be evaluated before being given final approval. In developing countries capital is a scarce resource requiring careful management. Controlling the cost of a project is in the recipient country's own interests. This makes the untying of loans a necessity. If loans are tied, projects become more expensive and it might even be better business to seek other sources of financing. OECF loans, in such a case, may not be advantageous, especially if the present high value of the yen is taken into consideration.

A third factor in the two-way trade is the way in which OECF processes are established. OECF loans are request-based. The recipient decides what is needed and chooses the projects that it will request. The recipient has its own long-term plans, its own view of the best way to develop and its own processes through which requests are formulated. They are also in charge of the tendering process. Notwithstanding, the recipient must still accommodate the wishes of the donor. OECF cannot force a recipient to submit a certain request but the decision-makers, the Four Ministries, can always say 'no' and will reject projects that they do not agree with. This guides the type of requests that are brought forward and works in favour of economic infrastructure projects. Often the donor can also make a choice between several projects submitted by the recipients. This makes aid two-way.

PROJECT ORIGINS

Examining the origins of the projects in these case studies shows that a variety of options existed. The classical image of 'upstream project preparation' done by Japanese engineering consulting firms holds true for the Renun case in Indonesia. An engineer from Nippon Koei, who was working on another project in the area, found a perfect spot for a hydroelectric power plant. Ten years later JICA granted a feasibility study for the project. Renun is strongly connected with another Japanese hydroelectric power plant, the Asahan, also partly financed by OECF. Renun in itself was not a feasible project but the combined generating capacity of Renun and Asahan made Renun worthwhile. The two were also connected with an aluminium smelter in the area (PT Inalum[1]) which OECF also invested in and which demanded substantial energy for its operation.

In the Thai case, the road was first proposed in a master plan for road development in the central region, the last of a number of such plans that JICA prepared for Thailand. The reason the Chonburi–Pattaya New Highway was the first one to be realized in this plan was obvious. It was part of the infrastructure for the Eastern Seaboard area, an industrialized zone in which there were several other OECF and JICA financed projects as well. The Chonburi–Pattaya New Highway had a spur road which extended to Laem Chabang, a new deep-sea port that OECF was financing. Without a road of sufficient capacity to handle the increased port traffic, that project was likely to be a failure.

Calaca II, the coal-fired thermal power plant in the Philippines, was originally included in the drawings for Calaca I. This was a project ordered by the Philippine National Power Corporation and paid for by loans from the Exim Bank of Japan. The feasibility study for Calaca I was prepared in 1979 by three consultant companies of which one was Philippine, one British and one was Japanese. This project seemed to be the perfect solution when the Japanese government wanted to very quickly show immediate support for the Aquino government through a substantial aid package. This could be achieved in one stroke through Calaca II. This power plant was also located in the CALABARZON area which was envisioned to be the centre of all future industrialization and due to a JICA financed regional master plan was widely identified as the Japanese project CALABARZON.

In the China cases, both projects were originally Chinese plans. A survey conducted by the Chinese as early as in 1953 identified the spot at Yantian bay as perfect for a port. At that time it did not proceed due to lack of funding. In 1985 JICA granted money for a Chinese–Japanese feasibility study. Yantian bay is located close to the Shenzhen economic zone which is currently one of the most explosive economic high growth areas in China. It is a general export zone that has attracted many Hong Kong, Taiwanese, Japanese and other foreign companies.

The Hengshui–Shangqiu Railway was part of the Little Jing-Jiu railway project in the 1980s and was approved by the State Council as part of the Great Jing-Jiu railway between Beijing and Jiulong (that is, Kowloon, Hong Kong) in 1990. For the Chinese it is a top priority project within their five-year plan and, therefore, financed by OECF loans.

In all of the projects, except the Hengshui–Shangqiu railway, there are strong and clear connections to other Japanese projects or to export oriented economic zones. At first, this might seem like a plot to assist Japanese companies in the area, but it can also be regarded as concrete steps to help the recipients to develop through industrialization and promotion of export oriented industries – something that in the long run will give benefits to Japan as well through increased trade and possibilities to locate production abroad where wages are lower. All these projects were in high-priority sectors of the recipient countries and most also located in geographical areas that were considered important.

With the choice of projects, namely, economic infrastructure, it also seems fairly natural that they are mostly located close to economic zones. This is where power plants and highways are mostly needed. Since Japan is the major bilateral donor to Asia it is not strange that it would have more than one project in such areas. Neither is it difficult to understand why Japanese companies established themselves in geographical areas where major initiatives are being taken to develop the infrastructure and where there may also be considerable tax incentives. Companies from other foreign countries choose these areas as well.

HOW THE CASES PROCEEDED

These case studies were all conducted in countries which are regular recipients of Japanese ODA. In all of the countries annual consultations for loan aid are convened between representatives of the donor government (in this case the Four Ministries) and representatives of the recipient government. These consultations are well prepared. The recipients submit a list of request several months in advance. OECF have informal contact with the officials in the recipient countries both before and after this and are also in contact with the decision-makers in Tokyo.

Projects other than those on the list can be inserted during this process, like the case of Chonburi–Pattaya New Highway. The road was not on the list from the begining but, due to its urgency was inserted during the process. To a large extent loan aid projects are selected at the working level and annual consultations usually disclose few surprises but are more of a formal nature. This is obvious from, among other things, the short time spent on each project, which makes treatment by necessity superficial at the annual consultations. The Japanese government has a stable policy in which roughly the same proportion of money is given to each country every year, except when special political considerations are made. Of course there might be variations, depending on the number of 'suitable' projects available, but Japan usually does not give huge amounts one year and then nothing at all the following year to the larger recipients in Asia. Generally, the recipients have a number of 'suitable' projects available.

The donor and the recipients know each other well on the working level. They know what their priorities are and based on this they hold discussions. Still there are always many more projects requiring financing than there is money available, and there are a considerable number of considerations that have to be made. These might cover everything from natural disasters, such as the Pinatubo eruptions in the Philippines, to mass media reports about certain projects. Other topics could include the likelihood of an oil crisis,[2] and general trends, or common agreements between DAC countries on how aid should be distributed. Different events are likely to affect both the requests from the recipients as well as the preferences of the donor.

An amazing amount of flexibility was demonstrated in the Japanese processes. The operational manual of OECF, although describing how projects should proceed, was not always followed. One of the probable reasons for this was that it did not appear until 1991 and before that time there was a considerable lack of clarity regarding different loan approval procedures. Many of the cases studied had loan agreements predating 1991. Another reason why rules were not always followed was that sometimes political considerations superseded OECF's regular procedure. Once politicians have made oral commitments it is difficult not to fulfil them, even if priorities have changed and it is considered that the projects chosen might not be the most appropriate.

Political considerations also affected the appraisal of Calaca II. An Environmental Compliance Certificate was not made a requirement for the appraisal nor a condition before a binding Japanese commitment, although it was required. Instead, the appraisal mission acted pragmatically and honoured the political circumstances and the spirit of the time with an approval that was needed to show support for the Aquino government.

Time constraints may be another factor that makes regular procedures difficult to follow. The Chonburi–Pattaya New Highway is an example of this. There was simply not time to wait for the feasibility study to be formally completed. Neither the Thai nor the Japanese side would have gained popular support for such a policy once the port in Laem Chabang and the industrial estate around it opened and the public discovered that there was no adequate road available. The road was badly needed and something had to be done quickly.

The Chonburi–Pattaya New Highway Project also indicates that considerable unofficial consultations can occur prior to the more formal decision-making events. By the time the second loan agreement for the Chonburi–Pattaya New Highway was signed, Thailand's Department of Highways had already completed the tendering process and signed contracts with the construction companies. If it had not received an indication that the financing problem would be resolved this would have been difficult to accomplish.

The Indonesian case also clearly shows that consultations and other preparations occur in certain areas before formal decisions are made. In the case of Renun, loans for engineering services were, in principle, already approved by the time the feasibility study was ready.

Time constraints which lead to unusual procedures do not necessarily have to be detrimental. Sometimes these actions might represent the only practical solution to an urgent problem. It is a factor that also affects the procedure on the recipient side. However, it can lead to surprises later when it might be discovered that decisions were made without sufficient information. In the case of the Chonburi–Pattaya New Highway, costs became much higher than expected, partly because of price increases but probably also due to the fact that the feasibility study was not available, which made cost estimates difficult.

If a case suddenly has to return to regular procedures this might also cause problems. This was what happened in the case of Calaca II. A Philippine agency did not react to the public outcry over the situation in Calaca nor stop the process due to a missing licence. Instead, OECF stopped the process in order to protect its own interests, once the case became an issue in the media as well as in the parliaments of both countries.

The processes of the recipients were also found to be flexible. In the case of the Philippines, where legal requirements and administrative procedures had been eroded during martial law and where administrative guidelines, in general, were understood more as 'targets', flexibility was an expectation and this was accepted by OECF until the project ran into trouble.

Yet, the way that NPC used foreign consultants and established a system to check their work at every step demonstrated that the Philippines were in control of the process. The refusal to accept flue gas desulphurization, unless the extra expense was covered by a grant, is another proof of the Philippines ultimate control. What was also demonstrated by the Calaca case was that OECF, with its loan conditions, was able to intervene in the process of the recipient country and to ensure that certain rules and regulations were followed.

Flexibility by the recipient was also clearly found in the case of the harbour project in China, which appeared to be facing a financial disaster. Dongpeng Industries had failed to attract any traffic to the harbour and, was not surprisingly, worried about the future and loan repayments. Something had to be done to save the situation. The solution was to sell the right to operate and maintain the harbour.

In case of the Hengshui–Shangqiu railway, the Chinese considered this part of the Great Jing-Jiu railway which was a top priority within their five-year plan, while to the Japanese it was a separate project. Here it is interesting to note that the Japanese never mentioned the railway in connection with the Great Jing-Jiu railway but presented it as a railway project intended to strengthen the coal transport capacity of China. This is an example of how motivation for projects can be reformulated to please all parties and that way be able to pass through the pipeline.

There are standard regulations for how the aid process should occur both by OECF and by the various recipients. These are obviously not strictly followed. There seems to be a considerable amount of pragmatism from all parties involved to move projects through the pipeline. The regulations can be very flexible or very strict, depending on the situation. Regular procedures on both sides are affected by political considerations, time constraints, public opinion and by what seems practical to the actors involved at the time.

BIDDING PROCESS

With regard to the bidding process, OECF has issued *Guidelines for procurement under OECF loans* as well as *Guidelines for the employment of consultants by OECF borrowers*. It should also agree the tendering documents, the evaluation of the tender and finally the contracts. Yet, depending on in which country it occurs, this tendering process produces very different results. This is to a certain extent caused by the fact that the recipient is in charge of the process. Each recipient has a different system for handling tenders. This includes different people in charge as well as different traditions on how ICB should be prepared. In China there are three different procurement agencies in charge of all the ICB for projects financed by OECF. In Thailand procurement for the road project was handled by the Department of Highways. In each country the number of people involved and the process for procurement was country-specific.

Calaca II was divided into three main contracts for bidding and the Chonburi–Pattaya New Highway project into eight, but the Hengshui Shangqiu Railway was divided into more than 90 contracts. To a certain extent the tender documents and the number of contracts are also dependent on the type of projects. Some are more easily divided than others but certain countries also tend to favour the division of projects into as many sections as possible while others do not.

Similarly, the evaluation of tenders should be conducted in a prescribed way which OECF always has to concur with. According to the regulations the borrower may not ask a company which has submitted a bid to change the substance or price of that bid. Yet companies in China state that the bargaining process continues after the opening of tenders. In Thailand the administration must prepare a 'Government Medium Estimate' to ensure that prices are reasonable. In cases where prices are too high the tender price is negotiated with the companies submitting bids. In Indonesia alliances with companies controlled by Suharto's children are a plus in order to obtain major government contracts and in the Philippines a certain senator needed to be 'enlightened' twice in order to cease accusations of bribes in the parliament.

These irregularities do not always happen and it is not something particular to ODA loans in general or OECF loans specifically. This is just part of regular business practice in which each country has its own customs. Because the recipient is in charge of the bidding process it is important to understand local practices. OECF cannot do much to affect the process. Neither is it OECF's job to conduct thorough investigations into every contract. It has neither the staff nor the interest in doing so. As long as there is nothing blatantly illegal and the regular process is at least formally followed, OECF will concur. OECF's interest lies in disbursing the money as quickly and as effectively as possible.

ROOM FOR OTHER ACTORS

OECF's limited number of staff leads to a preferences for big projects but it also has a number of implications for the implementation process, one of the most important being that OECF cannot do everything itself. This allows considerable room for other actors. Their identity and the amount of influence they wield is dependent on the country, the project and the issues involved.

The role of the Japanese trading houses is not only emphasized by themselves but also by the media and public discussion. To a certain extent they become involved through 'upstream' project preparation, as well as through being well informed and firmly established with good contacts among Japanese and Asian decision-makers. Their 'influence' as well as 'interest' in the loan aid business has decreased with the gradual untying of OECF loans. There was no evidence of special favours being granted to Japanese trading houses or other Japanese companies working in this area. In the case of Yantian Port, a Finnish company working through an agent in Hong Kong was awarded the main contract, ahead of well established companies, such as Mitsubishi, Mitsui and IHI.

In Indonesia a Korean company won the main order for construction and through OECF loans was able to establish itself in the hydroelectric power sector in Indonesia. In the Philippine case, Japanese trading houses were much involved but the picture was still far from the regular image of 'Japan Inc.' in which Japanese companies work hand in hand with government officials to secure business opportunities for Japan. In the Calaca case, the Japanese trading houses were busy accusing each other of bribery. Another interesting fact was that both of the two main competing Japanese trading houses were working with other non-Japanese companies. Moreover, the trading houses' strength in moving the project along the pipeline in the Calaca case did not seem to be particularly successful. When the project ran into trouble there was nothing that they could do to speed up the process.

The gradual untying of the OECF loans has shifted the responsibility of the bidding process to various agencies in the recipient countries. They evaluate all tenders and decide who is awarded the contract. Their main interest is to choose the lowest possible bid conforming with the tender documents. They must be careful with money since it must be repaid and there exist no logical reasons for favouring Japanese companies.

If the OECF loans were tied, it is not certain that the governments in the recipient countries would be interested since prices would then be much higher. Other alternatives in the form of other official flows or building infrastructure through BOT or BOO might then be just as attractive. According to the trading houses the problem is not the untying of loans but rather the general loss of competitiveness due to the high value of the yen.

The role of the Japanese engineering consulting firms is often mentioned. They do play a role in a number of countries. This is clearly demonstrated by the Indonesian case study. In many other cases the feasibility study was also prepared by Japanese consultants on a grant aid basis. While 97 per cent of the procurement for OECF loans is untied, this figure is not as high for the employment of consultants. Although there has been a gradual untying for the employment of consultants, this still varies according to the country as well as the project. In Indonesia consultants are not employed on general untied conditions, while China simply does not spend money on such services. It never uses any Japanese engineering consultants and they are not even allowed to open offices in Beijing and can only work in China on a grant aid basis. This fact points to another group that plays an important role in the process, namely, the politicians and the administrators in the recipient countries. Their wishes will be reflected in the request that they make. Their laws and regulations affect the process. They submit requests for projects and are responsible for the bidding process, for the project implementation, and for the repayment of money after some years. If they know the OECF processes well enough there is considerable room for them to act within the system. To a certain extent this is, of course, dependent on their educational level but also on their administrative skills.

Chinese politicians and bureaucracy are very good in this respect. Requests are in principle limited to what is in their own five-year plans. At every step of the implementation process China has its own experts readily available. Besides MOFTEC, all the ministries involved with OECF loans have their own special sections dealing with the loans. They are all knowledgeable about the process, many of them speak Japanese, have considerable experience and have good negotiating skills. However, this is not only applicable to the Chinese, several of the Asian countries have experience in this field.

One of the things that varies from country to country is the amount of financing that is available for each project. While in some countries OECF loans fund the major part of projects, in others they do not. This influences the way projects are viewed in the recipient countries and the way that they are handled. In Indonesia, OECF financed most of the cost for the power project Renun, except for land acquisition. In China, 60 per cent of the projects are usually funded by the Chinese themselves leaving only a minority share for Japanese ODA which makes it less visable.

Another important group are the opinion makers, both in the recipient and in the donor countries. This could be NGOs, sending petitions to the parliament or working through the mass media to create opinions in both the recipient and the donor countries. It could also be journalists and parliamentarians actively participating in certain projects. Even if the Philippine authorities did not take notice of enviromental campaigns in the beginning they were forced to do so by the Japanese authorities when these complaints reached as far as the Japanese media and even into the Diet. In addition, Japanese ODA loans do not exist in a vacuum. They affect and are affected by general trends among the wider donor community.

A common feature among many of the actors in the Japanese loan aid process is that they tend to overestimate their own role. Politicians think that they are in charge, the bureaucrats of the Four Ministries all believe that the role of their ministry is the most important. OECF officials, with considerable knowledge in the field, claim that their influence is substantial.

On the recipient side, politicians as well as bureaucrats claim that they are the ones governing the process. The business community says that it has considerable influence behind the scenes. The mass media and the general public, in terms of mass opinion, also claim that they have influence.

Each can see their own actions and influence in particular projects but what appears to be lacking among most of them is an overview of how the whole process works. A considerable amount of variation was found at the implementation level and different actors had different amounts of influence depending on the case, the project-specific factors and the country-specific factors.

As shown from these case studies, Japanese loan aid is not just a business for the Japanese. The processes are fairly open. It can be governed in a number of ways depending on the actors involved and their skills. Therefore, it is important for the different actors to learn how the processes work.

Lack of financial resources is one of the main obstacles to development in the third world. In 1993 almost $6 billion was disbursed through OECF loans. How it is used, its results, who is to profit and who is to lose all depend on the actors involved both in the recipient and in the donor country. The processes are open, within certain limits, and anyone interested in participating should learn how they work.

NOTES

1 PT Inalum is a joint venture between the Indonesian and the Japanese governments as well as 12 Japanese companies. The Renun plant has become even more important when the financial difficulties and recent bail-outs for PT Inalum are considered.

2 Which strengthens support for projects to secure natural resources.

Index

Index

Laos 57, 100
Latin America 34, 40, 28–9
Laurel, Salvador 162
LCB (local competitive bidding) 140
LDCs (Less Developed Countries)
    61, 109, 136, 149n, 205n, 231
Li Ka-Shin 236, 239
Liu Dingtong 222
LLDCs (Least among Less
    Developed Countries) 42
loan agreements 68, 69; China 226–
    7, 228–9, 234–5, 252, 259, 276;
    India 34; Indonesia 140, 146;
    Thailand 90, 109–10, 114
Lombok Straits 129
Los Angeles 118n
Luzon 152, 177, 178

Macau 213
Maersk 242n
MAI/PAP see USA ('mini-Marshall
    plan')
Makati 197
Malacca Straits 129
Malawi 45, 278
Malaysia 22, 57, 75, 200n
Manchuria 127, 213, 249
Manila 151, 152, 153, 163, 169,
    203n; battle over (1945) 156–7
manufacturing 93, 130, 131
Marcos, Ferdinand 152, 163–4, 182,
    185, 202n
market oriented economy 45, 46
Marubeni 139, 163, 166; consortium
    with Babcock & Wilcox 185
Mekong River 100
MEWA Enterprise 141
Mexico 83
Middle East 34, 38, 40; see also
    Gulf; Kuwait
military expenditure 45, 49n
Mindanao 177; Mount Apo
    geothermal project 179
MITI (Ministry of International
    Trade and Industry) 47, 55, 56, 72,
    84, 88n; administrative control of
    OECF 51; China 218; grants 79;
    interests 48; meeting to decide on
    ODA amounts 136; 'New Asian
    Development Plan' 94;

Philippines 171; six biggest
    trading house representatives meet
    with officials from 80; Thailand
    108, 120n
Mitsubishi 139, 166, 184, 185, 187,
    206n, 236, 286
Mitsui Bussan 80, 82–7, 88n, 181,
    184, 185, 205n, 236, 286; illegal
    payments to Marcos 163;
    kidnapping of general manager 162
MOA (memoranda of agreement)
    189–90, 192, 206n
MOF (Ministry of Finance) 47, 55,
    56; administrative control of
    OECF 51; China 218, 240n;
    government coalition's desire to
    restrict the power of 58; interests
    48; meeting to decide on ODA
    amounts 136; Philippines 167; six
    biggest trading house
    representatives meet with officials
    from 80; Thailand 108, 120n
MOFA (Ministry of Foreign Affairs)
    35, 47, 49n, 56, 57, 71n, 84, 88n;
    administrative control of OECF
    51; approval of grant assistance
    43; China 218; interests 48;
    meeting to decide on ODA
    amounts 136; Philippines 163,
    167, 168, 171, 197, 201n, 203n;
    six biggest trading house
    representatives meet with officials
    from 80; Thailand 108, 120n
Mongolia 22–3, 46, 57, 85–6, 269n
multinationals 131

Nagasaki 156
Nakamura, Yukio 50n
Nakasone, Yasuhiro 161, 162
natural resources 35, 173, 183;
    abundance of 131; assistance
    extended to protect 134; projects
    to secure 289n; stable supply 34
Netherlands 132, 227; Indies
    Government 141
'networking' 80
New York 162
New Zealand 43
NEWJEC (consortium of
    consultants) 166, 169, 183, 202n

ports/shipping 44, 99–102, 116, 168, 221–44, 283, 286
poverty 128, 134, 161
power sector *see* energy
pricing mechanisms 247
private sector 77–8
privatization 103, 235–6
procurement process 67, 68–9, 71n; China 219, 227–31, 252, 260–6, 268, 273n; Indonesia 139, 140, 146, 148; Philippines 166–7, 182–7; Thailand 112
productivity 160
profits 81–2, 86, 92, 239; larger and easier 117; railways 247, 252

railways 44, 236, 245–76
Ramos, Fidel 152, 205n
rates of return 144, 226
'rational story assumption' 153, 197
raw materials 157, 246
recession 73, 81, 82, 131
Renun Hydroelectric Power Project 9, 71n, 127, 141–9, 150n, 279–80, 283, 288, 289n
rescheduling 60, 71n, 102–3, 158
research 85
respiratory diseases 188
Rio *see* UNCED
risk 66, 85, 198
roads 9, 44, 89–91, 99–126 *passim*, 280, 282–3, 285

savings 40
scandal 47
Self Defence Forces 31, 49n
'self-help' 2, 33, 40
semi-government organizations 66
Semirara 165, 181, 188
Shanghai 221, 246, 256
Shenzhen 9, 211, 221–44; *see also* Dongpeng
shipping *see* ports/shipping
Siemens 139
Sierra Leone 45, 278
Singapore 57, 118n, 231, 240n
South Africa 83, 86
South Korea 22, 31, 75, 231, 240n, 286; Japanese companies increasingly beaten in bidding

process by companies from 77; newly established relationship with Japan 51; OECF and 57; war reparations 33; *see also* Daewoo; Hyundai; Korea Power Company
Soviet Union (former) 85, 132, 141
Spain 42, 49n, 114, 156
Sri Lanka 24–5
stock markets 31
Stockholm 10
structural adjustment 64, 128, 201n
Suharto, Thojib 127, 128, 285
Sumatra: Asahan river 127, 141, 143, 144, 148, 149, 279–80; Lake Toba 127, 141, 143, 144; *see also* Renun
Sumimoto 139, 266, 273n
supply and demand 66
Sweden: content of aid 44; Embassy in Beijing 269n; Export Council 13–14nn; Export Invest company 241n; ODA contribution 36; prime minister 31–2; project study teams 141; untied aid 43
Syria 27

Taiwan 75; China's treaty with (1952) 214; investment in China 213; Japanese companies increasingly beaten in bidding process by companies from 77; road construction companies 114
Tanaka, Kakuei 92, 129, 162
taxes 40, 189, 191, 221
technical assistance 5, 95, 101, 133, 143, 220; agency which deals with 47; co-operation between loans, grants and 76; money pledged 134; tied 43, 77
technology 139, 153; non-performing 181; old, heavy 231–2; standard, coal-blending approach using 183; transfer of 183
telecommunications 64, 101, 133, 135
Thailand: aid distribution 42; contracts 25–7, 81, 95, 100, 103, 109, 114, 117, 118; human rights principles not reflected in implementation of ODA 45; Japanese exports 75; Japanese ODA to 94–8; Ministry of Finance